Sydney Box

BRITISH FILM MAKERS

MANCHESTER
1824

Manchester University Press

Brian McFarlane, Neil Sinyard *series editors*

Allen Eyles, Philip French, Sue Harper,
Tim Pulleine, Jeffrey Richards, Tom Ryall
series advisers

already published

Tom Ryall ANTHONY ASQUITH

Roy Ward Baker GEOFF MAYER

Jack Clayton NEIL SINYARD

Lance Comfort BRIAN MCFARLANE

Terence Davies WENDY EVERETT

Terence Fisher PETER HUTCHINGS

Launder and Gilliat BRUCE BABINGTON

Derek Jarman ROWLAND WYMER

Joseph Losey COLIN GARDNER

Carol Reed PETER WILLIAM EVANS

Michael Reeves BENJAMIN HALLIGAN

J. Lee Thompson STEVE CHIBNALL

Sydney Box

Andrew Spicer

Manchester University Press
MANCHESTER AND NEW YORK

distributed exclusively in the USA by Palgrave

Published by Manchester University Press
Oxford Road, Manchester M13 9NR, UK
and Room 400, 175 Fifth Avenue, New York, NY 10010, USA
www.manchesteruniversitypress.co.uk

Distributed exclusively in the USA by
Palgrave, 175 Fifth Avenue, New York NY 10010, USA

Distributed exclusively in Canada by
UBC Press, University of British Columbia, 2029 West Mall,
Vancouver, BC, Canada V6T 1Z2

British Library Cataloguing-in-Publication Data
A catalogue record for this book is available from the British Library

Library of Congress Cataloging-in-Publication Data
A catalog record for this book is available from the Library of Congress

ISBN 13: 978 0 7190 6000 7

First published by Manchester University Press 2006

First digital paperback edition published 2011

Printed by Lightning Source

Portrait of Sydney Box as Managing Director of Gainsborough Pictures, 1947

For Sean

Contents

List of plates

Series editors' foreword

The aim of this series is to present in lively, authoritative volumes a guide to those film-makers who have made British cinema a rewarding but still under-researched branch of world cinema. The intention is to provide books which are up-to-date in terms of information and critical approach, but not bound to any one theoretical methodology. Though all books in the series will have certain elements in common – comprehensive filmographies, annotated bibliographies, appropriate illustration – the actual critical tools employed will be the responsibility of the individual authors.

Nevertheless, an important recurring element will be a concern for how the oeuvre of each film-maker does or does not fit certain critical and industrial contexts, as well as for the wider social contexts which helped to shape not just that particular film-maker but the course of British cinema at large.

Although the series is director-orientated, the editors believe that reference to a variety of stances and contexts is more likely to reconceptualise and reappraise the phenomenon of British cinema as a complex, shifting field of production. All the texts in the series will engage in detailed discussion of major works of the film-makers involved, but they all consider as well the importance of other key collaborators, of studio organisation, of audience reception, of recurring themes and structures: all those other aspects which go towards the construction of a national cinema.

The series explores and charts a field which is more than ripe for serious excavation. The acknowledged leaders of the field will be reappraised; just as important, though, will be the bringing to light of those who have not so far received any serious attention. They are all part of the very rich texture of British cinema, and it will be the work of this series to give them all their due.

Acknowledgements

I would like to thank the Arts and Humanities Research Board, which supported the preparation of this book through a Research Leave Award. I also wish to acknowledge the support and encouragement of Professor Paul Gough, Dean of the Faculty of Art, Media and Design (now Bristol School of Art, Media and Design) at the University of the West of England, and of my colleagues in Visual Culture: Angela Partington the Field Leader, Gary Peters and Clare Johnson.

Warm thanks must go to those who kindly agreed to be interviewed about Sydney Box: Ken Annakin, Lord Attenborough, Sylvia Box, Vivian Cox, Leonora Dossett, John Franks, William Gell, Jean Kent, William MacQuitty, Jan Read, Peter Rogers, Dinah Sheridan, Carolyn Whitaker and Googie Withers. I am sensible of a particular debt to Bill Gell, who, over the course of two days – Bill and his wife Biddy were the most kind and generous of hosts – taught me much about the workings of the film industry, and provided priceless guidance about Box's later career and much important documentation. I am also very conscious of the wholehearted encouragement I received from Box's daughter Leonora Dossett, who was a gracious host on several occasions and lent me a mass of invaluable material, including Box's unpublished autobiography. She also kindly supplied many of the photographs for this volume.

I must acknowledge the assistance of the staff at a number of institutions: Bristol Central Library; Bristol University Theatre Collection; the British Board of Film Classification; the British Film Institute Library (especially Tessa Forbes and David Sharpe, and Janet Moat and her assistants in Special Collections); the British Library; the Centre for Cartoons and Caricature, University of Kent (Nicholas Hiley); the Co-operative College, Manchester (Gillian Lonergan); the Imperial War Museum (Matthew Lee); the Irish National Archives, Dublin (Tom Gilsenan); the National Film and Television Archive (Kathleen Dickson); the National Library of Australia (Paul Livingston); the Public Record Office, Kew and the Theatre Museum London. Above all I must thank the staff in the Bower Ashton Library at the University of the West of England, with special thanks to Iain Osborn, who handled a multitude of inter-library loan requests with great forbearance.

Various colleagues helped with advice, copies of films, or by generously sharing notes or unpublished material: Tony Aldgate, Alan Burton, James Chapman, Ian Conrich, Robert Murphy, Steve Neale, Jeffrey Richards, Anthony Slide and Sarah Street. In addition, I'm grateful for information from David Caute, Clare Deutsch and the late Alexander Walker. I should also like to thank Matthew Frost at Manchester University Press. As always in writing about British cinema, I am conscious of my indebtedness to Professors Sue Harper and Vincent Porter, whose advice, encouragement and friendship over a number of years have been a great source of support and inspiration, and who have contributed much valuable advice and information for this study. My principal debt is to one of the series editors for British Film Makers, Dr Brian McFarlane, who allowed himself to be persuaded that a producer would qualify for inclusion, and who has supported this project throughout its long gestation with endless enthusiasm, patience, sage advice and many points of detail. The manuscript has benefited from his judicious comments, but I remain entirely responsible for any faults that remain.

My partner, Joyce Woolridge, gave, as always, her complete support, and colluded with my sustaining fantasy that Sydney Box was the most important person ever to have lived. Her comments on various drafts of the chapters were characteristically trenchant and perceptive and helped me shape the final version. Our son Sean seems to have grown up alongside the project, though his progress was infinitely more important. This book is dedicated to him.

In praise of producers

1

If Sydney Box is remembered at all now it is as the producer of *The Seventh Veil* (1945), the tenth most successful film ever at the British box office according to a recent authoritative survey.[1] And yet, as this study will seek to demonstrate, over a quarter century (1940–65) Box was a highly influential presence in the British film industry. Box's career encompassed spells as contract producer (1943–44); independent producer (1944–46, 1951–59); executive producer – of both documentaries (Verity Films, 1940–45) and feature films (Gainsborough Pictures, 1946–49); and film and television impresario – he came close to gaining control of British Lion and London Weekday television in 1964. He was also an accomplished and successful playwright, and he had periods as a journalist, advertising scenarist, writer and producer of operettas, screenwriter, publicist and novelist. It is an impressive range of achievements, and I confess freely that in preparing this study my admiration for Sydney Box has risen sharply. But this is neither biography nor special pleading, rather it is a full and, I hope, objective analysis of the nature and significance of Box's career and what it reveals about the British film industry during a period of turbulence and profound change. It is both a contribution to and an extension of the British Film Makers series, which has so far concentrated solely on directors.

This lack of attention to producers is largely the result of the long shadow of the *auteur* theory, which, in its conventional form, has elevated the director as the key creative influence within film-making, expressing a personal vision with an distinctive aesthetic 'signature'. As a consequence, the producer has been relegated to the role of organiser and financier, concerned only with a saleable product and often actively hostile to creativity, or, at best, a trimmer, fearful of the radical or the experimental, seeking an acceptable compromise.[2] Unlike the director, cinematographer, set-designer, scriptwriter or composer, the producer does not need to possess any particular skills, or even any professional training. It seems that anyone can become a producer and therefore any achievements appear unpredictable and fortuitous. In addition, there is a general uncertainty about the producer's actual function because the term itself, as Duncan Petrie observes, 'is rather ambiguous in that it covers a range of very different tasks and responsibilities'.[3] Petrie distinguishes a producer, defined as 'someone who is responsible for developing a project and approaching potential investors for a financial commitment', from an associate producer, who supervises the day-to-day running of the production, and from an executive producer, who is 'usually connected with the company who [sic] has put up the money'.[4] As this study will make clear, the boundaries between these roles are often fluid and Box could find himself performing all three functions, though he usually delegated the day-to-day running of a film to a production manager.

In addition to clarifying the complex and shifting nature of a producer's role, this study seeks to demonstrate why it might be important to understand and appreciate its significance. For Michael Balcon, the producer's key function was twofold: to have a comprehensive overview of the entire film-making process, to be the one person who could apprehend, 'a film as an entity and be able to judge its progress and development from the point of view of the audience who will eventually view it'; and to be the mediator between commerce and creativity, a 'dual capacity as the creative man and the trustee of the moneybags'.[5] Box understood the potential tensions between the two roles, but he also felt that they were not necessarily contradictory:

> A film producer has two responsibilities: to the public and to his backers. If he is an imaginative and courageous producer, the two may coincide. The ideal producer, it seems to me, must always look ahead and try not merely to acquiesce in box-office trends but to lead public opinion and gauge future audience requirements.[6]

The creativity of a film producer may therefore express itself not in a fudged and timorous compromise, but in being able to make films that are both profitable and challenging, ones which extend the boundaries of conventional taste and attitudes. And, in order to be a successful mediator, the producer needs to have wide experience of film-making and the ability to organise and control financial, technological and human resources, to be an all-rounder who possesses 'the ability to recognize ability, the knack of assigning the right creative persons to the right creative spots', and the ability to 'manage, placate, and drive a variety of gifted, impulsive, and egocentric people'.[7]

This conception of the producer as a mediator and facilitator with an overview of the whole production necessitates that the focus of this study should be on the *film-making process itself*, in order to be clear about the nature of the choices that were open to Box, as well as the constraints under which he laboured at any given moment, rather than on the textual analysis of specific films. This is a question of emphasis rather than exclusiveness, and I have provided substantial discussion of films deemed to be representative, or thematically rich, or very little known – such as *The Man Within* (1947), one of several films made during his period at Riverside Studios, for which I think high claims can be made. However, I do not engage with (the point is worth stressing) later critical or academic interpretations of his films, as these are not relevant to my concern with why those films came to be as they were, or with their contemporaneous reception by critics and the public, in so far as the latter can be inferred from box-office data.

In making the film-making process the centre of attention, the context of production, I am following the lead of Vincent Porter, who argued that, rather than looking for a producer's signature on individual films, analysis should be focused on the longer term relationship between four key factors: the producer's estimation of public taste, the ability to obtain adequate production finance, an understanding of whom to use in the key creative roles and on what terms, and the effectiveness of the overall control of the production process.[8] I would add that the production sector as a whole needs to be understood in relation to distribution and exhibition, which are in turn profoundly affected by changing economic and social factors. Box's importance resides therefore not simply in the 61 feature films and 100 plus short documentaries for which he was responsible – though that, by any measure, is a sizeable corpus of work – but in the overall contribution he made to the development of the British film industry.

In order to assess that contribution systematically and in detail, this study is organised chronologically, each chapter dealing with a major phase of Box's career, beginning with a chapter that discusses the formative influence of his childhood. Chapter 2 discusses his early career, locating the origins of Box's restless ambition and determination to succeed in whatever he turned his hand to in the circumstances of his childhood: his poverty, lack of educational opportunities, enforced assumption of adult responsibilities at a young age and, most of all perhaps, his consciousness of a disability (a limp caused by a malformed hip) that set him apart from others but helped create the astonishing mental energy that compensated for his lack of physical prowess. Chapter 3 considers his achievements in running Verity

Films, which produced over 100 propaganda shorts for the government and the services during the Second World War. Chapter 4 traces his initial efforts as a feature-film maker, and the important period (1943–45) when he was based at Riverside Studios, producing a coherent corpus of six challenging films that need to be distinguished (as they have not been hitherto) from his work as head of Gainsborough Pictures. Two chapters, 5 and 6, are devoted to his tenure at Gainsborough – the most complex, and the most important, period in his working life. Chapter 7 explores the struggles he experienced as an independent producer in the 1950s after he left the Rank Organisation following the closure of Gainsborough Studios in 1949, forming London Independent Producers and then the more ambitious Sydney Box Associates at the end of 1958, an initiative prematurely concluded by Box's ill health. Chapter 8 examines his return to film production, his role in the notorious 'sale' of British Lion in 1964 and his parallel bid for the London Weekday television franchise.

Chapter 1 also charts his early career as a writer in some detail, because Box's consciousness of himself as a writer shaped his entire career. His first job in the film industry was as a scenarist for Publicity Films, a role he continued when head of Verity Films, and he went on to write twenty-four feature-film screenplays. These were mostly adaptations, but one of four original screenplays, *The Seventh Veil*, received an Oscar. In an article Box wrote in 1947, 'A New Deal for Film Writers', he deplored the writer's lack of status within the film industry and declared: 'However long I go on producing films, I shall continue to think of myself as a writer'.[9] As a producer, his practice was to privilege the script over everything else, including the director's contribution, and his innovative adaptations of W. Somerset Maugham's short stories, beginning with *Quartet* (1948), may be said to have constituted a writer's cinema. In retirement, Box looked forward to an 'era of the creators' in which the writer would be 'king'.[10] There were often tensions between the two roles of writer and producer – though there were important synergies as well – and these are highlighted in the course of this study.

Of course, almost all Box's screenplays, including *The Seventh Veil*, were written in collaboration with his wife Muriel. Therefore any analysis of Box's career must, of necessity, give close consideration to their thirty-year partnership. Is it possible to separate the two? I argue that it is. The sources detailed below make it possible, with some degree of accuracy, to distinguish their respective writing contributions; but more importantly, their roles of director and producer were separate. It was Sydney Box who ran Verity Films, Gainsborough Pictures, London

Independent Producers and Sydney Box Associates, taking all the crucial decisions. Indeed, his career as an impresario led to an increasing separation between their working lives – Muriel Box played no part in Sydney's bids for British Lion or London Weekday television – which contributed to a growing emotional estrangement that ended in their divorce. In many ways Box was temperamentally closer to his younger sister, Betty Box, but although their careers were frequently interconnected it remains possible to define clearly their respective roles.

Betty Box's autobiography, *Lifting the Lid*, acknowledges her brother as a guiding and sustaining force throughout her career; but it was Muriel Box's autobiography, *Odd Woman Out*, published twenty-five years earlier and containing a not altogether flattering portrait of the man who deserted her, that has shaped the accepted image of Box.[11] In Muriel Box's account, the young creative writer bursting with ideas declined into a dreary, absentee businessman, obsessed with ever more complex and convoluted deals. The detailed Diaries which she kept throughout their partnership, and which are preserved in the Muriel and Sydney Box Collection held at the British Film Institute, were the basis of *Odd Woman Out* and contain a similarly partial portrait of Box. And of the two, it has been Muriel who has commanded scholarly attention and respect. There have been several accounts of her career that rightly celebrate the substantial achievements of a woman writer-director working in a thoroughly misogynist industry.[12] The regrettable consequence of this attention has been to obscure and occlude the nature and significance of Sydney Box's achievements, both as a writer and as a producer. The one account of Box that has been published, by Charles Drazin, is impressionistic and finishes in 1950.[13]

In preparing this account of Box's career, I have made extensive use of Muriel Box's Diaries – which are indispensable because of their meticulous detailing of the minutiae of particular productions – but have also drawn upon new primary material kindly lent to me by Box's daughter, Leonora Dossett. This includes unpublished writing, letters regarding censorship issues, costings of films, clippings files, four volumes of journals, and extensive correspondence relating to various projects and the British Lion bid. It also included Box's unpublished autobiography, *The Lion That Lost Its* Way. Had this witty and engaging account found a publisher when it was completed in 1977, it might have done much to redress the emphases and imbalances of his wife's account, though, of course, it cannot be treated as objective.[14] I was also fortunate to be given further papers and correspondence, particularly relating to Box's bid for British Lion and to the operations of Sydney Box Associates, as well as several unpublished screenplays, by William Gell, who worked very closely with Box during his later career (from 1959 onwards).[15] Gell's recollections of this period, in which Box controlled so many intricately interwoven companies, were of enormous help, as were those of the thirteen people interviewed specifically for this study. In addition to these private papers and oral testimony, I have consulted all the relevant material in the public domain: other primary documents in the Muriel and Sydney Box Collection, Broadcasting, Entertainment, Cinematograph and Theatre Union (BECTU) interviews, the trade press, contemporaneous film reviews, PRO files and records of Box's companies held at Companies House. Gaps remain, especially in relation to Box's work as a television producer. In particular, it would have been of great value to have had a copy of Box's detailed bid for the London Weekday franchise, which William MacQuitty, who worked with Box for over twenty-five years, regarded as 'the best application he had ever put together', and which Box stated contained a credo that ran for eight pages.[16] This appears to have disappeared and has not, or not yet, resurfaced in the ITC collection currently being catalogued by the BFI.

With this proviso in mind, I hope to have constructed an accurate, balanced and comprehensive account of Box's career, one that can restore him to his rightful place as one of the key figures in the British film industry. Beyond this aim, I would like it to act as a spur to further studies of British film producers. This work is important, not only to respond to Alexander Walker's observation that 'The tendency to ignore the role of the producers or production chiefs has to be resisted if films are to make sense as an industry that can sometimes create art'[17] but also because, as John Caughie has argued, producers have occupied a central role within the British film industry: 'Outside of a studio system or a national corporation, art is too precarious a business to be left to artists: it needs organizers. The importance of the producer-artist seems to be a specific feature of British cinema, an effect of the need continually to start again in the organization of independence.'[18] It is therefore vital to undertake a systematic and comprehensive survey looking at the changing nature of the producer's role, from the beginnings of British cinema to the present day, and this study of Sydney Box is offered as a contribution to that larger project.

Notes

1 Ryan Gilbey (ed.), *The Ultimate Film* (London: BFI, 2005), pp. 44–5.
2 For further discussion, see Andrew Spicer, 'The Production Line: Reflections on the Role of the Film Producer in British Cinema', *Journal of British Cinema and Television*, 1:1 (Autumn 2004), 33–50.

3 Duncan Petrie, *Creativity and Constraint in the British Film Industry* (Basingstoke: Macmillan, 1991), p. 181.
4 *Ibid.*
5 Michael Balcon, *The Producer* (London: British Film Institute, 1945), p. 5.
6 Sydney Box, 'Sadism – It Will Only Bring Us Disrepute', *Kinematograph Weekly* (hereafter *KW*), 27 May 1948, 18.
7 Leo Rosten, *Hollywood: The Movie Colony, the Movie Makers* (New York: Harcourt, Brace and Co., 1941), pp. 238–9.
8 Vincent Porter, 'The Context of Creativity: Ealing Studios and Hammer Films', in James Curran and Vincent Porter (eds), *British Cinema History* (London: Weidenfeld and Nicolson, 1983), pp. 179–80.
9 Sydney Box, 'A New Deal for Film Writers', *Penguin Film Review*, 3 (August 1947), 49.
10 See Duncan Graham, 'Let's Forget the "Art" of Film Making', *The Bulletin*, 31 January 1970, 44.
11 Betty Box, *Lifting the Lid* (Lewes: The Book Guild, 2000); Muriel Box, *Odd Woman Out* (London: Leslie Frewin, 1974).
12 See Louise Heck-Rabi, *Women Filmmakers: A Critical Reception* (Metuchen, New Jersey and London: Scarecrow Press, 1984), chapter six, pp. 135–94; Caroline Merz, 'The Tension of Genre: Wendy Toye and Muriel Box', in Wheeler Winston Dixon (ed.), *Re-Viewing British Cinema, 1900–1992* (New York: State University of New York Press, 1994), pp. 121–31; Sue Harper, *Women in British Cinema: Mad, Bad and Dangerous to Know* (London: Continuum, 2000), pp. 175–82, 193–6; Justine Ashby, 'Odd Women Out: Betty and Muriel Box', unpublished Ph.D. thesis, University of East Anglia, 2001. *Gainsborough Melodrama*, edited by Sue Aspinall and Robert Murphy (London: BFI, 1983), contains an extensive interview with Muriel Box.
13 Charles Drazin, 'Sydney Box', in *The Finest Years: British Cinema of the 1940s* (London: Andre Deutsch, 1998), pp. 200–12. There is also a short analysis of Box's tenure at Gainsborough by Robert Murphy, 'Gainsborough After Balcon', in Pam Cook (ed.), *Gainsborough Pictures* (London: Cassell, 1997), pp. 148–52; and there is a brief but incisive analysis of Box's work as an independent producer in the 1950s in Sue Harper and Vincent Porter, *British Cinema of the 1950s: The Decline of Deference* (Oxford: Oxford University Press, 2003), pp. 159–62.
14 A new edition has been prepared, with an introduction and notes by the present writer published by Scarecrow Press in 2005.
15 This material, together with the documents supplied by Leonora Dossett, has been donated to the BFI for scholars' use as the Sydney Box Papers (hereafter SBP).
16 William MacQuitty, *A Life to Remember* (London: Quartet Books, 1991), p. 347; Sydney Box, *The Lion That Lost Its Way: And Other Cautionary Tales of the Show Business Jungle*, edited with an introduction and notes by Andrew Spicer (Lanham, Maryland and Oxford: Scarecrow Press, 2005), p. 9.
17 Alexander Walker, *Hollywood, England: The British Film Industry in the Sixties* (London: Harrap, 1986), p. 17.
18 John Caughie, 'Broadcasting and Cinema 1: Converging histories', in Charles Barr (ed.), *All Our Yesterdays: 90 Years of British Cinema* (London: BFI, 1986), p. 200.

The self-made man

2

Forging the entrepreneur

Frank Sydney Box was born on 29 April 1907 at Ravenscroft Road, Beckenham. Despite living in this rather genteel suburb, on the outskirts of south-east London, the Boxes were poor. Box recalled in his autobiography that their two-roomed cottage was 'a cramped, inconvenient apology for a home, with a leaky slate roof and wooden walls'.[1] Box gravitated towards his mother, a head gardener's daughter who had worked as a housemaid from the age of twelve until she married, because she 'never lost her defiant resolve to better the lot of herself and her family' and tried to ensure that 'her children were to have the best education available [and] the right to work at the careers they thought most appropriate for them' (p. 142). By contrast, his father was not ambitious, either for himself or for his children. Frank Box was a nurseryman and market gardener who also ran a florist's shop 'in a little glass house on an empty plot of land in the main street' (p. 138). But he would often neglect this in favour of his real passions: cricket and football. When the business failed, he joined the local Volunteer Corps and was sent to Belgium as part of the Royal West Kent Regiment soon after the outbreak of the First World War in September 1914. Almost immediately the family's situation deteriorated, as Frank Box's separation allowance was not paid when his papers went missing. There were no savings because he had been made a bankrupt before the war, and Box's mother was forced to take in lodgers (three Belgian refugees) and turn her hand to dressmaking.

While she went out to fit her customers, Box, in his father's absence, assumed the role of head of the household, which included doing the shopping and cooking and minding his two younger brothers, John and Norman. To supplement the family income, Box took two paper rounds (though he was under age) and served each evening in a tobacconist's until closing time (p. 138). At weekends he took any job he could find. These early years therefore saw the birth of Box the entrepreneur, precociously self-reliant, turning his hand to whatever might make money, but always with a governing sense of his responsibilities towards the family, including his two younger brothers. These increased when his mother gave birth to twin girls, Kitty and Betty, in 1915. Betty Box recalled: 'to me he was all things wonderful. He acted as father, guardian, tutor and guiding light'.[2] As Box's responsibilities grew, so did his intimacy with his mother, who began to rely on Sydney as her 'close companion and confidant', an intimacy abruptly ended when his father returned from the army. This served further to alienate him from his shy, unconfident father, who always seemed to be 'withdrawn and incapable of intimate communication' (p. 140). Frank Box's health had been affected by bad shrapnel wounds in his chest, and he was only able to earn a meagre living as a landscape gardener, which ensured that his eldest son's priority remained earning a living.

Box always acknowledged that the memories of his impecunious upbringing – 'I still shudder at the memory of one period of two weeks when our diet consisted solely of porridge, boiled sweets and cocoa' (p. 138) – were a formative influence, and the determination never to experience poverty again often guided his conduct: 'I have to admit that the scars remained and conditioned my actions on many occasions in later life when I would apply to any decision-making the test how much will it pay? instead of how good is it?' (p. 139). Box always kept £200 in his pocket for reassurance, remarking, 'I've always got this.'[3]

Box's ambition and restless mental energy were also the product of his intense desire to overcome his disability: 'a dislocated and malformed right hip which causes me to limp heavily and walk with the rolling gait of a drunken sailor' (pp. 135–6). His condition was first diagnosed when he was two years old, but surgical techniques were not advanced sufficiently for the condition to be corrected at this time. Although he was subject to cruel verbal abuse at school – other boys shouted 'dot and carry one' in mockery of his walk – Box argues that he had never 'felt deprived or hard done by because of my deformity', because it 'kept me out of the wars in which many of my school friends lost their lives [and] prevented me from frittering away my time and substance on sporting pursuits, as my father did' (p. 137). However, Box remained conscious of his disability throughout his life. He never walked anywhere, always ensured that he entered a room last, and drove large American automatic cars with wide doors; he was also reluctant to go on the studio floor for fear of falling over the cables, which perhaps was one of the reasons why he was never tempted to become a director.[4]

Birth of the writer

At his father's insistence, Box left school at sixteen to become a junior clerk for the Antofagasta (Chile) and Bolivia Railway Company at its transfer office in Finsbury Circus, rather than staying on to sit for a university scholarship. However, his salary of fifteen shillings a week was only a quarter of what he was already earning in his spare time as a writer (p. 144). Box's writing career started through an act of characteristically quick-thinking opportunism. When his father declined the offer of providing a 'weekly column of sports news and gossip' for the *Kentish Times* in 1920, Box, then thirteen, stepped in and wrote the column himself without his father's knowledge. His mother colluded in the deception, and when his father found out, she persuaded him that the income was useful. Box therefore continued to write and his column led to further work as a 'stringer' sports reporter for other local papers, branching out into local affairs as well as play and film reviews. His success as a journalist enabled him, at the age of seventeen, to leave his job as a clerk to take up a position on the *Beckenham and Penge Advertiser*. He also worked as a weekend sub-editor on the *Sunday Graphic* and the *Daily Sketch*, and later sustained a three-year stint as editor of the weekly *Christian Herald*, where he increased the circulation by 'revitalising the lay-out and bringing its turgid style up to date' (p. 146). From 1935 onwards he wrote regularly for *Play Pictorial*, a monthly theatre magazine (which he also edited for a brief period), and *Theatrecraft*, another monthly journal, devoted to amateur theatre. Box had a lucid and concise prose style, but journalism was not his preferred form of writing, nor, after 1935, his principal source of income, which was derived from his plays.

It was Box's mother, ever anxious to encourage him to realise his ambitions and seize the opportunities that had been denied to her, who first nurtured Box's literary ambitions, which were sustained by his English teacher at Beckenham County School, Tom Williams. Box had his first play, *Pathways*, performed while still at school in 1926 and he produced shows for the Beckenham Dramatic and Operatic Society, and nativity plays for the Methodist church, which was the centre of the Boxes' social life.[5] His breakthrough into professional theatre came when his one-act drama *Murder Trial* was performed at the Little Theatre in October 1934 by Nancy Price's People's National Theatre, an organisation devoted to presenting the best modern and classical plays, regardless of their commercial possibilities.[6] It accompanied Pirandello's *The Life I Gave You*, with Alastair Sim playing the lead in both plays. *Murder Trial* is an expressionist satire that attacks the hypocrises of the law and the press. As an aspiring dramatist, Box argued that the one-act play was developing into an independent art form, able to take on large issues and to break free from the tyranny of the well-made three-act play, with its polite middle-class ambience.[7]

The majority of Box's early plays are serious satires, cautionary morality tales about the failings of mankind and the parlous state of society, with the press and big business as particular targets. *Self-Made Man* (1934), set in the United States, was a coruscating account of the all-consuming drive for success and wealth, while *Twentieth Century Lullaby* (1936) and *Dirge without Dole* (1937), both written under the pseudonym Cedric Mount, painted a bleak picture of a British society that had gone disastrously wrong. *Not This Man* (1934), which won first prize at the National Drama Festival at the Old Vic in 1935, presents a 'world tottering on the edge of an abyss', in which greed and fear drive a group of influential people to murder a Gandhiesque figure and so stifle his dangerous creed of universal brotherhood. *Not This Man* attracted a certain notoriety when it was the subject of a court case for blasphemy. Box, defending himself, lost his case, but the trial gained him and the play a great deal of publicity.[8]

Box's uncompromising radicalism aligned him with various left-wing theatrical groups – including the Workers' Theatre Movement (1926–35) and Unity Theatre – which made a considerable impact on British theatre during this period, though he was never part of any collective or movement and did not espouse a doctrinaire socialism. His work may be understood as part of a broader movement to which one could give the label 'theatres of conscience', defined as a 'progressive, artistically accountable and democratic theatre'.[9] The central idea was that drama could educate and inspire, as well as entertain, by exposing the injustices of a corrupt and uncaring society – Box called *Twentieth Century Lullaby* 'an SOS' – and also warn about the rise of fascism and the threat of a further world war, the central concerns of the Popular Front. The social consciousness and left-wing idealism evident in these plays were to stay with Box throughout his life, though they became attenuated in some of his more nakedly commercial enterprises.[10]

Box was well aware that in writing these fluid, flexible 'expressionist' one-act plays, with small casts and limited demands for staging and scenery or lighting effects, he was targeting the burgeoning amateur-dramatic movement, whose rapid development in the 1930s was an important cultural phenomenon, with a huge array of groups performing and competing with each other at festivals up and down the country. Box estimated that there were probably as many as 20,000 amateur-dramatic societies, with an overall membership of nearly a million.[11]

The movement's impetus came partly from the retreat of the professional stage into large cities propelled by the wholesale conversion of provincial theatres into cinemas.[12] Many people's sole contact with live drama came from amateur productions. Although hundreds of authors supplied this market, Box became one of the select few who could earn a modest living from his royalties.[13] For three years running (1934–36) he was the second most performed playwright in the national British Drama League Festival. Box adopted the pseudonym Cedric Mount in 1936 precisely because he sensed that his name was being over-exposed in the one-act play market (pp. 149–50). His plays appeared in several anthologies, including three Box edited himself. Box was quite prepared to tailor his plays to the marketplace, rewriting the dream scene from *Bring Me My Bow* to avoid the ambitious stagecraft required by his original directions. As an astute critic as well as practitioner, Box was also much in demand as an adjudicator at various drama festivals.

It is important to acknowledge that Box achieved recognition, popularity and status in his own right as a writer, but his career from 1934 onwards was intimately bound up with his partnership with Muriel Baker. They first met in 1932 when she tried, unsuccessfully, to get *Murder Trial* taken up as a film project. As Muriel records in her autobiography, she became increasingly attracted to this 'broad-shouldered amiable journalist of twenty-five who looked thirty-five (his fair hair already thinning above the temples) bursting with ideas like a coruscating catherine wheel and impatient of the follow-through'.[14] They were married on 3 May 1935 at Holborn Register Office. Their only child, Leonora, was born on 5 November 1936. This was Box's second marriage. The first had been in 1929 to Katherine Knight, a very beautiful young actress who had appeared in West End shows and who was desperate to escape from 'an unbearably unhappy home life'.[15] The marriage was a disaster: 'Next morning we sat up and looked at one another and realised we were strangers ... mentally we had not an idea in common'.[16] The pair went their separate ways before divorcing in 1933.

In the early 1930s, Box's collaboration with Muriel took the form of a steady production of one-act plays for all-women casts. Box regarded this strategy as 'one of my brightest and most rewarding ideas. I had observed that up and down the country regiments of women, organized in Women's Institutes, Townswomen's Guilds and similar groups, were constantly looking for plays which needed as few men as possible in the cast' (p. 149).[17] They clearly fulfilled a need: several become staples of amateur productions up and down the country and Box was able to have six plays published as *Ladies Only* in 1934, a lively mixture of styles and genres from the high-flown sententiousness of *Peace in Our Time*, another 'play of conscience', to the broad burlesque of *Amazons on Broadway*, about an all-female gang. As in Box's single-author plays, casts were kept small and sets minimal. *Ladies Only* sold well and was followed by *Petticoat Plays* (1935), containing a further six original one-act plays with the same shrewd mixture of genres.

The third strand to Box's writing career was more nakedly commercial. He had written numerous revues and lyrics for radio performance and, at the suggestion of Hugh Quekett, the owner of *Play Pictorial*, branched out into operetta. Quekett knew that amateur societies were fed up with producing Gilbert and Sullivan and other standard material and wanted new musical comedies (p. 127). Box's inspired idea was to adapt well-known and much-loved classics because they offered exactly what amateur societies wanted: the freshness of something apparently new combined with a scenario and songs the majority of which were deeply familiar to both cast and audience. In the first instance he adapted *Goodnight Vienna*, a radio operetta written by Eric Maschwitz (as Holt Marvell) with a score by George Posford, which had been made into a highly successful film by Herbert Wilcox in 1932. Having secured the performance rights from Maschwitz and Wilcox, Box was able to persuade Posford to write some extra numbers, because the two had worked together on some of Box's revues, while the experienced Harold Purcell wrote the lyrics.

Goodnight Vienna! (exclamation mark added) received its world premiere at the Scala Theatre in April 1936 and its huge success led to an adaptation of *Blossom Time*, the 1934 film about the life of Schubert (itself based on the 1922 operetta *Lilac Time*); *Glamorous Night*, a Ruritanian romance with melodious songs based on Ivor Novello's 1935 Drury Lane hit; and *Castles in Spain*, packed with over thirty musical numbers and set in Parabola, a fictitious South American republic. In what was to become the familiar pattern of his career, Box left the day-to-day running of *Castles in Spain* to others, while he devoted his energies to producing three similar shows: *The Fleet's in Port Again*, a naval extravaganza; *The Lady in Red*, another South American show; and *Night on the Nile*, an operetta based on *Antony and Cleopatra*, all of which used numbers familiar from recent shows at the London Palladium and elsewhere. Box sank all his savings into this triple venture, but just as the shows were ready to be staged, in September 1939, the outbreak of the Second World War ended all forms of amateur theatre for ten years.

Entering the film industry

Although he enjoyed writing for the theatre in various forms, and experienced considerable success, Box had long cherished ambitions to become part of the 'glamorous world of films', writing 'more screenplays on spec than I care to remember' (p. 23). There was far more money to be made in the film industry, always an important consideration for Box, though it is likely that, at this stage, his thoughts did not extend beyond writing. His only pre-war success in feature films came in 1935 when he and Muriel co-wrote the original screenplay for *Alibi Inn*, a 53-minute crime thriller produced and directed by Walter Tennyson for MGM-British. The screenplay does not exist, nor is the film available for viewing, but plot summaries make it sound an entirely typical 'quota quickie'.

However, if Box made little impact in feature films, he did have a significant pre-war career in British cinema through his work at Publicity Films, which he joined in 1934. Box's entrée to the company came through Muriel, who introduced him to Ralph Smart, with whom she had worked at British Instructional Films, a company which specialised in scientific, educational and industrial films, but which ceased production in 1933 when it was taken over by British International Pictures. Smart was looking for someone to replace him in Publicity's script department so that he could direct films (p. 23). Publicity Films had been established in 1920, as a subsidiary of the London Press Exchange, to produce advertising shorts, working from a small studio at Merton Park. It developed rapidly in the 1930s to become the largest producer in the field.[18] This expansion was created by the growth of corporatism; large firms invested heavily in advertising both their products and themselves in order to boost sales and to promote a modern, socially progressive image.[19] By the late 1930s, major firms were allocating over £10,000 a year to the production and exhibition of increasingly sophisticated advertising films.[20]

Box wrote a wide range of advertising shorts for Publicity that 'were shown in cinemas just before the newsreel and were supposed to consist of four minutes or so of entertainment, followed by thirty seconds of hard sell for the sponsor's product' (p. 24). But he also rapidly established himself as an astute salesman who became increasingly involved in soliciting commissions. He was successful in gaining several valuable accounts for the company, including Ford Motors.[21] In 1937, *Advertiser's Weekly* included a portrait of Box, describing him as the man who 'will make you a film as good as Grierson. He is studio chief, quiet, rubicund, competent. His ample, nerveless frame is surely ideal for the distracting life of a film studio. Waves of trouble must break upon him as they do upon Alfred Hitchcock without effect of any kind.'[22]

Box attempted to elevate his status, and establish himself as an authority in what was a rapidly expanding business, through the publication of *Film Publicity: A Handbook on the Production and Distribution of Propaganda Films* in 1937, a lucid and informative analysis which soon became the standard book in its field. Box instructively divides propaganda films into various categories, but the main value of *Film Publicity* is its detailed account of the preparation, distribution and exhibition of these films, including detailed information about the calculations the 'publicist' must make in order to decide on the budget to be allocated.[23]

Box's own screenplays display a keen awareness of form and function. *Sweet Success* (1937), an instructional film written for Cadbury's and designed to be road shown to groups of shopkeepers up and down the country, addresses its specialist audience through a straightforward scenario in which an experienced salesman guides a new recruit in the most effective way to run a confectionery shop, giving detailed advice about such matters as the importance of window displays and how to handle the goods without damage. *The Window Dresser's Dream*, made to advertise Co-operative Wholesale clothes for women and aimed at a general audience, deploys Box's skills in revue writing, helped by Posford's musical score, to create a miniature operetta in which various window displays come to life. Unfortunately, the film appears not to have been released, but it created a good relationship between Box and the CWS that was to have important repercussions.

Box's most prestigious commission was *The World Rolls On* (1938), a public-relations film for Dunlop Tyres, costing £6,000, which shows a progressive corporation meeting the needs of a complex, modern society through a historical account of changing transportation.[24] The scenario narrates, in a droll, amusing fashion, the story of the wheel from the first crude wooden roller placed under a heavy stone to the pneumatic tyre invented by Frank Dunlop. It culminates in the firm's slogan, 'Where there's a wheel there's a Dunlop!', and in an uplifting celebration of its success: 'From the vast aeroplane to the child's scooter there's a Dunlop tyre for each of them, defying the roads and the miles as the world rolls on.'

Although Box was highly successful at Publicity, like everyone else at the company he lost his job when the Second World War broke out and commercial firms cancelled their contracts. This, together with the cancellation of his operettas and the cessation of his income from the performance rights of his plays, meant that 'a pretty certain income of £1,000–£1,800 per annum from royalties suddenly disappeared completely'.[25] Temporary respite from this parlous financial situation came from selling the copyright on all his and Muriel's plays to Samuel French for £1,000 and, another ingenious Box stratagem, from *The Black-Out Book*, published under the pseudonym of Evelyn August. This was a miscellany written to amuse people after the blackout, containing games, *pensées*, puzzles, jokes and literary snippets, designed to 'provide the average family with amusement and entertainment for one hundred and one black-out nights'.[26] It was a joint publication with Muriel, but based largely on material that Box had used in his articles for the *Christian Herald*. Working with characteristic speed, to catch the moment, the Boxes were rewarded when *The Black-Out Book* sold out within a few months of publication in November 1939.

The writer-producer

These early years formed Box's character, its most notable traits being an enormous capacity for hard work and a restless desire to succeed, spurred by the determination never to experience poverty again. Box's talents were varied: he was at once a creative writer with a strong social conscience, a quick-thinking journalist able to turn his hand to whatever came his way, an astute self-publicist, a gifted salesman able to woo clients, and someone with an acute sense of how the film industry (or at least one branch of it) worked as a business and with a keen understanding of the qualities that a producer required. In *Film Publicity* he noted that because 'a large number of unconventional, temperamental and often brilliant people are herded together in one room all day and every day for weeks on end, normal disciplinary methods are useless', therefore success is achieved through a producer's tact and charm as well as technical skill.[27] In addition to gaining extensive experience, Box had made a wide network of contacts that was to prove invaluable in what lay ahead.

Notes

1 Box, *The Lion That Lost Its Way*, p. 138. Subsequent references to Box's autobiography are cited in the text.
2 Betty Box, *Lifting the Lid*, p. 1.
3 Author's interview with William Gell, 28–29 July 2003.
4 *Ibid.*

5 Betty Box, *Lifting the Lid*, p. 17.
6 See Elspeth Grant, 'The Woman Behind the People's National Theatre', *Play Pictorial*, 66:397 (1935), 14.
7 Sydney Box, 'Preface', *One-Act Play Parade* (London: Allen & Unwin, 1935), pp. 9–10.
8 For full details see Box, *The Lion That Lost Its Way*, chapter 12, pp. 123–6.
9 Peter Billingham, *Theatres of Conscience 1939–53* (London: Routledge, 2002), p. 7.
10 In 1961 Box supported the efforts of Unity Theatre, then in dire financial straits, to acquire the freehold of its premises. Asked to be one of the ten guarantors whom the bank required to grant an overdraft, Box agreed to stand the sum of all ten guarantees himself; see Colin Chambers, *The Story of Unity Theatre* (London: Lawrence and Wishart, 1989), p. 369.
11 Box, 'Preface', *One-Act Play Parade*, p. 9.
12 See Fay Compton, 'Preface: The Theatre of Today and Tomorrow', in Muriel and Sydney Box, *Petticoat Plays* (London: Harrap, 1935), pp. v–vi.
13 See Edward Lewis, 'The Lure of the Footlights', *Yorkshire Evening News*, 2 September 1937.
14 Muriel Box, *Odd Woman Out*, p. 138.
15 Betty Box, *Lifting the Lid*, pp. 21–2; Box, *The Lion That Lost Its Way*, p. 148.
16 Letter from Sydney Box to Muriel Baker, n.d., quoted in Muriel Box, *Odd Woman Out*, p. 136.
17 In 'A Letter to a Young Actress', published as a foreword to Muriel and Sydney Box, *Ladies Only* (London: Harrap, 1934), Flora Robson estimates that 'women actively interested in drama in this country outnumber men by something like ten to one' (p. 8).
18 Rachel Low, *Film Making in 1930s Britain* (London: Allen & Unwin, 1985), p. 132.
19 Ian Aitken, *Film and Reform: John Grierson and the Documentary Film Movement* (London: Routledge, 1990), pp. 152–6.
20 See 'The Use of Poster, Cinema and Radio', *Newspaper World*, 18 July 1938, 9.
21 Muriel Box, *Odd Woman Out*, p. 142.
22 *Advertiser's Weekly*, 16 September 1937, 5.
23 Sydney Box, *Film Publicity: A Handbook on the Production and Distribution of Propaganda Films* (London: Lovat Dickson, 1937), p. 30.
24 The £6,000 was made up of £1,125 for production costs and £4,875 to book *The World Rolls On* into 404 'Grade A' cinemas; *ibid*, pp. 30–1.
25 The Muriel and Sydney Box Collection (hereafter MSBC), BFI Special Collections, boxes 7–10, Muriel and Sydney Box diaries, 1943–65 (hereafter Diaries), 13 April 1943.
26 Evelyn August, 'Preface', *The Black-Out Book* (London: Harrap, 1939), no page number.
27 Box, *Film Publicity*, pp. 114–15.

The documentarist: Verity Films

3

At the beginning of the Second World War, an impecunious Box had been reduced, as he put it himself, to 'hack journalism of the worst type for nine months and some ineffective story writing for Don Taylor at Strand Films, who wanted to make features without knowing how'.[1] Box's solution to his financial and creative problems was a typically bold move: to strike out on his own. He formed Verity Films in March 1940, in partnership with Jay Gardner Lewis, in order to make short propaganda films for the government and other agencies. Lewis had worked as an assistant director and production manager at Gaumont-British, before joining Strand Films in 1938 as a scenarist, becoming an editor then director. Lewis had worked with Muriel at Gaumont-British and she helped engineer the alliance.[2] Both men were dissatisfied with Strand's organisation and competence. Lewis brought to the partnership technical know-how and experience, while Box had extensive knowledge of how the non-fiction film industry worked, proven skills in soliciting commissions and writing scenarios, and numerous business connections.

A competitive marketplace

Box's decision to launch a new company was based on a shrewd assessment of a radically changed market, in which the Ministry of Information – which, after very uncertain beginnings and obvious muddle and confusion, had gradually established a reasonably effective structure and organisation – looked to outside companies to meet its voracious demand for propaganda shorts, some 1,887 of which were produced during the course of the war.[3] These consisted of two-minute trailers and 'flashes' for specific publicity campaigns or urgent messages, and an extensive programme of five-minute shorts begun in July 1940. Such shorts were replaced at the end of 1942 by longer, fifteen-minute films which allowed an extended treatment of more complex subjects. The MoI also commissioned shorts for non-theatrical distribution, aimed at those who would have found going to the cinema impossible, such as factory workers on shifts or those in remote towns and villages, or targeted at specific groups, such as civil defence workers, who might need detailed instructional films.[4] In addition, a large number of propaganda films were sponsored by the services. Three-quarters of the 150 films commissioned each year by the Army Kinematograph Service were usually made by outside contractors.[5] Finally, a number of shorts were commissioned by large organisations such as the CWS, with which Box already had established connections. Verity had frequent commissions to make precise film records of factory processes for firms such as Ford and Dunlop in case their works were completely destroyed by bombing.[6]

There was a high demand for propaganda films, but Verity had to vie with numerous other small independent documentary production companies in what was a highly competitive marketplace. These included Strand Films, Realist Films, Technique Film Productions and Greenpark Productions, all of which were established firms, as well as the government run Crown Film Unit, which had first pick of personnel, equipment and film stock and was usually given the longer, more prestigious and generously funded commissions.[7] In such a crowded marketplace, Box had to fight hard to get Verity established as a company that the MoI and the services were prepared to do business with. Companies had to submit a detailed synopsis to the Films Division in order to get the MoI's approval and, although Box had extensive contacts within the non-fiction film industry, he was not known to Jack Beddington, who had succeeded Kenneth Clark as Head of the Films Division. Box wrote to Beddington in August 1940 trying to sell Verity as a company that could make short propaganda films cheaply and quickly, in under four weeks if necessary. Verity had 'a great deal of experience of the straightforward instructional film' Box wrote, 'we can produce it at a figure considerably below your standard rate of £1 per foot'.[8] Box had earlier written to Beddington's script adviser, John Betjeman, to express his eagerness for Verity to become one of the MoI's five-minute-film programmers, intimating that he was anxious to discuss a number of ideas he had worked out.[9]

Betjeman asked Box to produce examples of the company's work, and Box was forced to fall back on three advertising shorts made by Publicity for the Lever group. Betjeman reported back to Beddington that, while he was impressed by their ingenuity and humour, they lacked visual polish: 'the sets & dissolves & camerawork are mediocre'.[10] Thus although a Ministry of Food official, A. D. Peters, had judged Box's idea for a five-minute film starring Jack Warner called 'A Rill Mill' (one of Warner's wartime catch-phrases, the Cockney pronunciation of a 'real meal') suitable for its campaign to encourage good, non-wasteful food preparation habits, neither Beddington nor Betjeman were persuaded that the project should go ahead. Betjeman was instructed to write to Box declining his proposal.[11]

The rejection of 'A Rill Mill' demonstrates the difficulties Verity was under as a new and unproven company and was a blow to Box's hopes of making propaganda films with box-office potential. However, he had much more initial success with straightforwardly instructional films, including the series that effectively launched Verity as a viable company, 'Cookery Hints'. This was a series of five six-minute films – *Oatmeal Porridge, Potatoes, Casserole Cooking, Steaming* and *Herrings* – for non-theatrical distribution, directed by Lewis for the Ministry of Food in December 1940. The *Documentary News Letter* (*DNL*) enthused: 'it is good to welcome a new company which can immediately take its place in technical competence alongside other and older-established units'.[12] *Kinematograph Weekly*'s reviewer was also impressed: 'Each one in a simple, yet forceful, manner delivers its message and they are certain to have the desired effect on the housewives of Britain ... The commentary ... is concise without being condescending.'[13]

Despite this success, Verity had to struggle to survive, working under enormous pressure on a hand-to-mouth basis, hiring, borrowing or buying second-hand equipment and usually assembling a crew only when Box gained a commission. Verity had severe difficulties obtaining material from the Board of Trade and also suffered from the dilatory system by which ministries made payments. These were always in arrears because they were made on receipt of trade invoices long after the film had been completed. This arrangement ignored the need of small companies to pay wages, hire equipment and pay interest on any overdraft.[14] And, like any other organisation, Verity was subject to the hazards of war. Box arrived at the company's offices on the Charing Cross Road one morning in 1940 to find that they had been severely damaged by a bomb. He wrote to Muriel, evacuated with their daughter to Scotland: 'The window behind my desk was blown out, glass all over the floor, desk and chair, and at least an inch of dust and rubble everywhere. We just grabbed cheque book, portable typewriter, stationery, and about £200 worth of camera gear, which had been left there and was happily untouched and then slammed the door behind and left it.'[15]

The pressures told and, at the end of its first year in production, Box had a bitter row with Lewis over the company's finances, which ended with Lewis's departure, leaving £2,000 of debts.[16] Box turned to his former employers, Publicity, now part of the Sound Services Group, to pay off the debt, and the company was refloated as Verity Films in 1941. From this point, under Box's sole direction, Verity went from strength to strength. By the end of 1942 it had a turnover of £75,000 and the £2,000 debt had been turned into £2,000 profit even after 'paying handsome salaries to me and others, of £5,000'.[17] In January 1943, *Kinematograph Weekly* referred to Verity as 'by far the largest documentary film organisation in Great Britain'.[18] By 1944, Verity maintained eight to ten units in the field and could advertise itself in the trade press as 'The largest short film production organisation in Europe, incorporating the Greenpark Unit, the Technique Unit and Donald Taylor's new Gryphon Unit'. In August 1944 the company became part of the Film Producers' Guild, an umbrella organisation for different companies operating from Guild House in Upper St Martin's Lane.[19]

Verity's success irked Sidney Bernstein, controller of the Granada chain of cinemas and one of Beddington's advisers, who wanted Box to hand over four units for his use. Box was able to refuse, since all his units were fully occupied, but he had to ensure that they remained so.[20] Box also benefited from Establishment prejudice. He wrote to Muriel that the Air Ministry was willing to work with him because it was 'apparently looking for an extra company to add to their lists and they won't do business with Jews'.[21] Work for the Air Ministry resulted in six or seven film commissions per year. Overall, Verity produced well over 100 films during the war.[22] Verity used Merton Park Studios in South London, leased by Sound Services, but conditions were cramped and difficult with inadequate soundproofing. Occasionally Box rented the superior facilities at Riverside Studios in Hammersmith.

Verity Films: organisation and personnel

Box's ability to develop such a successful company from nothing is a tremendous testimony to his energy, organisational ability and skill in coordinating the efforts of a diverse range of people. Box worked as a scenarist or co-scenarist on a number of Verity films (frequently acting as a script adviser and 'doctor') and as producer or co-producer on many others, but his principal function was to conceive and initiate projects, then to solicit commissions from various agencies. In his autobiography, William MacQuitty, who joined Verity as an associate producer in 1943, gives a vivid picture of Box encamped in the Two Brewers at Seven Dials, (the local pub) where he 'worked out ideas for films on the backs of envelopes with a stubby pencil and passed them to his accountant, Alfie Burlinson, to check costings'.[23] It is a powerful image, encapsulating wartime austerity (the 'stubby pencil'), the need to think rapidly, with Box's quicksilver mind at full stretch, and the importance of translating those ideas into workable and cost-effective projects, all in an atmosphere of social camaraderie. Although Verity worked to specific commissions, like other companies, it enjoyed a degree of creative freedom, with the opportunity to generate ideas and formulate projects as well as suggest how a subject might be treated.[24] Producers had considerable freedom in creating films with a non-theatrical distribution, which were not subjected to the same kind of scrutiny as those released in cinemas.

After Lewis's departure, James Carr – who had previously worked as a freelance writer, director and cameraman on numerous documentaries – was placed in charge of production, where he remained until his departure in December 1942 to found World Wide Films with Box's support. His duties were then taken over by Box's sister Betty, who characterised her role as that of Girl Friday, having to provide the documentary units with transport, accommodation, cameras, film, sound equipment and studio space, as well as keeping an eye on costs in conjunction with the chief accountant, A. E. 'Alfie' Burlinson. It was also her unenviable task to try to obtain rationed materials from the Board of Trade.[25] Returning to London, Muriel Box joined Verity as a scriptwriter and director (under her maiden name), one of eighteen writers and directors working for the company by January 1943. These also included Maxwell Munden, an experienced screenwriter (a former staff scenarist at Publicity) who, as principal scenarist, scripted and directed a wide variety of Verity's films; Alfred Travers, who had experience in feature films as an editor and screenwriter; Henry Cass, an accomplished theatre producer; and Daniel Birt, who had been in the industry since 1929 as a cameraman and editor. Birt's wife Louise worked for Verity as both screenwriter and director. Ray Elton (who also directed) was one of the main cinematographers, along with the experienced Reginald Wyer, Bernard Browne, Erwin Hillier, and Eric Cross who had worked at Fox-British. The supervising editor was Peter Tanner, who had worked for Ealing and Fox-British.

With the exception of Browne, who died when his ship was torpedoed making a documentary about a Russian convoy, all these talented film-makers went on to have post-war careers in the feature-film industry. They were drawn to Verity because of Box's ability to secure a steady stream of commissions, which allowed him to offer long-term contracts; this not only ensured a regular income but exemption from military service. It was also an attractive company for new recruits to the industry, and Box, in what was to become his lifelong habit, did his best to encourage and nurture fresh talent. This included Ken Annakin, who was sent to Verity by Beddington because: 'They're doing some good stuff for us and are very short-handed'.[26] Annakin started in a lowly position, as camera assistant to Reginald Wyer, but gradually became one of the company's most important writer-directors. Another was Julian Wintle, who joined the company later in the war as an editor before going on to direct several films.

Verity's films

Verity's output of over 100 films was an achievement in itself, and the range of subjects covered was impressive. The majority were straightforward instructional films, the field in which Verity had made its reputation with 'Cookery Hints'. This reputation was sustained by such films as *A Way to Plough* (1942), a fifteen-minute instructional short made for the Ministry of Agriculture, which shows a group of land girls being taught the correct method of ploughing a field to save land, fuel and time. It was singled out for praise from the *DNL* whose reviewer thought the 'treatment is extremely simple and lucid ... as an aid to training, excellent. On subjects such as these a film is worth far more than its weight in text-books.'[27] The director/cinematographer, Clifford Hornby, had been an experienced technician before the war, and the film was co-produced by Box and Carr with assistance from Edgar Anstey. Verity also produced detailed instructional films for particular audiences; for example, *Decontamination of Streets* (1943), also produced by Box and Carr and directed by Louise Birt, was made for the Ministry of Home Security and the Home Office. It showed how to make an area safe from contamination by liquid-gas bombs and was screened to civil defence workers, who were expected to sit through the full twenty minutes several times in order to absorb all the precise details.

Verity's output included instructional films for private companies – including two, *Fuel and the Tractor* and *Harness Your Horsepower*, for Ford in 1944, about the correct care and maintenance of tractors – and for the services. The latter included *HM Minelayer* (1941), produced for the Admiralty about how to lay mines, and *The Soldier's Food* (1941), a 63-minute film commissioned by the army, produced by Box and directed by Lewis, which was regarded as a first-class film about the education of chefs and the correct methods of storing and preparing food. It was enlivened by a strong cast, with Ralph Richardson as an avuncular, pipe-smoking commanding officer, Hubert Gregg as the anxious-to-please Messing Officer, and Ronald Shiner and Hay Petrie as disgruntled privates.

By 1944, Verity had become more adept in the imaginative treatment of apparently dull subjects. One of the best examples was *You Too Can Catch Malaria* made for the army and produced by Box. Private Bill Smith (Jimmy Hanley) has a profound contempt for the interfering regulations about health – 'I'm a soldier not a hot-house rose' – and ignores malaria precautions. He falls ill with the disease just before an important action and, in a feverish hallucination, imagines being put on trial, appearing as his own judge sentencing himself to the 'full torments' of malaria. This sequence is shot by Reginald Wyer in a *noir* visual style, which vividly dramatises Smith's feelings of guilt and paranoia. After recovery and recuperative training, he is shown lecturing new arrivals on the dangers of the disease.

The company contributed to a number of important government campaigns, including the call to working women to retrain. *Jane Brown Changes Her Job* (1941), a nine-minute film for the Ministry of Labour directed by Harold Cooper, shows a middle-class secretary, Jane Brown (Anne Firth), responding to a newspaper appeal to produce more aeroplanes. She goes to a government training centre to learn both the theoretical and practical skills needed to produce aircraft components. In the factory to which she is taken after training, women are shown working alongside men as mechanics, electricians and riveters. Although the factory is unsparingly depicted as a harsh, noisy and uncomfortable environment, Jane's line is a no-nonsense pragmatism – 'It's hard work standing on your feet all day or crouching in position, but you soon get used to it' – inspired by the knowledge that her work is 'of national importance'. In the final sequence a finished Spitfire is towed out of its hangar; Jane is filled with pride but also the sense that 'many more women are needed'. James Chapman argues that, in being addressed to young, single, middle-class women, *Jane Brown* targets a group that would not normally consider a blue-collar occupation rather than the more fashionable services like the ATS. However, as he notes, it sidesteps the contentious issue of conscription (Jane volunteers for factory work), which was one of the more difficult issues that the government faced after legislation enabling the conscription of female civilians into war jobs had been introduced in December 1941.[28]

We Serve (1942), a recruiting film for the ATS directed by Carol Reed, marked Box's increased stature in that he could secure Reed's services;

the director's reputation also persuaded a clutch of distinguished actresses – Joyce Carey, Penelope Dudley-Ward, Celia Johnson, Ann Todd and Googie Withers – to appear for only £5 a day.[29] *We Serve* broaches the issue of the nature of femininity in wartime, but the emphasis falls on the responsibilities of the middle-class. In one of the central incidents, the rather uptight Siddeley (Todd) fails to show the compassion and patience expected of an officer, having sent one of her subordinates out on duty in a storm despite her complaints that she feels sick. After she contracts pneumonia, the MO (Carey) admonishes Siddeley for her lack of imagination, opining that 'high ideals of industry and efficiency are not enough without humanity and understanding'.

Verity made several films that contributed to one of the longest-running MoI campaigns, against 'careless talk', which had been initiated as early as November 1939 with the famous Fougasse posters, including 'Keep Mum She's Not So Dumb'.[30] Its first contribution to this campaign, *Telefootlers* (1941), a five-minute short directed by John Paddy Carstairs in which an ordinary greengrocer is shown to be a fifth columnist who gathers information from careless telephone conversations, was rather ham-fisted. But later efforts, such as *Other Men's Lives* (1944), directed by Henry Cass and intended for munitions workers, were more assured. The most accomplished was *Jigsaw* (May 1943), a naval instructional film produced for the Admiralty, also directed by Cass, which, with a running time of thirty-two minutes, was the type of reconstructed narrative-documentary in which the Crown Film Unit specialised and was therefore a prestigious project for Verity. Clearly modelled on the highly successful *In Which We Serve* (1942), *Jigsaw* begins with a dramatic montage of action shots of the sinking of the cruiser *HMS Hibernia* and proceeds through flashbacks which span the lives of Captain Carlin (Harold Warrender), an older crewman, Bert, and the principal focus, Leading Seaman Dick Erskine (Jimmy Hanley), who is married to Ann (Dinah Sheridan), a WREN. The film's central motif is the Nazis' slow but inexorable piecing together of apparently inconsequential items of information, such as the captain's chauffeur talking about a 'rush job' or a remark to the laundress that the officers' uniforms need to be returned quickly, in order to create a complete picture of the exact time and place of *Hibernia*'s movements and the convoy she is protecting. When the jigsaw is completed, twelve U-boats lie in wait for the convoy and the film returns to *Hibernia*'s sinking and Dick's death, falling off a life-raft in thick fog. As she hears the news of his death, Ann denounces 'Those talkers. Those slack minds and silly blabbering mouths. Those men of ours were drowned in a sea of idle, stupid talk.'

Verity also made a substantial contribution to the promotion of the ideology of the 'people's war', a shift towards the celebration of ordinary men and women that had profound social and cultural repercussions. Several films detail the work of groups and institutions, including *Mobile Canteen* (1941), directed by Jay Lewis for the Empire Tea Bureau and the MoI, which showed YMCA mobile canteens, staffed by women volunteers, being driven from street to street to bring refreshments to ARP workers, firefighters and shelterers. Unusually, and to good effect, no commentary is used, allowing the images and snatches of dialogue to provide a record of tireless service in the midst of devastation. The *DNL* enthused: 'While politicians declaim, it is films like these that help bring people together and show that an ounce of service is worth a ton of speeches'.[31] Equally effective was Louise Birt's *WVS* (1942), produced for the MoI, which ran for twenty-two minutes and boasted music by William Alwyn played by the London Symphony Orchestra. It has some vivid actuality photography of many different locations, helping to emphasise the extraordinary variety of tasks that the Women's Voluntary Service encompasses: getting salvage, sorting and mending clothes, fixing blackout material, looking after evacuee children, sheltering the homeless or displaced servicemen, tending the sick and wounded. The deft editing from scene to scene gives vivid force to these 'quiet, unspectacular women doing unspectacular jobs, maids of all work in green uniforms'.

A number of Verity's other 'people's war' films depicted individual workers. *Dai Jones* (1941), a five-minute short for the MoI directed by Daniel Birt, describes how a South Wales miner, the victim of a world recession that has necessitated his moving to the city, rescues a trapped boy in a blitzed house through his expert tunnelling skills. He realises his new vocation, joins an air raid rescue squad and is 'now digging for souls'. The *DNL* thought *Dai Jones* broke new ground in telling a particular rather than a generalised story, one that was 'allowed to stand on its own feet', and therefore treated its audiences with respect, asking them to make relevant connections and inferences rather than having this done for them through an overemphatic commentary.[32] The *New Statesman and Nation* thought: 'Every detail is tensely and simply shown with an emotion which never topples over.'[33]

Even more accomplished was another five-minute MoI short, *Shunter Black's Night Off* (1941), produced by Box and Carr and directed by Munden, which also tries to create an authentic dramatic space for the ordinary worker, and which was based on a true story. Rather than an anonymous voice-over, railwayman Joe Black, played by a non-professional actor, narrates his own story, written by Munden and spoken by

John Slater. Black's mundane job is as a 'wagon-chaser' in the marshalling yard, running alongside trucks and putting the brake on so that when they reach the yard they do not smash too hard into the other trucks. On his night off, he cycles back to the yard when he notices that falling incendiaries have ignited some trucks next to an ammunition train. In a feat of skill, daring and imagination, he commandeers a locomotive, gets a signalman to clear its passage across a main line, and shunts the now blazing explosives wagon under a water tank, quenching the blaze just in time. The pipe-smoking, phlegmatic and unflappable Black possesses all the usual attributes of the middle-class hero, the dominant image of admirable masculinity at the time.[34] He cycles in to work the following day as usual, reflecting that 'a little thing like a Blitz doesn't hold up a marshalling yard for long'. *Shunter Black* has some accomplished night-time photography (by Bernard Browne), and, although the editing is slightly ragged in places, is a well-constructed, tense and exciting film, which, within its brief compass, conveys the key values of the 'people's war'.

This ideological construct, essentially emphasising endurance and 'seeing it through', modulated into a concern that there should be a better world after the war, a change of emphasis which became part of the MoI's policy once its new chief, Brendan Bracken, sensed that the public's mood was turning away from survival and the prosecution of hostilities towards social reform and reconstruction.[35] Here too, Verity made a significant contribution, reflecting Box's socialist idealism. *Country Town* (1945), directed by Julian Wintle, uses a newspaper editor (Philip Robinson) to narrate the story of a community that is moving towards a more co-operative, progressive and harmonious future in which its citizens are conscious of a purpose behind all their actions. *The Second Freedom* (1945), also directed by Wintle, celebrates the vision of the Beveridge Report (December 1942) through the story of Jack, nurtured by a caring state. An Infant Welfare Centre – 'available to all children, not just those who can afford it' – provides him with the orange juice, milk, cod liver oil and food concentrates full of vitamins he needs to grow, while his state school provides 'the best possible education for all'. In his first job, Jack is secure from the threat of sickness and loss of income through the benefits of National Insurance. Free to marry young, Jack takes his equally healthy and happy bride off to the planned environment of a suburban housing estate.

More ambitious was *Public Opinion* (1945), made for the Army Bureau of Current Affairs, which explores the individual's responsibility for helping to shape the future. It takes the form of an encounter between ordinary citizens at a post-war exhibition about communication.

A sceptical and non-committed Everyman (Jimmy Hanley, in his customary persona for Verity) derides a propaganda leaflet he picks up as an interference with his right to make up his own mind. He is gently schooled into the need for change by a better-informed visitor (Hubert Gregg), who takes on the role of narrator, explaining the power of the spoken and printed word and of the modern forms of communication, radio and film. He argues that progressive change has been achieved, not by governments, but through collective action by ordinary individuals, creating organisations such as the NSPCC, which complement the great British non-conformist tradition of radical thinking that produced reformers including Wilberforce, Fry and Shaftesbury, culminating in the Beveridge Report. Everyone must take his or her part in creating the new Britain, 'demand what you want, and damn well see to it that you make your opinions felt'. *Public Opinion* manages, through accomplished editing and lucid presentation, to encompass many aspects of a complex issue and reflects the groundswell of opinion that elected the Labour government of 1945, which Box supported.

The celebration of ordinary people and the drive for a better tomorrow was evident in the most prestigious and ambitious of Verity's films, *Men of Rochdale* (1944), which dramatised the foundation of the Co-operative Movement. It was the centrepiece of the Co-operative Wholesale Society's centenary festivities, which included large and small pageants up and down the country and a Joan Littlewood play, *Pioneers*, broadcast on the BBC.[36] Despite wartime restrictions, the CWS was determined to mark the event handsomely, and the relatively huge sum of £15,000 was allocated to the film, enabling a running time of thirty-eight minutes and an impressive score composed by John Greenwood and played by the London Symphony Orchestra.[37] Box secured this important project for Verity through his earlier work for CWS while at Publicity and the reputation which Verity had built up during the war.[38] *Men of Rochdale* recounts the establishment of the first co-operative store at Toad Lane, Rochdale in 1844, narrated through the words of George Jacob Holyoake, the great nineteenth-century historian of the movement. Although the Rochdale Society of Equitable Pioneers was imbued with Owenite ideals of creating a self-supporting community, what was new 'was the businesslike way in which the Rochdale men organised and ran their society. There was no credit. Book-keeping and cash control were closely supervised.'[39] This collective socialist entrepreneurialism mirrored Box's own ideology, but the screenplay was largely the work of Reg Groves, an experienced screenwriter who had moved to Verity from Strand in 1943.[40] Compton Bennett, who had worked on several Verity films as an editor, was given his first chance to direct, and he handles the actors and much of the action with aplomb. The most dramatic scene is the pivotal moment when the Treasurer, William Cooper (John Boxer), exhibiting all the *sang-froid* of a professional poker player, bluffs his way through the demands of an agitated crowd which has gathered at the shop because of rumours, orchestrated by local businessmen, that the society has over-extended itself and cannot pay its creditors.

Men of Rochdale culminates in a vivid montage of the contemporary Co-operative Movement, with its 1,200 societies, 200 factories and membership of 9,000,000. This modulates into Holyoake's interrogation of the shades of the original five pioneers, superimposed over a cloudy sky, asking if they are satisfied with the progress that has been made. Each expresses disappointment that more has not been achieved and exhorts the movement to continue its fight against the injustices of war and capitalism. To William Cooper's question whether 'poverty, crime and meanness' have been abolished, Holyoake responds: 'There are men still to be found. Men who seek the Co-operative way of life. Men who will finish the work you men of Rochdale started.' At this point there is a concluding montage of houses, factories and harvest-gathering while dawn breaks behind the clouds.

The *DNL* objected to the 'cathedral atmosphere' of the final scene being at odds with the rest of the film.[41] But *Men of Rochdale* is a highly stylised film, derived from Soviet models, and can accommodate this elevated rhetoric. The *DNL*'s carping was not shared by *Co-operative News*, which enthused about a film that:

> Ought to be seen by audiences of the type that rarely attend Co-operative gatherings. It should be seen by trade unionists, shop stewards, socialists, youth groups, service men and women. To them it would be a revelation of the true story which lies behind the local Co-operative Store and the possibilities which are open for the newer pioneers of the 20th Century.[42]

Box went on to produce *Song of the People* (1945) for the CWS, also scripted by Reg Groves, a musical pageant celebrating the achievements of British workers, culminating in lessons for future unity and world co-operation.

Verity's achievements

Although the qualities of many of Verity's wartime shorts are demonstrable through analysis, any propaganda film needs to be considered in terms of its effectiveness in persuading or informing its target audience. Apart from the well-documented example of *Men of Rochdale*, which was very popular and proved to be an important ambassador for the CWS, the success of Verity's propaganda films, or those of any other company, is very difficult to judge, as there was very little monitoring of their reception.[43] Some work was carried out by Mass-Observation, whose workers made detailed observation of audience responses in cinemas, and also recorded conversations as patrons left the cinema, supplemented by informal interviews.[44] In one of its preliminary reports, dated 24 July 1941, *Dai Jones* and *Mobile Canteen* were amongst a small group of shorts that were frequently praised.[45] The main report, released on 1 April 1942, argued that although a large majority liked the MoI shorts, which 'command an extensive goodwill', an appreciable minority were critical.[46] Mass-Observation concluded that the public was more appreciative of films, such as the two Verity films mentioned above, which informed and explained, rather than exhorted or relied on an emotional appeal; those which were most enjoyed showed ordinary people 'as part of the war effort in an interesting, informative, informal way'.[47]

It seems from Mass-Observation's findings that, on balance, the short film was an effective medium of propaganda and commanded a broad degree of public approval, a conclusion corroborated by both *Kinematograph Weekly* and *Sight and Sound*.[48] In his authoritative study, James Chapman concludes that these films filled a particular niche in the MoI's overall strategy, the need to put across 'more direct, immediate and urgent messages that were deemed necessary by the government', and thus met short-term objectives even if their overall effect is difficult to gauge.[49] Verity's films made a substantial contribution to this strategy and to the non-theatrical programme where the effects may have been more direct and positive. For Box himself, Verity ensured a comfortable livelihood and the chance to develop the reputation he had started to acquire at Publicity as not only a gifted scenarist but also an ambitious and capable entrepreneur, able to co-ordinate and inspire a range of creative personnel and to promote new talent.[50] Under Box's leadership, Verity was able to produce a remarkable volume of films throughout the war, and to espouse, where possible, a broadly socialist agenda that reflected Box's ideals.

Notes

1 Diaries, 13 April 1943.
2 Muriel Box, *Odd Woman Out*, p. 151.
3 Frances Thorpe and Nicholas Pronay, 'Preface', *British Official Films in the Second World War: A Descriptive Catalogue* (Oxford: Clio Press, 1980), p. ix.
4 For further details see The Arts Enquiry, *The Factual Film* (London: Political and Economic Planning/Oxford University Press, 1947).
5 James Chapman, *The British at War: Cinema, State and Propaganda, 1939–1945* (London: I. B. Tauris, 1998), p. 140.
6 Betty Box, *Lifting the Lid*, p. 29.
7 For details see Paul Swann, *The British Documentary Film Movement, 1926–1946* (Cambridge: Cambridge University Press, 1989), pp. 107–11.
8 Public Record Office, London (hereafter PRO), INF 1/207, Sydney Box, letter to Jack Beddington, 12 August 1940.
9 *Ibid.*, Sydney Box, letter to Betjeman, 7 August 1940.
10 *Ibid.*, Betjeman, note to Beddington, 10 August 1940.
11 *Ibid.*, Betjeman, letter to Box, 18 September 1940.
12 *DNL*, 1:12 (December 1940), 7.
13 *KW*, 26 December 1940, 9.
14 Muriel Box, *Odd Woman Out*, p. 157.
15 Box's letter to Muriel Box, quoted in *Odd Woman Out*, p. 154.
16 Diaries, 13 April 1943.
17 *Ibid.*
18 'Progress and Future of Verity Films', *KW*, 14 January 1943, 131.
19 See *KW*, 11 June 1945, 7.
20 Box, *The Lion That Lost Its Way*, pp. 26–7.
21 Box, undated letter, quoted in Muriel Box, *Odd Woman Out*, p. 155.
22 It is impossible to be exact about the total number of films produced by Verity, as records do not exist for all the films that were made. The filmography lists all those I have been able to verify.
23 MacQuitty, *A Life to Remember*, p. 280.
24 Helen Forman, 'The Non-Theatrical Distribution of Films by the Ministry of Information', in Nicholas Pronay and D. W. Spring (eds), *Propaganda, Politics and Film, 1918–45* (London: Macmillan, 1982), pp. 222–3.
25 Betty Box, *Lifting the Lid*, pp. 28–9.
26 Ken Annakin, *So You Wanna Be a Director?* (Sheffield: Tomahawk Press, 2001), p. 17.
27 *DNL*, 3:4 (April 1942), 54.
28 Chapman, *British at War*, p. 207.
29 Annakin, *So You Wanna Be a Director?*, pp. 18–19.
30 Marion Yass, *This Is Your War: Home Front Propaganda in the Second World War* (London: HMSO, 1983), p. 25.
31 *DNL*, 2:3 (March 1941), 7.
32 *DNL*, 2:4 (April 1941), 67.
33 Quoted in a Verity advertisement in *DNL*, 2:4 (April 1941), 66.
34 See Andrew Spicer, *Typical Men: The Representation of Masculinity in Popular British Cinema* (London: I. B. Tauris, 2001), pp. 8–16.
35 Yass, *This Is Your War*, pp. 57–60.
36 Sir William Richardson, *The CWS in War and Peace 1938–1976* (Manchester: The Co-operative Wholesale Society Limited, 1978), pp. 147–8.
37 Alan Burton, *The People's Cinema: Film and the Co-operative Movement* (London: National Film Theatre, 1994), pp. 30–1.

38 Alan Burton (ed.), *The British Co-operative Film Catalogue* (Trowbridge: Flicks Books, 1997), p. 61.
39 Richardson, *The CWS in War and Peace*, p. 37.
40 Box ordered a production meeting about the script when the film was running into difficulties and smoothed over the problems; see Diaries, 1 March 1944.
41 *DNL*, 5:5 (October 1944), 53.
42 Quoted in Burton, *People's Cinema*, p. 31.
43 Mass-Observation was critical of the MoI's 'ad hoc and largely aesthetic approach' to audience reception; see Len England's report, 'Fifteen Ministry of Information Shorts', in Jeffrey Richards and Dorothy Sheriden (eds), *Mass-Observation at the Movies* (London: Routledge & Kegan Paul, 1987), p. 426.
44 See Tom Harrisson, 'Films and the Home Front – The evaluation of their effectiveness by "Mass-Observation"', in Pronay and Spring (eds), *Propaganda, Politics and Film*, p. 236.
45 Mass-Observation, 'Preliminary Report on Opinion about Ministry of Information Shorts' FR 709, (July 1941), in Richards and Sheriden (eds), *Mass-Observation at the Movies*, pp. 442–3.
46 Mass-Observation. 'Report on Ministry of Information Shorts' (FR 1193, 1 April 1942), in Richards and Sheriden (eds), *Mass-Observation at the Movies*, pp. 445–58.
47 *Ibid.*, pp. 451–2.
48 *KW*, 3 October 1940, 4; *Sight and Sound*, 9:35 (Autumn 1940), 39.
49 Chapman, *British at War*, p. 113.
50 Box managed to persuade Two Cities to finance *Out of Chaos*, an important wartime information film exploring the work of war artists, written and directed by Jill Craigie, which had been turned down by the British Council and the Arts Council.

1 Working for Publicity Films: Sydney Box waits for the reaction of an unidentified client

2 Jimmy Hanley (seated) in *You Too Can Get Malaria*, Verity Films (1944)

3 Gordon Harker, Jill Evans and Betty Balfour in the 'dirty picture', *29 Acacia Avenue* (1944)

4 Francesca (Ann Todd) entering the bachelor domain of her guardian Nicholas (James Mason) in *The Seventh Veil* (1945)

5 The world premiere of *The Seventh Veil* at the Leicester Square Odeon in October 1945. Sydney Box with Ann Todd and co-producer John Sutro and his wife

6 J. Arthur Rank and Sydney Box discuss business at the Gainsborough children's party, 1948

7 Sydney Box in earnest conversation with Phyllis Calvert at the jubilee party to celebrate Box's twenty-fifth Gainsborough film, *The Bad Lord Byron* (1949). In the background is Clive Morton

8 Sydney Box in a more jovial mood with Margaret Lockwood in front of the cake at the jubilee party to celebrate Box's twenty-fifth Gainsborough film, *The Bad Lord Byron* (1949)

9 Jack Warner and Kathleen Harrison as Joe and Ethel Huggett in *Holiday Camp* (1947)

10 Hollywood, England: spectacular set design by Maurice Carter for *Christopher Columbus* (1949)

11 [*left*] A pensive and passive Lord Byron: Dennis Price poses on location for *The Bad Lord Byron* (1949)
12 [*right*] The writer whom Box most admired, W. Somerset Maugham, in the library of his home in the South of France, the Villa Mauresque, *c.* 1948

13 Jean Simmons serving Rank's producers. Left to right: Earl St John, Michael Balcon, Lord Archibald, Sydney Box, *c.* 1950

14 London Independent Producers: William MacQuitty and Sydney Box, *c.* 1951

15 Muriel and Sydney Box on set, possibly for *The Happy Family* (1952)

16 Lion hunt: Cartoon by Vicky (Victor Weisz) in the *Evening Standard*, 6 January 1964

17 Sydney Box in retirement with Sylvia Box beside their camper van, 1976

18 Sydney Box at home, c. 1965

'I had something they wanted to buy': the feature-film producer

4

It would have satisfied most people to create, from nothing, the largest producer of documentary films in Europe, but Box always had designs on breaking into the more glamorous and lucrative world of feature-film making. In January 1943 he announced that A. E. Burlinson had been promoted from chief accountant to joint managing director as 'part of a new production policy for my company which will eventually embrace both feature films and shorts. Mr. Burlinson's appointment will relieve me from preoccupation with the financial and organizational side of the business and leave me free to concentrate on production.'[1] In December 1944, Box resigned from Verity and Burlinson succeeded him as managing director.[2] Box was fully conscious that Burlinson, assisted by Betty Box, who had proved to be an extremely capable and efficient organiser, would continue to run the company as he has fashioned it.

Box sensed his opportunity had come to move into feature-film making because he had established himself as an efficient and capable documentary producer who could command the services of a number of talented personnel; as he put it succinctly in a diary entry at the time: 'I became known to feature film interests as a person who had the goods they wanted to buy.'[3] Characteristically, Box's motives for the switch were both financial and creative. He had always been attracted by the glamour of features and the possibility of making large sums of money, but they also offered far more possibilities for Box, both as a writer and as a socially conscious film-maker, to develop the ideas that had preoccupied him in his plays and to engage fully with topical issues, notably the psychological and emotional reverberations of the Second World War. As he stated at the time, his aim was to use Verity's technical staff to produce 'at the earliest possible moment' a number of feature films 'produced in a similar fashion to the French films of the nineteen-thirties ... that, without undue loss of entertainment value ...

will give expression to the new spirit which is abroad in Great Britain today, particularly with reference to post-war reconstruction'.[4] Box's analogy with French film production of the 1930s, was presumably referring to what Colin Crisp characterises as the 'producer-package system', in which the producer was the central decision maker in an 'intimate' mode of production where each film was an autonomous enterprise, in contrast to a system dominated by a few large vertically-integrated companies.[5] However, the film industry in Britain was rather different from the French model, and although Box was able to promote the 'new spirit' of renewal and reform in a number of Verity's documentaries, the feature-film industry proved to be far less tractable and the transition was difficult and fraught with compromises. These included a number of aborted attempts to make controversial 'adult' crime thrillers – including adaptations of Patrick Hamilton's *Rope*, Max Catto's *They Walk Alone* and Legh St John Clowes's *No Orchids for Miss Blandish* – all rejected at the scenario stage by the British Board of Film Censors.[6]

'I learned a hell of a lot': *On Approval*

The first person to approach Box to produce a feature film was the star actor Clive Brook, who contacted Box in October 1942 through the intermediary of their mutual agent, Christopher Mann.[7] Brook was looking for a producer for *On Approval*, an adaptation of Frederick Lonsdale's 1927 acerbic comedy of manners which had undergone a highly successful revival during the war. It offered Brook the possibility of escaping the shackles of playing stiff-upper-lipped patriots, and reminding the public of his skills as a light comedian.[8] Brook was very much the key creative force on this production, as star, co-screenwriter (with Terence Young) and co-producer. Box's role was to arrange the finance and to oversee the budget, for the modest fee of £2,000.[9] As a new and as yet untested producer, Box was kept under the closest scrutiny by the Rank front office once finance had been agreed, presented with daily costing sheets that itemised every expenditure.[10] In addition, he was Brook's whipping boy. When Brook decided to fire the director, Brian Desmond Hurst, and the cinematographer, Günther Krampf, after the first week of shooting, it was Box's unpleasant task to break the news to them. Brook's decision was based on a clash of temperament with Hurst and frustration at Krampf's meticulous and time-consuming lighting decisions, which inclined towards the abstract and expressionist – according to William MacQuitty, he took three days to light the first scene to be shot[11] – and which were both expensive and inappropriate for the brittle, sophisticated comedy of Lonsdale's play.

Although Box managed to commandeer Claude Friese-Greene from a neighbouring stage as the new cinematographer, he reluctantly decided to co-direct with Brook because Hurst had to be recompensed in full and there was no money to pay a new director. However, this arrangement only lasted a few days before Brook took over completely. At this point, Brook recalled in his autobiography, he felt free for the first time to implement all his own ideas, including the crucial decision to transpose 'the story to the gay nineties, when it would seem not only daring but also shocking' and therefore overcome the play's apparent datedness for cinema-goers.[12] However, it was Box who managed to persuade Cecil Beaton, then at a loose end, to design the costumes. These, together with Tom Morahan's handsome sets, contributed much to the overall polish and sophistication of the production.

But the Box-Brook partnership was at best an uneasy alliance: Box characterised his relationship with Brook as the clash of two strong personalities.[13] This came to a head when the production, which always remained behind schedule, had to be moved from Denham to the much smaller, far inferior but much cheaper facilities at Merton Park.[14] After an acrimonious altercation, Box left the production for its final week and removed his name from the film except as executive producer.[15] Initially this was of little consequence, because *On Approval* was kept on the shelf for almost a year as Rank's executives pronounced it 'worthless' and were uncertain how it should be promoted.[16] However, when it was finally released in March 1944, *On Approval* was warmly reviewed. One representative plaudit came from Elspeth Grant in the *Daily Sketch*, who found that although '[m]ost film versions of plays are marred by traces of their theatre origins. This delicious Edwardian period piece is not', and bemoaned the fact that 'it has taken the best British light comedy film 18 months to reach the screen'.[17] In fact, *On Approval*'s notices were so good that Box wrote in his diary: 'I'm almost beginning to wonder whether I was wise in giving up full production and direction credits to Clive!'[18]

Reviewers were responding to a consistently inventive adaptation and excellent performances from a highly talented cast. The witty prologue, devised and shot by Brook towards the end of the production, uses a droll commentary by Gaumont-British's newsreel narrator E. V. H. Emmett to transport the audience away from the battle images of 'another war film' to a vanished age, a performance of Lonsdale's play, inviting viewers 'to find out just why they were called the naughty nineties'. In calling attention to the play's apparent datedness, the adaptation emphasises the risqué modernity of its ideas: two couples deciding to spend a month together 'on approval' before committing themselves to marriage. Brook gives a bravura performance as the self-centred and often-boorish George, matched by Beatrice Lillie, in a rare film role, as George's inamorata, the shallow and mean-spirited Maria Wislak. Lillie conveys marvellously a world of menacing innuendo each time she sits down at the piano and starts the refrain: 'I'm just seventeen and I've never been ...' Roland Culver, retained from the stage revival, and Googie Withers play their good-natured foils, Richard and Helen, unselfishly. Although Brook was careful to retain a great deal of Lonsdale's crisp and incisive dialogue, if the pace of the action is about to slacken or become too wordy, he uses nimble montage sequences to compress time and create humorous juxtapositions, or fantasy sequences – shot like scenes from an early silent film with speeded-up action and histrionic gestures – to retain the necessary drollery and lightness of touch.

In retrospect, Box claimed that it had been his idea to transpose the setting of this comedy, but his letter to Brook, written after the production was concluded in March 1944, conceded:

> I learned a hell of a lot from working with you and the peculiar circumstances of the production enabled me to gain experience that I could not have got from a dozen run-of-the-mill pictures.
>
> I would also like you to know that I am quite honestly and sincerely satisfied with the credit position. The real controlling force throughout the picture was always yours and I freely admit that I would not have made it in anything like the same way if I'd been doing it on my own. The fact that your way has proved so completely successful makes me all the happier that the credits give credit where credit is due.[19]

Thus, if *On Approval* was Brook's creative triumph, it acted as a crash course in feature-film production for Box, which gave him the confidence to take the decision to become an independent producer later that year.

Contract producer: tribulations at Two Cities

However, before that decision was made Box spent an unhappy period as a contract producer for Two Cities. Box joined the company in May 1943, one of several producers hired by studio head Filippo Del Giudice in order to manage an ambitious production programme financed by Rank, largely on the basis of the success of *In Which We Serve*. Box was highly envious of a contract worth £2,000,000 a year, which also gave

Del Giudice complete creative freedom.[20] Although Del Giudice proclaimed that he now wished to concentrate on prestige pictures with the 'Rolls Royce stamp', he was shrewd enough to leaven such productions with the more modest topical comedies and patriotic thrillers with which Two Cities had started out in 1939. Box worked on three of these: *The Flemish Farm* (August 1943), *English without Tears* (August 1944) and *Don't Take It to Heart* (October 1944). *The Flemish Farm*, produced at the same time as *On Approval*, celebrated the courage and daring of the Belgians under Nazi occupation. It starred Clive Brook in one of his stiff-upper-lipped roles as Major Lessart, and Clifford Evans as Jean Duclos, the pilot who smuggles the flag of his squadron out of the country and over to Britain as a symbol of resistance and a free Belgium. *The Flemish Farm* was written and directed by Jeffrey Dell, as was *Don't Take It to Heart*, a mildly socialist satire about the English class system thrown into confusion by the war, starring Richard Greene. It was Del Giudice's policy to give writer-directors (his 'talents') creative freedom, but Box, who had been hired on the basis of his ability as an administrator and because he brought with him technical personnel from Verity, including cinematographer Eric Cross, found his role was closely circumscribed, limited to keeping the productions on time and within their modest budgets, again closer to that of a production manager than a creative producer.

He also played a subordinate and managerial role on the slightly more prestigious *English without Tears*, a 'sequel' to *French without Tears* (1939), Two Cities' outstanding pre-war success. The key creative decisions were taken by the writer Terence Rattigan and co-writer and senior producer Anatole de Grunwald, who had collaborated on the earlier production. However, *English without Tears* was a troubled production and the preferred combination of Rex Harrison as star and Anthony Asquith as director had to be replaced with Michael Wilding and Harold French respectively. French recalled that the film was a 'mishmash', and that the script was largely the work of de Grunwald and lacked Rattigan's polish.[21] It was at this point that Box was taken off *The Way Ahead* and moved to this production to help retrieve the situation. William Sassoon was also drafted in as another co-producer, but his was a junior role to gain experience.[22] Box thought the script needed attention but, although Del Giudice agreed that cuts were necessary, he was not prepared to back Box's contention that it was fundamentally flawed and should be replaced by a different story, *Close Quarters*, which the Boxes had written.[23] Clearly frustrated and unhappy at what became a lengthy production, Box twice threatened to resign but eventually saw the film through to completion.[24] *English without Tears* –

an affectionate satire on English eccentricities with accomplished performances by Wilding and Penelope Dudley-Ward as the romantic couple, ably supported by Roland Culver and Margaret Rutherford – was quite favourably reviewed on its release in August 1944. The *Daily Telegraph*, in particular, admired this 'outstanding comedy with faultless acting and direction', which moved 'naturally from one sparkling situation to another'.[25] However, the Boxes held the film in sour contempt: 'A pretty useless film except as a highly polished bromide to accompany back-stalls petting parties'.[26] Box tried to negotiate a five-film contract with Del Giudice that would give him much more creative freedom, working under the Verity label.[27] When this failed to materialise, he left Two Cities shortly after completing *Don't Take It to Heart*. Box understood that the only way to realise his ambitions was to become an independent producer: 'I wanted to have my own company and choose my own subjects and stand or fall by their success or failure at the box office.'[28]

In order to realise his ambitions, Box had discussions with other Two Cities producers – John Sutro and William Sistrom – about the possibility of collaboration. In partnership with William MacQuitty, he also engaged in talks with Charles McConnell, an Irish publicist and advertising expert, about launching a production company called Irish Film and trying to acquire studios in Dublin.[29] But it was Box's acquisition of a long lease of Riverside Studios, after protracted negotiations with its owner, the impresario-star Jack Buchanan, which facilitated the move into independent production. Box recalled: 'That lease of Riverside Studios turned out to be my most potent weapon. Studio space was at a premium and, while others were struggling for precious space, I had control of Riverside for roughly thirty-six weeks a year.'[30] Riverside was hired through Theatrecraft Holdings, a new company Box had formed to avoid the Board of Trade's veto on established companies securing any more space for feature production.[31] Riverside had two adequate sound stages with a total area of 12,675 feet, and was also conveniently located in West London, though it was rather more at risk from bombs than studios further out such as Denham or Pinewood.

The 'dirty picture': *29 Acacia Avenue*

As an independent producer trying to work 'on French lines', Box was able to entertain plans for an ambitious range of projects that reflected the interests and aspirations of Muriel and himself. A lengthy diary entry in February 1944 revealed details of his intentions, which encompassed original film treatments such as *Blessed Are the Dead*, about a bomber crew shot down over Germany, in which the souls of the men return to their families or relatives to resolve the problems of hope and despair and their relationship to death; the story of a slum evacuee going to a public school; and biographies of Shelley and Byron. He also had plans to adapt the work of others: J. B. Priestley's *Time and the Conways* and Elswyth Thane's 1933 biography of the young Elizabeth I, *A Tudor Wench* – both somewhat unconventional works. Longer-term projects, once the war ended, included a film about women in parliament and one about Elizabeth Blackwell, the first woman doctor, as well as a puppet film and a modern revue.[32]

However, as Box acknowledged, his independence was still highly circumscribed: 'I wanted to be my own master, insofar as anybody who needs to borrow hundreds of thousands of pounds ever can be.'[33] He had control of precious studio space at Riverside, but no guarantee of either production finance or distribution. Box's choice of his first film as an independent was therefore necessarily circumspect. Box bought the rights to Mabel and Denis Constanduros's *Acacia Avenue* in February 1944 for the relatively modest sum of £2,000. Their play had enjoyed a long and successful run at the Vaudeville Theatre in 1943–44, which indicated its box-office potential, and its witty satire of suburban mores would have appealed to Box's sensibility. The Boxes' adaptation, *29 Acacia Avenue*, retained Gordon Harker in the central part of Charles Robinson, the archetypal London suburban paterfamilias, a role that had been partly created for him.[34] Box also invited the play's director, Henry Cass, who had made several documentaries for Verity, to direct his first feature. In what became his usual practice, Box teamed Cass with an experienced editor, Compton Bennett, and cinematographer, Reginald Wyer, to help guide his efforts. Box managed to persuade Betty Balfour to take the role of Charles's wife, Clara, making a return to the screen after an absence of nearly ten years.[35] The popular Jimmy Hanley, a Verity regular, was cast as Robinson's son Peter, and the adaptation invented a role for Hanley's wife, Dinah Sheridan, as Peter's long-suffering girlfriend, Pepper.

However, despite these clear indications that the film had definite box-office appeal, Box could not obtain either production finance or a distribution deal. *Kinematograph Weekly* commented, 'people are always suspicious of the new boy'.[36] Box's achievements as a documentarist were no automatic guarantee of his ability to make commercially successful features. Box had to sink £10,000 of his own capital into the production to hire equipment and buy costumes and sets so that filming could begin in August 1944.[37] An unexpected setback occurred when Barclays Bank, with which Box had done business for several years, refused to loan the further £30,000 necessary to fully finance this very modestly budgeted production.[38] Without this money, the production was plunged into crisis. Harker, sensing he might be robbed of an important window for his talents, invested £2,000, while William MacQuitty, looking to gain experience in features, advanced £5,000. But it was Alfred Shipman, part owner of the Shipman and King cinema circuit, also looking to enter feature film production, who rescued *29 Acacia Avenue* by investing £20,000, on the understanding that his money would be recouped first.[39]

Although the production suffered no further setbacks and was completed by the end of October, Box had yet to find a distributor. In order to interest Rank, Box negotiated a sneak preview of *29 Acacia Avenue* at the Tooting Astoria, where the audience gave the film very high approval ratings on the lobby cards.[40] This persuaded Rank to consider the film for circuit release, a final decision to be taken after a further preview screening for the notoriously 'tough' audience at the 3,000 seater Edgware Road Odeon, where it was inserted in place of the second feature. Rank himself had agreed that if the reaction of this audience was favourable, it would be booked on the Odeon circuit.[41] However, despite its being received with continuous laughter and a 'hand' at the end, a rare occurrence, Rank's Methodist sensibilities were outraged at what he considered to be a highly immoral film. Summoned to a personal meeting, Rank told Box: 'It's a dirty picture and I'm not going to have my name associated with it.'[42]

Rank's reaction was an extreme response to the film's mildly risqué subject matter, which the BBFC had approved without fuss. Charles Robinson lives in dread that his neighbours, the more cosmopolitan Wilsons, look down on him. Clara is less in awe, as Mrs Wilson is 'the sort of woman who uses mats instead of a tablecloth', but in order to impress the Wilsons, the Robinsons decide to go on a Mediterranean cruise rather than returning to their habitual holiday choice of Bognor. After their departure, their daughter Joan (Jill Evans, a Box 'discovery' who had been in *Men of Rochdale*) invites her fiancé Michael (Hubert Gregg) to stay at the house. At the same time their son Peter, having quarrelled with Pepper, decides to go away for the weekend with his 'fast' new girlfriend Fay (Carla Lehmann). Joan and Michael, having finally decided to sleep together, are forestalled by the early return of the Robinsons, who have got cold feet about going abroad – 'so much further away and full of foreign types' – and have spent a contented fortnight in Bognor. Peter's lovemaking with Fay is interrupted when they discover her husband (Guy Middleton) is on board the houseboat to which they have repaired. In a protracted aftermath, with many recriminations, the Robinson family eventually recovers its stability.

Although the Boxes' adaptation makes the aborted affair between Peter and Fay more salacious than in the Constanduros's play, this was hardly sensational material, even for 1945. But it was enough for Rank, a strict Methodist, to consider that it encouraged young people to have illicit affairs. In order to preserve them from harm, he offered to reimburse Box the whole £45,000 that had been spent on the production in order to take the film permanently out of circulation.[43] This would have had a highly deleterious effect on the careers of the principal cast and technicians, including Cass, directing his first feature, and it would have permanently damaged Box's reputation as an independent producer. Box therefore felt he had no option but to reject Rank's offer and to try to get *29 Acacia Avenue* exhibited on another circuit; without a circuit release, a film stood no chance of becoming profitable.[44] Robert Clark, in charge of production at ABPC, which controlled the ABC circuit, would not handle the film because, conscious of Rank's position, he felt ABPC could not afford to play a film that would compromise its position as purveyors of family entertainment.[45] Alfred Shipman, no doubt anxious to recoup his investment, rescued the production for a second time by persuading Joseph Friedman, London head of Columbia Pictures, to include *29 Acacia Avenue* in the company's portfolio of films, a package that neither the circuit managers nor independent cinemas could afford to turn down.[46] Almost a year after shooting started, *29 Acacia Avenue* gained its West End premiere, before being played on all three circuits under the Columbia banner in May 1945. In December 1945, *Kinematograph Weekly* reported that it 'looks like grossing more than double its production costs'.[47] Columbia also handled *29 Acacia Avenue*'s worldwide distribution and, rechristened with a more sensational title, *The Facts of Love*, it ran for over a year on Times Square, recouping its budget in that one cinema alone.[48]

All is revealed: *The Seventh Veil*

The delays and difficulties Box encountered with *29 Acacia Avenue* meant that it could not provide a bargaining counter with which to negotiate financing of his next production, which he needed to make swiftly in order to take up the space he had rented at Riverside. Given his precarious financial position, it was a bold move for Box to choose to make a film from an original screenplay he and Muriel had written. This script was the one in which he had tried to interest Del Giudice under the title *Close Quarters*; it was announced in the press as *Close Up*, but later retitled *The Seventh Veil*. It was inspired by a documentary that Box had produced for Verity, *The Psychiatric Treatment of Battle Casualties*, which explained new forms of therapy, including truth drugs which helped unlock the patient's suppressed fears, which had begun to be used in the rehabilitation of soldiers suffering from psychological trauma.[49]

Box initially took the project to Columbia, which turned it down because of the failure of what the company considered to be a somewhat similar subject, *A Song to Remember* (1944), about George Sand and Chopin.[50] But, in a role reversal which encapsulated the unpredictable capriciousness of the British film industry, Rank came to the rescue. While his Board of Directors prevaricated about the script's merits, Rank gave his personal go-ahead for a script that was in many ways much more controversial than *29 Acacia Avenue*, because of his wife's admiration for an 'original, jolly good story'.[51] However, although Rank had agreed to guarantee £75,000 of the film's costs, this money would not be forthcoming until nine months after delivery of the film.[52] Box, whose own money was tied up in *29 Acacia Avenue*, was only able to start production with £15,000 provided by John Sutro, another Two Cities' producer trying to break into independent production as Ortus Films.[53] Box managed to keep the production going on such slender funding 'by a process of financial jugglery at which [he] excelled'.[54] Betty Box recalled that, as assistant producer, her job was to ward off 'the howling wolves who wanted their money and wanted it without delay' with a series of well-practised stalling devices.[55] Once a rough-cut had been produced, Box was able to approach Shipman again, now reassured that he would recoup his money from *29 Acacia Avenue*. As Shipman was enthusiastic about what he saw, and knew that this production was assured of a release on one of the Rank circuits, he invested £40,000, which enabled Box to pay the cast and crew and prepare the final version.[56]

In outline, *The Seventh Veil* depicts the emotional coming-of-age of Francesca Cunningham, whom we first glimpse escaping from a clinic and trying to take her own life by throwing herself off a bridge. She is placed in the care of Dr Larsen, a psychiatrist, and under treatment reveals the events which led to this drastic act in a series of extended flashbacks. After a traumatic incident at school, in which she fails to pass a piano examination because she has been caned on her hands, Francesca develops a morbid fear of injuring her hands and loses confidence in her musical abilities. She leaves school to take up residence in the house of her severe, older bachelor cousin, Nicholas. A lover of music, Nicholas is prepared to encourage her considerable aptitude as a pianist, but when she announces her intention to marry Peter Gay, an American saxophonist, Nicholas takes her away with him to continue her studies in Paris. From then on he masterminds her career as a concert pianist, rarely letting her out of his sight. But when she has her portrait painted by Maxwell Leyden, the pair become romantically involved and Francesca again tries to break free from Nicholas's domination. Enraged, he crashes his stick down on her hands and she runs way with Leyden. They have a car accident and her hands are damaged. Although she is assured she will make a full recovery, Francesca is unwilling to play again and attempts suicide. This returns the action to the present. Larsen, convinced that in recounting her story Francesca has now recovered and is free from the grip of the past, assembles the three men, Nicholas, Peter and Maxwell, so she can make a free choice of the one she really loves.

This version of *The Seventh Veil* was the result of several significant script revisions, which demonstrate how its original conception had to be adjusted to the marketplace. Muriel Box's original outline had focused on a traumatised female violinist, who was changed to a concert pianist because Gainsborough had announced plans to make a film about Paganini.[57] Box then wrote a fresh outline, incorporating a portrait of a pianist obsessed with her hands, which was based on someone he had interviewed in his Fleet Street days.[58] The character of Francesca was also written with Ann Todd in mind. The Boxes had admired her performance as a headstrong but fragile and vulnerable woman in the title role of *Lottie Dundass*, then playing on the West End stage. In their opinion Todd 'possessed all the physical attributes needed for the part, i.e. small stature, fine bones, and a personality hinting of maturity beyond her years'.[59] The first finished screenplay no longer exists, but Ann Todd recalled that it was radically experimental: 'the girl was the only person who appeared on the screen. The other characters were to be filmed in shadow voices-off and reflections in the piano or mirrors.'[60] In many ways this resembles the 'expressionist' style of Box's early plays. However, although a relatively experienced film actress, Todd was 'frightened' by this avant-garde approach, and a more conventional treatment was prepared, in which the three men with whom she becomes romantically involved are actual characters with whom she can interact.

The screenplay was further transformed when, ten days into production, Box became aware that James Mason had become available for casting having been unable to take the starring role in the Archers' *I Know Where I'm Going* (1945).[61] Although casting Mason added £10,000 to the production costs, Box opined that his name 'ensures good release of the picture', i.e. a West End premiere.[62] Ann Todd was not at this point a star and so Mason's name was worth the fee, especially since Box could expect a handsome box-office return because Mason was the most popular British male star.[63] Mason was attracted by the quality of the script, despite being warned by 'the know-it-alls at Gainsborough [who] glanced at me in pity when it became known I was to play a part in a film which had been dreamed up and modestly budgeted by Sydney Box, who was known only as a producer of documentaries'.[64] However, Mason's stature meant that he was able to insist on further script revisions, whereby his part was enhanced. Working with some suggestions from Mason's wife, Pamela Kellino, the Boxes added or lengthened scenes between Nicholas and Francesca, and made Mason's character more complex, enigmatic and much more romantic.[65] However, in what was the third full screenplay, the youngest suitor, Peter Gay, is the man Francesca chooses after she has recovered from her trauma, and the screenplay ends on the veranda outside Dr Larsen's consulting room with the couple planning their future life together. Nicholas is not present, having been left in the previous scene gazing at Francesca's portrait over the fireplace: 'The camera goes back to Nicholas. He has tears rolling down his cheeks.'[66] In fact this was one of three endings that the Boxes prepared, which were not revealed to the cast until the final day of shooting.[67] In the second, Francesca descends the stairs towards the three waiting men but without making it clear whom she will choose. The decision to go with a third ending, in which she embraces Nicholas, was based on card votes taken at a sneak preview.[68] Some final adjustments were made and the length reduced slightly after a second try-out in London, before *The Seventh Veil* received its West End premiere on 22 October at the Leicester Square Odeon.

Despite minimal publicity – the budget had been completely spent – *The Seventh Veil* was phenomenally successful, becoming the most popular film of 1945, beating even the major American releases. Rank's managing director, John Davis, announced that it 'has broken the all-time record on its London general release. In our 80 London theatres, the "Veil" has taken over ten per cent more than any picture we have played, either British or American, and at 41 theatres created an all-time individual record for the theatre.'[69] It made a record £78,000 on its London release, before grossing a phenomenal £300,000 in the British market alone.[70] *The Seventh Veil* received Royal imprimatur when a private screening was arranged for Queen Mary at her request; she apparently approved of Francesca's choice.[71] *The Seventh Veil*'s British success was capped by an impressive box-office take in America. It was easily the most popular British melodrama (as opposed to prestige epics such as *Henry V*, which were very carefully promoted) screened by Eagle Lion, Rank's US distribution subsidiary; *The Seventh Veil* could play in Cincinnati as well as in the metropolises.[72] By February 1948, *The Seventh Veil* had grossed £750,000 worldwide and its box-office receipts exceeded £2,000,000.[73] It became a celluloid ambassador for British cinema, one of eight films chosen for the British Films Festival in Prague in 1946 and one of six British pictures shown at Cannes the same year.[74] In the 1947 Bernstein questionnaire, conducted for Sidney Bernstein's Granada chain of cinemas, *The Seventh Veil* came second only to *The Way to the Stars* in popularity, judged as 'outstanding' by 69 per cent of those who responded.[75]

How can the extraordinary success of *The Seventh Veil* be explained? The answer lies in a combination of four factors: fortuitous timing; archetypal generic elements shrewdly deployed; star charisma; and high production values in scripting, direction, cinematography, music and sets, achieved despite the strict economies in its construction. The release of *The Seventh Veil* coincided with the high point of a pronounced popular interest in war trauma and Freudian psychoanalysis that has been well documented.[76] *The Seventh Veil* was in the vanguard of feature films which focused explicitly on forms of psychotherapy, including *Spellbound* (1945), *The Dark Mirror* (1946), *The Locket* (1946), *Possessed* (1946) and *The Snake Pit* (1948). In these films, the protagonist is affected by an unacknowledged childhood trauma overlaid by further emotional crises from his or her adult life, but can be cured, or at least understood, by the new wonder-science of psychotherapy, capable of healing deep emotional wounds accentuated by the stresses and dislocations of war. In *The Seventh Veil*, Dr Larsen (Herbert Lom) plays the stereotypical analyst, middle-European, omniscient, compassionate, judicious and effective. Nicholas would have been recognised, metaphorically, as a damaged veteran, in need of understanding and compassion. Two other enormously popular films, *I'll Be Seeing You* (1944) and *Spellbound*, had focused on this figure, and many others followed; *The Seventh Veil* thus mobilised widely shared concerns, its conclusion registering a general hope for reconciliation and atonement as the war ended.

The Seventh Veil's topicality is set within the framework of the 'woman's film', a staple Hollywood sub-genre throughout the 1930s and 1940s, which was very popular with British audiences. As Molly Haskell characterises it, the woman's film has an embattled or victimised middle-class heroine at its centre, who is bound by a rigid moral code in which her options are strictly limited. Although she suffers emotional and sometimes physical cruelty, her strong-willed refusal to give in allows her to be rewarded with the 'right' male partner.[77] Within this overarching sub-genre, *The Seventh Veil* can also be seen as part of the wartime revival of the Gothic romance, inaugurated by Thorold Dickinson's *Gaslight* (1940) and Hitchcock's *Rebecca* (1940). In the latter, the victim-heroine has a relationship with an enigmatic older man by whom she feels intensely attracted but also repelled; she feels helpless, confused, frightened and despised. She has a desperate urge to know the man's secret, but is terrified about the consequences of that knowledge. In *The Seventh Veil*, Francesca is intimidated and bullied by Nicholas, but also deeply attracted to him: 'He was a wonderful teacher. He instinctively knew how to get the best out of me.' Nicholas is recognisably a modern archetype, a Svengali, creating a protégé whose will is utterly subordinate to his own. He also has the dark, menacing eroticism of the Byronic hero, exhibiting the type's characteristic contradictions: a brooding loneliness based on a secret sorrow (his faithless mother ran off with a singer) which often breaks out in cruel, sadistic violence, but also an ineradicable nobility and refinement that inspire love and devotion. Nicholas even has a pronounced Byronic limp. Francesca's transformation from diffident, dowdy schoolgirl into a refined and captivating woman has clear elements of the Cinderella fairy tale; while her final choice between the three suitors is an inversion of the judgement of Paris. Thus within its clear generic framework, *The Seventh Veil* mobilises deep-rooted cultural topoi that would have had a potent appeal for cinema-goers.

The Seventh Veil also benefits from charismatic star performances. The casting of Ann Todd, who was not an established screen star at this point, was an astute decision. Nearly all reviewers were enthusiastic about her performance, particularly about the skill with which she negotiated the difficult task of transforming from a gauche, shy schoolgirl into an accomplished and sophisticated woman. They also responded to the convincing way in which Todd could suggest cerebral, artistic sensitivities combined with a refined sensuality. One thought she 'has a quality which the producers of this moving film have exploited with both skill and good taste. She can really convince an audience that she is a gifted pianist; and that she can live a life of the imagination remote from the sordid realities of the world.'[78] Ann Todd recalled that men responded strongly to her plight as the victim. The scene in which Nicholas crashes his stick down on her hands while she is playing, shouting 'If you won't play for me, you won't play for anyone else!', was capable, years later, of rousing a London taxi-driver to her defence: he still wanted to hit Mason back.[79] The enhanced role for Mason also shrewdly exploited his established persona, derived from Gainsborough's bodice-ripping melodramas *The Man in Grey* (1943) and *Fanny by*

Gaslight (1944); as the *Mirror*'s reviewer commented pithily: 'Mason registers another hit as a fascinating brute'.[80] Todd was equally direct, arguing that 'females thrilled to Mason's power and cruelty as women have thrilled to this since the world began, however much they may deny it'.[81] However, it was the mixture of elements of refinement and cultivation with sadism and cruelty which audiences liked most about Mason; *Picturegoer*'s readers adored him as Nicholas, the divided man, capable of love and devotion as well as a violent possessiveness.[82] If both Todd and Mason appealed to viewers separately, there was a strong on-screen chemistry between them, which gave a distinct frisson to the sublimated eroticism of their encounters. When Francesca first enters Nicholas's bachelor domain, he toys with her innocence as he does with the cat on his lap: 'Don't you want to stroke him?' he enquires.

If the final version of the Boxes' script, for which they won an Oscar, is not as innovative as their initial draft, it is still very effective, beginning with a highly dramatic opening scene in which an audience is plunged *in media res* as Francesca begins her headlong flight at night towards the bridge. Although extended 'confessional' flashbacks became a standard device of *film noir*, *The Seventh Veil* was in advance of the main development, so the device possessed a freshness for audiences. Most reviewers admired the polished dialogue, and here the Boxes show their accomplishment as playwrights, particularly in the crisp exchanges between Nicholas and Francesca. The screenplay is enhanced by James Carter's expensive-looking sets, including Nicholas's large town house, whose intimidating size helps inspire Francesca's fear and trepidation in an austerely classical bachelor domain where no woman has previously set foot.[83] The sets were also exceptionally well-finished, using exquisite ornamentation; the Italian chimneypieces worth £2,500 had been borrowed for the production.[84] The scale of the set when Francesca plays at the Albert Hall impressed most reviewers even though, on close inspection, very little of the space is revealed: its apparent grandeur is a tribute to Compton Bennett's deft use of camera angles. Here, as elsewhere in the film, Bennett, directing his first feature film, shows a good eye for evocative compositions; overall, his direction is remarkably assured. His smooth tracking shots, techniques of breaking down on-screen space and concentration on character interaction are the stuff of the Hollywood 'cinema of quality' with which audiences were thoroughly familiar. His work is complemented by Reginald Wyer's photography, which is capable of subtle gradations and is particularly effective in the opening scene. Here the soft, diffused lighting of the clinic creates an oneiric atmosphere before the arresting chiaroscuro of Francesca's headlong flight towards Hammersmith Bridge, where the intense light on her white smock gives a peculiar vulnerability to her terrified plunge.

All reviewers commented on the film's extensive and effective use of music: 'a feast for lovers of good music'.[85] C. A. Lejeune noted that this was part of the 'vogue of the moment [which] is to present classical music to the people in popular form with film stars playing famous composers', mentioning *Love Story* (1944), in which Margaret Lockwood plays 'The Cornish Rhapsody', Anton Walbrook playing the 'Warsaw Concerto' in *Dangerous Moonlight* (1941) and the Chopin music in *A Song to Remember*.[86] In *The Seventh Veil*, the use of Rachmaninov's piano concerto in C sharp major is particularly effective since some audience members would recognise that this was the piece whose initial failure caused Rachmaninov to declare he would never compose again, only to be persuaded otherwise after hypnosis, a fact which neatly tied the circumstances of the music's composition to the film's narrative. Todd had rehearsed at the Royal College of Music for three months in order to give an authentic impression of her accomplishment, though the music was actually played by Eileen Joyce.[87] *Film Music Notes* judged that 'the use of classical music beautifully cued in and performed, adds further distinction ... The piano playing of the concerto ... has real virtuoso feeling, a plus rarely conveyed in a picture', and also praised the ways in which the film conveyed the arduous drudgery of her training and 'the montage of the continual study required for a concert artist is marvellously conceived and executed'.[88]

The scale of *The Seventh Veil*'s success, in inverse proportion to its slender budget of £92,000, made the film a byword for post-war indigenous production. In *Kinematograph Weekly* 'Josh' Billings enthused: 'Beautifully acted, elegantly mounted and superbly directed, it establishes a new and exacting yardstick for the measurement of British box-office successes.'[89] The *Spectator*'s anonymous reviewer, reassessing the film six months after it was released, considered *The Seventh Veil*,

> belongs to a type of film which the British industry has never previously achieved. It is an example of the intelligent, medium-priced picture made with great technical polish, which has represented for Hollywood the middle path between the vulgar and the highbrow. If the British film industry is to satisfy a bigger proportion of the home market and then – having thus reduced our subservience to the American industry – is boldly to compete for markets overseas, I am convinced that businesslike films like *The Seventh Veil* which are sparing of time, studio-space and money should be our main stock in trade. And clearly, there are countless other (and more characteristically British) themes to be handled in a similar manner.[90]

With an eye on Rank's highly expensive 'prestige' productions, Joan Lester in *Reynold's News* commented: 'there seems to be an idea here for the maestros who stress the importance of spending a couple of years or so on their epics'.[91] In the polemical 'Whither Rank?', Frederick Mullally praised *The Seventh Veil* as the kind of modest feature film that could recoup its costs in Britain alone, and could therefore keep the studios working consistently and effectively and increase the British film industry's twenty-per-cent share of the home market, in contrast to expensive and space-consuming epics such as *Caesar and Cleopatra*, which was released in January 1946 having been in production for over a year.[92] *The Seventh Veil*'s success also recommended it to the architect of austerity Britain. Addressing a group of Rank executives, the Labour Chancellor of the Exchequer Sir Stafford Cripps congratulated Sydney Box on making 'an eighth wonder of production in the confined space of a small studio'.[93]

The coming man

In a rare profile of a producer in *Picture Post* in June 1946, Box was contrasted with the vulgar showman of the past, 'who drifted into movies in the early days, from circuses and travelling burlesque and dubious promotions', but who was now an 'outmoded type', lacking in culture and education. In his place 'A new sort of film-maker, a man with the same kind of cultural affinities and background which we find in any other sort of accomplished artist, is gradually emerging here in Europe. And perhaps the most interesting example of his type in this country is Sydney Box, producer of that brilliant success, *The Seventh Veil.*' Box, moreover, is uncorrupted by his achievement: 'Strangely enough, unlike most qualities that make success, they are extremely amiable and civilised ones. Calm integrity, and gentleness are here joined to wit, imagination, energy and taste. He works abominably hard.'[94]

Buoyed by the astonishing success of *The Seventh Veil* – which ultimately led to his appointment as head of Gainsborough Studios, the subject of the next two chapters – Box was swift to advertise himself as an important producer, the coming man who could revitalise the British film industry. In 'My Plan for Finding Film Talent', published in *Kinematograph Weekly* in December 1945, Box lamented the dearth of new young prospects in the industry and the lack of any system for the education and training of prospective actors and technicians, and argued that it was 'the duty of the Industry to set up its own nurseries'. Box argued that his own achievement in building Verity Films from scratch – a company 'which was capable of producing – and did, in fact, produce – 250,000 ft of completed film in a year' – was based on the cardinal principle of offering new talent a chance. He had given fourteen directors the opportunity to shoot their first feature: 'Eight of the 14 failed, but the other six have become valuable assets to the film Industry in this country'. In addition, Box had established a scheme to train actors – the Company of Youth – in which they would attend the studio every day, to absorb the atmosphere but also to be properly instructed in deportment, voice production, make-up and other technical requirements. Rather than wait around for an elusive role, the members of the Company would act as stand-ins to gain experience and take part in low-budget 'B' features that also used fledgling directors and new writers. During rehearsals Box and other experienced technicians would come in and comment on progress. Once they were satisfied, the film would be put into production. He argued that six such films could be made each year. These would be different from the despised pre-war 'quota quickies' because they would be the result of many weeks hard effort and represent 'the fresh and enthusiastic work of young brains and young ambitions'. British audiences would welcome such films as a contrast to the 'routine sausage machine product of Hollywood's second-raters'.[95] Box also gave preferential treatment to those returning to the industry from the services.[96]

At the same time as he outlined his master scheme to create a viable British film industry, Box announced ambitious plans to make fifteen films, three in Technicolor, over a two year period at an overall cost of £1,500,000.[97] One, *The Years Between*, was already in production, to be followed by three films with Ann Todd: the thriller *Daybreak*; *Romance with Music*, based on Elizabeth Vernon's popular story; and *Mantilla*, based on another original screenplay by the Boxes. This was to be 'a spectacular production with a great deal of dancing, and authentic Spanish fiesta scenes', in Technicolor, with extensive location shooting in Spain; Todd would play a 'penniless English girl who experiences a series of extraordinary adventures in Andalucia'. The success of *The Seventh Veil* was James Mason's entrée to Hollywood, which meant that he was no longer available.[98] Box had acquired the services of his nearest rival, Eric Portman, to star in *Daybreak* and another psychological thriller, *The Killer and the Slain*. Box also announced plans to produce *No Ladies, Please!*, a further original screenplay, and an adaptation of Box's own award-winning play *Self-Made Man*, described as 'one of the most important pictures in the programme'. The second spectacular Technicolor film was to be based on John Guthrie's *So They Began*, about the early period of New Zealand's history, while the third was to be an adaptation of Graham Greene's *The Man Within*. Box also mentioned plans to adapt Ronald Mackenzie's popular comedy *Musical Chairs* and a further film, *The Boy Who Came Back*, which would 'deal with an important social problem', presumably the returning veteran.

As with all producers, this announcement was partly bluff and chest-beating, and many of these projects came to nothing. But it gives a vivid insight into Box's determination to become an important presence in the British film industry, capable of making a range of films which included adaptations and original screenplays, topical and historical subjects, and a mixture of genres – comedy, thriller and melodrama.

In part these plans were truncated by the Gainsborough appointment, but before that occurred, Box produced a further six films at Riverside Studios, which, as several were released after he took up the post at Gainsborough, are often mistakenly thought of as Gainsborough films. However, they should be understood as Riverside films, a thematically and to a lesser extent aesthetically coherent group that explores the same territory as *The Seventh Veil*: psychological problems, fractured relationships and troubled masculinity, notably through the figure of the divided man whose impulses are contradictory.

The Riverside films

The Years Between

The film already in production, *The Years Between*, showed Box's determination to deal with significant social issues by resuming the exploration of the emotional and psychological fallout of the war. It was also the opportunity to realise the Boxes' ambition, announced in January 1943, to make a film with a strong feminist and socialist agenda about a woman MP, which, according to Muriel Box, 'gave a hint of the things we wanted to say politically'.[99] It was an adaptation of Daphne Du Maurier's play, provisionally entitled *The Return of the Soldier*, which had opened in November 1944. Although Box wanted Du Maurier to write the screenplay, she was too busy and 'never got involved with the film at all, [and] refused to be consulted over the script'.[100] However, although the Boxes experienced some difficulties with the length of their screenplay, which was significantly trimmed on three occasions, shedding over a half an hour in total, and hesitated over whom to cast in the central role of the returning serviceman, the production went relatively smoothly.[101] The main irritant seems to have been Ealing's rival production *The Captive Heart*, which had similar subject matter and also starred Michael Redgrave, and which was released in April 1946, two months before *The Years Between*, even though it had gone into production later. Box reflected ruefully that Michael Balcon had more editors at his disposal, five to Box's one, and Ealing enjoyed a far more privileged relationship with the Rank Organisation.[102] Not only did Box feel that *The Captive Heart* rather stole his production's thunder – *The Years Between* had been advertised as the 'most topical film ever made' – he was also annoyed at what he considered to be direct plagiarisms of the script, which he had given to Ealing's scriptwriters as a matter of courtesy.[103]

The Boxes' hard work in trimming and shaping the screenplay of *The Years Between* brought dividends, as it is one of their best. The film opens in June 1940, when Diana Wentworth (Valerie Hobson) receives the news of her husband's death. In flashback she relives the major events of their married life: their wedding, his election to parliament, the christening of their son and the happy and contented intimacy of their time together before he goes to war. Initially distracted by grief – she has night-time conversations with her husband's empty chair and refuses to have any of his things touched – Diana slowly comes to terms with her loss, taking over the running of their estate and her husband's place as the local MP. Gradually she becomes an effective and successful campaigner for her constituents and for woman's rights. In her maiden speech to the House (only vaguely sketched in Du Maurier's play), Diana departs from her notes prepared by the Party adviser and makes an eloquent and moving plea for the rights of Mrs Smith, the Everywoman, whose husband has been called up, whose children have been evacuated, who combines a twelve-hour shift in an aircraft factory with fire-watching, housework and queuing, and who wants a great deal from the post-war world: good housing, the best education, equal wages and an equal say in the government of the country. Her speech is a distillation of some of the key issues broached in Verity's films.

Diana also gradually disentangles herself emotionally from her husband's memory and falls in love with her neighbour Richard Llewellyn (James McKechnie). She is about to remarry when her life is shattered again by her husband's return – his death had been faked in order that he could fight a covert war helping the European resistance movement. Not only is Colonel Michael Wentworth (Redgrave) that potently disruptive figure, the man returned from the dead, he is a divided man, deeply resentful of the suffering and sacrifices that his country has asked of him, and yet clearly full of admiration for the brilliance of the operation that Intelligence planned and which he executed faultlessly. Michael is a man still emotionally organised for war, gaunt, shifty-eyed and perpetually tense, who is now plunged into the very different demands of peace. He displays an almost infantile craving for Diana's love and attention – 'You see, I woke up and you weren't there and I was frightened. You must always be there' – together with a surly scepticism that resents any show of affection. Above all, Michael cannot accept what Diana has become. He craves the certainties he left behind, a craving which expresses itself in a bullying demand to recreate the *status quo ante*: 'I'd like everything to be as it was before the war, as though the war never happened ... I want the wife I left behind ... I'm not the only one, there are thousands, millions like me.' Rather than the returning hero, Michael finds himself an interloper, unable to recreate a relationship with his son who has, like his wife, gravitated towards Richard. His abrasiveness only serves to push Diana further towards Richard, though she struggles to preserve their marriage despite being unable to respond to Michael's sexual needs.

In Du Maurier's play, Diana abandons her socialism and her spent marriage is only preserved by Michael's decision to accept a government post abroad. Vague hopes for a better future rest upon the son, Robin. Perhaps feeling that this would have been too bleak a conclusion for cinema audiences, the Boxes' screenplay opts for an upbeat ending, which is rather clumsily contrived. Nanny (Flora Robson) steps forward as a saintly mediator, castigating both parties for failing to make compromises and work at their new relationship, and exhorting her employers not to 'lose the peace', but to set an example to other families and nations by living together in harmony. This is symbolised in the final shot of the Wentworths smiling at each other from opposite sides of the House of Commons.

Box's casting was again well judged. Reviewers applauded Hobson's facility in making Diana admirable without being priggish and Redgrave's ability to emote 'a nervous tension and a kind of angry unreasonableness which belong to truth and not the stage', and to 'sharply convey the exhaustion and sardonic disillusion of the Colonel'.[104] If this is not one of the more celebrated of Redgrave's performances, it is one of his best. As in *The Seventh Veil*, Compton Bennett displays a shrewd eye for evocative composition and Reginald Wyer's limpid cinematography is uniformly good. In the expertly lit interiors and the satisfying use of location shooting, he manages a delicacy of tone that is rare in British films of the time. The sets, by James Carter, are also well designed, including an impressive reconstruction of the chamber of the House of Commons on which a full £25,000 was spent after the Speaker had refused permission to film in the chamber itself.[105]

Although some press reviews were carping – the *News Chronicle*, for instance, disliked its 'novelettish distortion of a contemporary problem'[106] – several film journals' reviewers were much more positive. The *Monthly Film Bulletin* thought:

> The end is rather unsatisfying, for the break-up of the marriage is the only correct solution. Otherwise this is a courageous portrayal of the rehabilitation and resettlement problems with which thousands of families in Britain, America and other countries are now faced. It is excellently done, with outstanding performances by Valerie Hobson and Michael Redgrave, and by Flora Robson.[107]

Film Industry called *The Years Between,*

> as near a flawless production as one is entitled to expect once in several years ... Everything which the characters say or do is incidental, because the important thing is that they act and talk like real people, expressing real and genuine and feasible emotions. This can only happen when the highest degree of co-ordination is reached between director, script writer and artist.[108]

The public's verdict was unequivocal: *The Years Between* performed well, indicating that once more the Boxes had understood the temper of the times.[109]

A Girl in a Million

A Girl in a Million, which went on the floor at Riverside on 10 December 1945, is an altogether slighter film than *The Years Between,* but the Boxes' original screenplay explores comically a similar set of issues, notably the male drive to dominate women who are seen as irrational and threatening, how women try to resist this control, and the ways in which the relationship between men and women is going through a difficult period of transition and renegotiation. Initially called *Love Is Dumb,* then *No Ladies, Please!, A Girl in a Million* was inspired by Anatole France's famous story *The Man Who Married a Dumb Wife* (1915), which ultimately derives from Ovid's *Pygmalion and Galatea.* Research scientist Tony Preston (Hugh Williams), engaged on important war work, is another divided male, a congenital bachelor who is absorbed in his work, but whose sexual drives are very strong. His marriage to the shrewish Molly (Yvonne Owen), which ends in divorce, drives him to seek a secluded retreat, shared by Prendergast (Naunton Wayne) and Fotheringham (Basil Radford), who are convinced that marriage is 'a wonderful thing for women'. This contented bachelor establishment is shattered when nineteen-year-old Gay Hardwicke (Joan Greenwood) arrives, having been rendered dumb when a torpedo struck her ship. Despite his protestations, Tony falls in love with a woman both beautiful and blissfully silent. But, once married, he longs for the 'dummy' to talk, to hear her say 'I love you'. When a mine threatens to explode against the pier on which Tony and Gay and hundreds of others have been listening to a concert (Eileen Joyce playing Cesar Franck's *Symphonic Variations*), Tony heroically descends to defuse it. In her anxiety for his safety Gay screams out, 'Tony!', and her voice is restored. Although initially delighted, Tony comes to loathe the sound of her incessant loquaciousness, feeling that his peace and tranquillity have once more been overturned. Gay, unable to fathom his change of heart, leaves. The couple are reunited when Tony is called to her bedside after the birth of their son. Gay is now only pretending to be dumb, and in the final shot, the camera dwells on her smile of satisfaction in reclaiming her husband.

Box was disappointed by Bert Mason's pedestrian cinematography, noting that the predominantly 'dark sets and low-key' lighting were inappropriate for a light romantic comedy, which should have the opposite treatment. He was even more dissatisfied with Francis Searle's direction, which he felt lacked both pace and subtlety, qualities that were essential to the film's success.[110] Although Box had given Searle his break from documentaries into feature films, he did not work for Box again but went into 'B' features. The most fundamental problem, however, lay in the Boxes' script. Although the *Monthly Film Bulletin* thought *A Girl in a Million* 'presents an amusing commentary on the inability of the average male to recognize and be satisfied with his heart's desire, even when he is so fortunate as to achieve it', the pronounced feeling among reviewers was that the film was an entertaining anecdote stretched rather too far.[111] The *Daily Mirror*'s reviewer commented sourly that it was 'an old-fashioned music hall joke that goes on for eighty-six minutes'[112] E. Arnot Robertson in *The Listener* judged it 'A farce with an idea, but no pace. And unfortunately a farce for an hour and a half needs pace to carry it successfully even more than it needs an idea.'[113] In retrospect, *A Girl in a Million* looks like a rather rushed and cut-price production, designed to be fitted in to a tight schedule; one that betrays Box's tendency to think of a script in terms of a one-act play rather than a ninety-minute feature, a penchant he had successfully avoided with *The Seventh Veil*.

The Man Within

The Man Within was an altogether more ambitious film, made in Technicolor, a rarity for a British picture at this time. Although it was an adaptation of a prestigious author, Graham Greene, it was from his first published novel; Box had acquired the rights from fellow documentarist Ralph Keene in February 1944 for only £400.[114] Keene had failed to interest anyone in Greene's convoluted mixture of psychological turmoil and historical adventure about smugglers on the Sussex coast in the early nineteenth century, but the Boxes were stimulated by Greene's 'strange, slightly surrealistic' novel, especially its delineation of the divided man – both novel and film begin with the epigraph from Sir Thomas Browne: 'There is another man within me and he is angry with me' – that would continue their metaphorical exploration of wartime trauma.[115] Muriel Box began work on a draft screenplay in June 1944 and Box finished a final version by the following May, but the project was shouldered out by their other productions.[116] The opportunity to make the film came in March 1946, when Rank offered Box space at Shepherd's Bush after Columbia had pulled a film.[117] Box wrote to John Davis that, although he received 'very friendly co-operation form the technical and floor crew' enabling his film to be completed for only £168,000, 'there is a great deal of obstruction on the executive side'.[118] The Ostrer brothers, in charge at Gainsborough, were no doubt reluctant to see this interloper use their studio, little realising that he was the cuckoo in the nest.

Although Box could not persuade Anthony Asquith to direct and opted for the less experienced but also less expensive Bernard Knowles, as he pointed out to Davis, he had assembled a strong cast.[119] Joan Greenwood, a Company of Youth player, was chosen for the major female role of Elizabeth, following her much admired performance in *A Girl in a Million*; Jean Kent, under contract to Rank, was the wanton Lucy. Richard Attenborough, whose performance as the 'windy' rating in *In Which We Serve* had been superb, was cast as the neurotic anti-hero, Francis Andrews. But the crucial casting decision was to have Michael Redgrave, who had been outstanding in *The Years Between*, play Andrews's guardian, Carlyon. Redgrave's stature meant that the role of Carlyon had to be enlarged and made much more central. Redgrave was even allowed to decide which of the two endings Box had written for the final screenplay was to be used.[120] *The Man Within* was also subject to some cuts required by the censors, but these do not appear to have been extensive.[121]

Characteristically, the Boxes' screenplay uses an intensely dramatic opening *in media res* – after a close-up of flames, the camera pulls back to reveal Francis Andrews being tortured and interrogated – followed by a series of flashbacks to reveal what had happened and the narrator's psychological working through of the trauma of those events. Although the novel focuses on Andrews's confused love for Elizabeth, the demure and courageous woman who offers him shelter, the emotional centre of the film is emphatically his relationship with Carlyon, who becomes his guardian after the death of his father and takes him on board his ship which is engaged in smuggling. But, unlike Andrews's hated father, who was a rough, tough, violent man at one with the smugglers he led, Carlyon is another divided man, able to instil respect and even fear in the crew but also cultivated, enjoying literature and music. To the bookish, over-sensitive Andrews, Carlyon's flute playing is 'like music from another world, like the whisper of an angel above the murmur of the sea', one of the qualities that makes Andrews feel that Carlyon is the man he would have chosen as a father. When Andrews, bullied at school, complains about his even rougher treatment by the crew, Carlyon invites him to move in to his cabin. Here an intense and clearly homoerotic relationship develops, conveyed by the exchange of looks and glances and by Andrews's voice-over: 'But the most wonderful thing about him was his charm. He could give you one look with those blue eyes of his and you would do anything for him, die for him if necessary.'[122]

This idyllic male bonding is shattered when one of the crew, Cockney Harry (Ronald Shiner), falsely implicates Andrews in thieving money that belongs to the whole crew and Carlyon, unable to disprove the accusation, flogs Andrews. Feeling humiliated and betrayed, Andrews informs against the crew to the authorities, who lie in wait for the smugglers on a deserted beach. During the ensuing fight, Andrews makes his escape and finds temporary respite in Elizabeth's isolated cottage. When he is spotted by Carlyon at the funeral of her stepfather, Andrews flees in panic. In the film's most expressionist and visually arresting scene, Andrews blunders around in the enveloping fog of a spectral forest, a pathetic fallacy of his distracted and confused state of mind. Even though he bears witness against the gang in court, he cannot bring himself to implicate Carlyon, who continues to haunt his every waking moment and even his dreams. It is Carlyon's knock that interrupts his lovemaking with Lucy, the mistress of the public prosecutor (Basil Sydney). Carlyon speaks to him through the closed door of the hurt and sorrow his betrayal has caused.

The two men are eventually brought together in the interrogation chamber at the end of the flashbacks. When Andrews refuses to betray Carlyon's identity to save himself, the two men exchange a look of love and forgiveness and Andrews collapses, falling forward on to Carlyon's bare chest. As Andrews walks free when Carlyon's confession exonerates him, he hears the flute playing for a final time. 'I thought perhaps you'd remember our tune', murmurs Carlyon. He confirms Andrews's manhood, no longer a coward but a man able to take responsibility for his own actions and protect those he loves, and therefore no longer divided or haunted by the debilitating grip of the past. But it is at the cost of Carlyon's life, whose look of mingled pride and longing through the bars of his cell as Andrews walks off is the final image of the film and the ending Redgrave chose.

The Man Within is an innovative and audacious departure from the norms of costume drama, radically different from the Gainsborough bodice-rippers that dominated the box office. In what was to be a characteristic of all Box's historical dramas, meticulous attention was given to authenticity, notably in the reconstruction of Lewes gaol by the set-designer, Andrew Mazzei, and in every detail of the ship that was used, 'down to the last piece of rigging in an exact replica of an 1820 sailing vessel'.[123] Geoffrey Unsworth's subtle Technicolor cinematography uses a deliberately restricted palette of subdued greens, browns and dark yellows, which lends a sombre, brooding tone to the whole piece, used 'not to make a brittle gloss but to enhance the poetic quality of Graham Greene's story'.[124] This complements the central thematic emphasis on psychological torment, paranoia, betrayal and homoerotic male bonding, which, together with the use of flashbacks, are more characteristic of *film noir*. But *The Man Within*'s emphasis on fear, cowardice and the eventual achievement of a courageous manhood are all characteristic of the war film. As Dilys Powell remarked of *In Which We Serve*, the emotional climaxes are between men.[125]

The Man Within's generic hybridity, its idiosyncratic singularity of theme and quasi-expressionist style, made it a difficult proposition for audiences; 'God knows what the public reaction will be to this odd picture' was the Boxes' diary entry just before its release.[126] If Jympson Harman in the *Evening News* saw it as 'a robust tale of olden Sussex' and thought Jean Kent's 'come hither' look worth the price of admission alone, most reviewers found it disconcerting.[127] Arthur Vesselo, in *Sight and Sound*, was the most censorious, judging it 'a curious film – a sort of introverted freak, with no apparent purpose and aimed at no clearly defined audience. If it were a nightmare, brought by a psychiatrist by one of his patients for analysis, it could be fitted into a Freudian framework without serious difficulty.'[128] In a more considered review for the *Spectator*, Basil Wright judged it 'a costume piece concerned with psychologically complex psychologies – or should I say psychological complexes? ... a curious and disturbing film, not easy to analyse, creaking a little at the joints, yet at moments most engrossing'.[129] Both Joan Lester in *Reynolds News* and Angela Milne in the *Observer* thought it the week's most important film, the latter wondering if a public used to

The Wicked Lady would accept such an intelligent film which made its audience think.[130] Little seen today, *The Man Within* needs to be recognised as one of Box's most interesting films, one that was prepared to widen the parameters of popular entertainment, even if it proved to be too singular to influence the development of the adventure genre or to attract a wide public.

The psychological thrillers

Box planned to make three psychological thrillers at Riverside – *Daybreak, The Killer and the Slain* and *The Upturned Glass* – all of which centre on the divided man and psychological trauma. *Daybreak* was the closest Box came to fulfilling his declared intention to emulate the style and theme of pre-war French cinema. Box had bought the rights to Monckton Hoffe's story *Grim Fairy Tale* in July 1945, seeing in it a choice part for Ann Todd.[131] *Daybreak* begins with a characteristically dramatic scene: Mendover (Eric Portman), a public hangman, breaks down when confronted by Olaf Tyson (Maxwell Reed) as he enters the condemned man's cell. Mendover confesses that he is Eddie Tribe, the man of whose presumed murder Tyson had been convicted. Mendover/Tribe then relates in flashback the events of the previous nine months that have led to this crisis.

They begin at the point when Tribe is informed of his father's death and returns to claim his inheritance, a fleet of barges on the Thames Reach at Gravesend. Tribe is another oversensitive, emotionally tormented protagonist, who has had a rootless life, having run away to sea and spent time in the army in order to escape his father's cruelty. He is also another divided man, with a second life as a public hangman. Shortly after gaining his inheritance, Eddie meets Frankie (Ann Todd), an attractive but insecure drifter, disillusioned with men's cruelty or indifference, whose shiny raincoat and cap echo the garb of the women in the pre-war French thrillers such as *Quai des brumes* (1938).[132] Frankie gradually comes to trust and love Tribe and experiences a settled happiness for the first time. Tribe, older, but far less emotionally experienced, cannot quite believe in her love or fidelity even after they are married. Fearful of losing Frankie, he never admits his second self, and the secret casts a shadow over their intimacy. Portman's insecurity and tormented longings echo those of Jean Gabin in the Carné-Prevert thrillers, and much play is made of Portman's anxiously suffering eyes, accentuated by heavy make-up and the shafts of light which fall across them, a technique copied from the Gabin films.[133]

To complement the central performances, careful attempts were made to create an authentic milieu for *Daybreak*. The *Agnes Mary*, the barge-cum-houseboat on which the main action takes place, was discovered derelict at Wandsworth wharf and towed to Riverside; a replica was constructed for studio use, occupying an entire stage, with synthetic fog pumped round to obscure the studio walls. In addition, Art Director James Carter 'visited the grimmest districts of the Thames waterfront in search of atmosphere'.[134] Reginald Wyer's cinematography attempts to emulate French poetic realism by alternating atmospheric studio shots with pellucid location photography. Setting and cinematography combine to render a waterside world cut off from normal social intercourse, often enveloped in an obscuring fog, in which motives become confused, actions obscure and the everyday world overlaid by a sinister pall.

In this miasmatic milieu, Frankie is gradually drawn, against her conscious will, into an affair with one of Tribe's workmen, Olaf Tyson. Tyson is another rootless figure, but Tribe's opposite: young, cool, assured, conscious of his muscular build and good looks, constantly combing back his hair, 'like an American film star'. Frankie warns Tribe to get rid of Tyson, but he is blind to what is happening and his duties as a hangman, disguised as business trips, take him away at crucial moments. Unable to resist Tyson's attentions, but much more a sympathetic victim of circumstances than a femme fatale, Frankie never loses the audience's sympathy. Discovering them together when he returns early from an aborted hanging, Tribe wrestles with Tyson and falls overboard. Tyson is arrested as a suspected murderer and Frankie commits suicide. After the scene in the condemned cell, Tribe, conscious that it was his deception that was the root cause of Frankie's death, returns to his former workplace, a barber's shop, to kill himself. His listlessly swinging body is discovered by his former assistant Ron (Bill Owen). This stark, terrifying conclusion, suffused with Gallic fatalism, was bold and uncompromising, and *Daybreak*, like *The Man Within*, shows Box's willingness to take considerable risks.

Daybreak is a moving and powerful film, but radically uneven in its execution, as a result of its troubled production and censorship wrangles. The diary entries during its making reveal that Box was very unhappy with the rough cut of the film that was ready in July 1946. He thought Todd's performance 'awful', and Compton Bennett's direction poor.[135] Box made numerous revisions to the script to get over these difficulties, but some six months later he was still working on the screenplay, in particular the opening and ending, which suggests that some of the difficulties lay in the script itself. The Australian Alan

Osbiston was asked to re-shoot scenes and to re-edit *Daybreak*, but as Muriel Box recorded in their diary in January 1947: 'neither Sydney nor I will ever be more than fifty per cent satisfied with it'.[136]

These difficulties were compounded by significant problems with the BBFC over the film, especially in the context of a debate in the Commons over whether or not the death penalty should be abolished. The censor demanded that almost all the key confrontation between Tribe and Tyson in the condemned cell be cut; all that could be salvaged, Box noted, was a 'miserable portion'.[137] Indeed, although the scene has evocative expressionist lighting and design, it is so truncated that Tyson's heartfelt appeal for Tribe to admit who he really is looks contrived and Tribe's breakdown absurdly histrionic. Box thought this intervention 'ruined the picture and cut out Max's best acting performance'.[138] Additional dialogue had to be shot to replace the gaps left by the censorship cut, making the scene rather wordy and wooden. The violent lovemaking between Tyson and Frankie was also cut, which Box also felt undermined the film's frank and adult treatment of sexuality. In a sympathetic article in *Reynold's News*, Joan Lester states that the death-cell scene was switched from the end to the opening and argues: 'The result of the cuts is to weaken the drama of the story and to leave the film a little disjointed and obscure.'[139] However, her account runs contrary to Box's own in his 'Open Letter' to the Critics (May 1948), where he protested that although the film 'has been mutilated in several places', these 'cuts have not altered the basic plot of the story, or the incidents of its development, in any way whatsoever. They have merely bowdlerised scenes which, in their original form, seemed to me to be examples of film craftsmanship at its best.'[140] Box also criticised the BBFC's ethical timidity: 'The final embargo placed upon the picture by the censor was the deletion of a title immediately preceding the opening scene. This title consisted simply of a quotation from the debate in the House of Commons on the abolition of capital punishment. The quotation appeared in nearly every national newspaper and, of course, in Hansard.'[141]

The censors' 'Minute of Exception', preserved in Box's papers, confirms his account, demanding the deletion of the whole scene of Tyson in the death cell (in reel one) and asking that Tyson's attempted rape of Frankie and her struggles be considerably reduced and the brutality of the fight between Tyson and Tribe be toned down considerably, but not asking for any restructuring.[142] As has been shown, it was a very characteristic Box technique to begin with a dramatic scene and have the rest of the action expounded in flashback. A shooting script (dated December 1945) also confirms Box's account and shows that there was to have been a final scene in which Tribe returns to the bar in which he first met Frankie. Having been drinking heavily, he imagines that a woman who arrives is Frankie, but realising he is mistaken slumps back into his chair.[143]

In its mutilated form, *Daybreak* was finally released in May 1948. For the most part, reviewers accepted Box's protestations, but the *Star* noted 'gaps and uncertainties, though they hardly relate to the scenes specified by Mr. Box'.[144] The *Daily Mirror*'s reviewer commented ruefully: 'Sydney Box is indeed an optimist if he ever thought the censor would allow him to make a true version of Monckton Hoffe's distinctly sordid drama of the Thames waterside.'[145] There was considerable praise for the 'sadly sensuous' Portman, but critics were generally quite scathing about this ham-fisted attempt to ape the French style.[146] The most positive comment came from the *Evening News*'s reviewer, who thought that *Daybreak* 'In its sombre way has an Eugene O'Neill atmosphere and some of the quality of the best French screen dramas'.[147]

The production of *The Killer and the Slain*, also announced in December 1945, suffered a worse fate. It was an adaptation of Hugh Walpole's controversial and highly acclaimed first-person novel, published in 1942, about a divided man, a murderer who gradually turns into the man he has killed, both physically and morally.[148] Several months and £15,000 were spent preparing the production, including commissioning a screenplay by Bridget Boland and hiring Henry French to direct. A mournful entry in the Diaries noted that the Rank board cancelled the film in May 1947 'on the grounds that it was too sadistic and gloomy for present day audiences!'[149] Not only did this decision mean that Box was denied the opportunity to further explore several key themes, the cancellation deprived Eric Portman of a marvellous acting opportunity. It demonstrates once again the limitation of the term 'independent' to describe Box's position because Rank, the distributor-exhibitor, still had ultimate veto over his projects.

The third psychological thriller was *The Upturned Glass*, another study of the tragic, doomed divided man. Michael Joyce (James Mason) is a cultivated brain surgeon, a man of sensitivity, depth of feeling and imagination, who becomes a killer in order to avenge the murder of his fiancée (Rosamund John) by her sister-in-law (Pamela Kellino). Unable to accept what he has done, Joyce commits suicide by driving his car over Beachy Head. This was a more formulaic and superficial treatment of the same themes, though with some highly accomplished cinematography by Reginald Wyer, and very much Mason's project rather than Box's. Its original screenplay was written in haste by Jno. P. Monaghan, the young American who was Mason's friend and biographer, after Mason's preferred subject, the life of the Brontës, had to be abandoned because of a rival Hollywood project.[150] When Box took up his position at Gainsborough, he handed the production over to Betty Box who co-produced with Mason himself and the film was finished at Islington and released in June 1947.[151]

The Brothers

The final film that must be considered as part of the Riverside group, even though it was shot at Shepherd's Bush, was *The Brothers*, because the project was brought to Box before his appointment at Gainsborough and released under the Triton label. Its origins go back to an agreement made in 1936 between the novelist L. A. G. Strong and the director David Macdonald that they would make a film of Strong's 1932 novel whenever the conditions were right.[152] Following demobilisation, after a distinguished wartime career as head of the Army Kinematograph Unit and director of some notable documentaries, Macdonald approached Box as the producer most likely to have the imagination to take on what is quite difficult material about murderous clan rivalries and sexual jealousies in a remote Scottish community at the turn of the twentieth century.[153] Box was keen to support another innovative historical drama based on a book he admired and to work with a director of Macdonald's stature. He announced *The Brothers* in his 1947 production schedules as 'strong-meat drama'.[154]

An added incentive for Box may well have been that much of the film was to be made on location, as a studio-based film would have been difficult to accommodate within the 1946/47 production schedules. One of the great strengths of *The Brothers* is its location work on the Isle of Skye. The often strikingly beautiful photography was under the direction of Peter Hennessey, whose cinematography on documentary films such as *The Crofters* (1945), made for Greenpark (one of the companies that Verity absorbed), had established a high reputation. The work was often difficult and painstaking: 'For two important sequences over four minutes unbroken sunshine was required. Every possible camera angle was used to heighten the dramatic effect of the scenes, from cameras slowly moving with the tide to cameras and crews lashed to cliff-tops for the thrilling lamb rescue scenes.'[155] The expansive, even lyrical exterior sequences are deliberately contrasted with Stephen Dade's studio work, which is sombre and often expressionist, using intense close-ups and looming shadows to suggest entrapment and fear. In keeping with his policy of trusting untried talent, Box also signed Cedric Thorpe Davie and Bernard Stevens to write the music after they had won first and second prize at a *Daily Express* symphony concert. Davie had knowledge of traditional Scottish music.[156]

Box was thus able to furnish the production with a top-notch technical crew, but unfortunately was unable to provide a comparably strong cast. Ann Todd refused to appear in the film and was suspended by Box; Michael Redgrave abandoned the central part of Fergus Macrae in order to star in *Fame Is the Spur* (1947).[157] Todd's replacement, the Rank contract star Patricia Roc, lacked emotional range in the role of Mary Lawson, in which she needed to be both femme fatale and victim. Redgrave's replacement, Maxwell Reed, had the physicality for the role, but also lacked emotional expressiveness. This was unsurprising as Reed, despite having an important role in *Daybreak*, was still very inexperienced, a Company of Youth hopeful suddenly catapulted to stardom. Another Company of Youth player, Andrew Crawford, fared rather better as Fergus's adversary, the boldly sensuous Willy McFarish, whose breezy sexual confidence contrasts with his rival's tortured gloom and guilt.

The Boxes' adaptation abandons the full sweep of Strong's novel, with its muted redemption of Fergus, in favour of an intense, concentrated narrative in which Mary plays a more pivotal role. The film opens with her arrival on the island, the poor orphan from a Glasgow convent now entrusted to the care of Hector Macrae (Finlay Currie), for whom she is simply a drudge. As another intruder into a male stronghold, her presence serves to intensify the Macrae/McFarish rivalry as Fergus and Willy battle over her. The rivalry is settled in time-honoured manner by a rowing contest. The Macraes are victorious, but Hector dies from an overstrained heart. His dying wish is that Fergus should marry Mary, but the scheming elder brother John (Duncan Macrae), keeps this command secret because he lusts after Mary himself. Told that he must obey John in all matters concerning the family, Fergus consistently represses his feelings for Mary, and is another divided man, his unquestioning loyalty to the family hierarchy fatally at odds with his sexual desire and his own inchoate urge to break free of the fearsome weight of tradition and custom.

Mary, baffled and confused by his attitude, turns again to Willy, but when Fergus whips her, at John's behest, the act turns into violent lovemaking. This convinces Mary of Fergus's passion, but Fergus is immediately plunged into guilty and bitter regret. The two are brought together again on a fishing trip by the avuncular Aeneas McGrath (Will Fyffe), but their happiness together is cut short when Fergus, trying to catch lobster in the rock pools, finds his thumb trapped in the throat of a conger eel. He is forced to cut it off in order not to be drowned by the rising tide. This graphic and shocking scene is a powerful metaphor for his fear of women and sexuality, and a symbolic castration.

John, whose advances are consistently rebuffed by Mary, convinces Fergus that she is the source of all the misfortune that has beset the family and must be removed. Fergus, blindly obedient, takes Mary out in his boat and kills her, but drowns himself in remorse, thus fulfilling the terrible legend that haunts all the lovers on the island. In the final stark and terrifying scene, the islanders, aware that John is responsible for what has happened, advance towards him bearing the weights that will root him to the sea-bed while a seagull dives for the fish tied to his head and cracks his skull. As this repeats the earlier ritual execution of an informer – the islanders smuggle whisky to supplement their fishing income and fear betrayal to the exciseman – it lends the film a grim, forbidding circularity, immensely powerful, but chilling.

The Brothers was another generic hybrid, part melodrama, part *noir* and part costume drama. But it was the film's corrosive fatalism that reviewers commented on most. *The Tribune* thought that it made 'few box-office concessions, except that passion is kept at fever pitch' and that though a work of art, it was 'grim and harsh, and shuts the gates of mercy on mankind'.[158] More positively, Reg Whiteley in the *Daily Mirror*, while he conceded the film's starkness, considered *The Brothers* to be a 'splendid essay in something new in the way of realistic drama ... another really top grade British picture'.[159] Dilys Powell was the film's most eloquent champion, arguing that she felt impelled to 'speak up for a film so courageous and so uncompromising' whose occasional flaws in characterisation did not obscure the power of the 'rough, strong images that persist in the mind's eye. If this were a French film we should, I fancy, be ready to excuse the weaknesses ... It is another proof of the coming of age of the British cinema that we in this country are able to recreate so grim a poetic tragedy.'[160]

However, in the *Evening News*, Jympson Harman, adducing *The Man Within*, as additional evidence, accused Box of fostering sadism in British films. In his reply the following day, Box robustly defended both films as faithful adaptations of prominent writers made by someone 'trying to raise the general standard of British films'. In responding to Harman's charge that the scene where Fergus has to cut off his own thumb 'exceeds legitimate dramatic limit', Box averred that he had asked readers of the novel which incident they remembered most clearly, and this had been their overwhelming choice. He went on to argue that although it would have been easy to give *The Brothers* a happy ending or to make comedies as an escape from austerity, such pandering to popular taste was a betrayal of the responsible producer's proper function: 'I believe that most people would prefer the avenue of escape to be that of good literature rather than cheap comedy. That is why you will find that many of our forthcoming films are based on the work of this country's best writers.'[161]

The Riverside films represent Box's most significant achievement as a writer-producer in the pre-war French mode. The success of *The Seventh Veil* ensured that the subsequent films were financed, distributed and exhibited by Rank, and Box was able to use this stability to produce films that were aesthetically and thematically innovative and challenging. They treat sexuality and relationships in an adult way and explore a range of social and psychological issues, which have their root, it can be argued, in the disruption caused by the war and the difficulties of the transition to peacetime. The principal focus is the troubled, divided male, riven by contradictory impulses and desires that he cannot control. But although women are often victims, their struggle to forge their own independence, to think for themselves and to make their way in a masculine world, is portrayed sympathetically. The emphasis is on change, the break-up of existing systems of thought and customs, and their replacement by ones that can accommodate a new relationship between the sexes where there is a greater degree of equality – an agenda that is broadly socialist-feminist. Although *Daybreak* and *The Brothers* show the failure of such impulses towards change, their stark, tragic power is a testimony to Box's willingness to confront difficult issues. To a remarkable extent these films fulfilled his ambitions to become a genuinely creative producer, making pictures that could engage with important issues and lead public taste. However, the problems surrounding *Daybreak* or *The Killer and the Slain* are a forceful reminder that Box worked under strict external constraints and that the independence he had won was often severely circumscribed.

Notes

1 'Progress and Future of Verity Films', 131.
2 'Sydney Box Gives Up Verity Post', *Today's Cinema* 1 December 1944, 1. Box continued to produce the occasional film for Verity, including two Shakespeare excerpts (*Julius Caesar* and *Macbeth*), made for the British Council in 1945.
3 Diaries, 13 April 1943.
4 *The Cinema*, 13 December 1944, 19.
5 See Colin Crisp, *The Classic French Cinema, 1930–1960* (Bloomington, Indiana: Indiana University Press, 1997), pp. 267–323.
6 For further details see Andrew Spicer, 'The BBFC Scenario Reports at the British Film Institute: The case of the macabre film', *Journal of Popular British Cinema*, 3 (2000), 121–4.
7 Box, *The Lion That Lost Its Way*, p. 27.
8 The Clive Brook Collection, BFI Special Collections, item 83, 'The Eightyfour Ages of Clive Brook: His Life and Times', unpublished autobiography, p. 242.

9 Box, *The Lion That Lost Its Way*, p. 32.
10 Muriel Box, *Odd Woman Out*, p. 165.
11 MacQuitty, *A Life to Remember*, pp. 281–2.
12 Brook, 'The Eightyfour Ages of Clive Brook', pp. 242–4.
13 Box, *The Lion That Lost Its Way*, p. 28.
14 Muriel Box, *Odd Woman Out*, p. 165.
15 Box, *The Lion That Lost Its Way*, p. 27.
16 Brook, 'The Eightyfour Ages of Clive Brook', p. 244.
17 Elspeth Grant, *Daily Sketch* (31 March 1944).
18 Diaries, 29 February 1944.
19 The Clive Brook Collection, BFI Special Collections, item 76, letter from Sydney Box to Clive Brook, 31 March 1944.
20 Diaries, 9 May 1943.
21 BECTU, collection of oral history interviews with union members, held at the BFI, tape 179, Harold French.
22 Diaries, 9 April 1943; 9 May 1943.
23 Diaries, 27 April 1943.
24 Diaries, 1 August 1944.
25 *Daily Telegraph*, 31 July 1944.
26 Diaries, 27 July 1944.
27 Diaries, 21 February 1944.
28 Box, *The Lion That Lost Its Way*, p. 38.
29 Diaries, 1 July 1944; 1 August 1944.
30 Box, *The Lion That Lost Its Way*, p. 38.
31 Diaries, 21 February 1944.
32 *Ibid.*
33 Box, *The Lion That Lost Its Way*, p. 38.
34 See Mabel Constanduros's autobiography, *Shreds and Patches: Autobiographical Memoirs* (London: Lawson and Dunn, 1946), pp. 125–6.
35 Balfour had been a major star in the 1920s, especially in the 'Squibs' comedy series produced by George Pearson. Her last film before *29 Acacia Avenue* had been *Eliza Comes to Stay* (1936).
36 *KW*, 27 September 1945, 28.
37 Muriel Box, *Odd Woman Out*, p. 167.
38 *Ibid.*
39 Diaries, September 1944 (no day specified).
40 Diaries, 22 January 1945.
41 Muriel Box, *Odd Woman Out*, pp. 177–8.
42 Box, *The Lion That Lost Its Way*, p. 44.
43 Diaries, 8 February 1945.
44 Political and Economic Planning, *The British Film Industry* (London: PEP, 1952), pp. 147–56.
45 Box, *The Lion That Lost Its Way*, pp. 45–6.
46 *Ibid.*, p. 74. Muriel Box's account is slightly different, see *Odd Woman Out*, pp. 177–8.
47 *KW*, 27 December 1945, 28.
48 Box, *The Lion That Lost Its Way*, p. 47.
49 *Ibid.*, p. 77. I have been unable to locate this film, but have no reason to doubt Box's veracity. Muriel Box does not name the film, but corroborates this account (*Odd Woman Out*, p. 169).
50 Box, *The Lion That Lost Its Way*, p. 47.
51 Muriel Box, *Odd Woman Out*, p. 171.
52 Diaries, 22 January 1945.

53 *Ibid.* 'Ortus' was a reversal of Sutro.
54 Muriel Box, *Odd Woman Out*, p. 171.
55 Betty Box, *Lifting the Lid*, p. 34.
56 Muriel Box, *Odd Woman Out*, p. 171.
57 *Ibid.*, p. 170. Gainsborough released the film about Paganini as *The Magic Bow* in October 1946, starring Stewart Granger.
58 Box, *The Lion That Lost Its Way*, p. 49.
59 Muriel Box, *Odd Woman Out*, p. 170.
60 Ann Todd, *The Eighth Veil* (London: William Kimber, 1980), p. 57.
61 James Mason, *Before I Forget* (London: Sphere, 1982), pp. 196–7.
62 Diaries, 22 January 1945.
63 See Andrew Spicer, 'Male Stars, Masculinity and British Cinema, 1945–60', in Robert Murphy (ed.), *The British Cinema Book*, 2nd edn (London: BFI, 2001), p. 94.
64 Mason, *Before I Forget*, p. 188.
65 Box, *The Lion That Lost Its Way*, p. 50; Mason recalled that before he became available Nicholas was seen as a 'straight Svengali figure' to be played by Francis L. Sullivan (*Before I Forget*, p. 198).
66 MSBC, box 1, item 1, third script, n.d., p. 74.
67 Muriel Box, *Odd Woman Out*, p. 174.
68 Alan Wood, *Mr Rank: A Study of J. Arthur Rank and British Films* (London: Hodder and Stoughton, 1952), p. 151.
69 *KW*, 13 December 1945, 12.
70 *Film Industry*, 4:20 (3 February 1948), 12.
71 Muriel Box, *Odd Woman Out*, pp. 184–5. Ann Todd's recollection was the opposite: 'Child, you didn't go to that horrid man at the end, did you? I couldn't quite see without my glasses' (*Eighth Veil*, p. 61).
72 Sarah Street, *Transatlantic Crossings: British Feature Films in the USA* (London: Continuum, 2002), pp. 94, 104, 114.
73 Figures quoted in Dennis Holman, 'Sydney Box', *Film Illustrated Monthly*, 3:2 (February 1948), 12.
74 Peter Noble (ed.), *The British Film Yearbook 1947–48* (London: Skelton Robinson, n.d.), pp. 134–5.
75 Bernstein, 'Film Questionnaire Reports, 1946–47', in Maud Miller (ed.), *Winchester's Screen Encyclopedia* (London: Winchester Publictions, 1948), p. 219.
76 See, *inter alia*, J. R. Rees, *The Shaping of Psychiatry by War* (London: Chapman & Hall, 1946). The *News Chronicle*'s reviewer thought *The Seventh Veil* was 'in the popular tradition of psychoanalytical melodrama' (30 October 1945).
77 Molly Haskell, *From Reverence to Rape* (Harmondsworth: Penguin, 1973), pp. 153–88.
78 *Evening Standard*, 19 October 1945.
79 Todd, *Eighth Veil*, p. 62.
80 *Daily Mirror*, 19 October 1945.
81 Todd, *Eighth Veil*, p. 58.
82 *Picturegoer*, 16 July 1946, 9. Mason gained 16.3 per cent of the vote, placing him second behind Laurence Olivier in *Henry V*, who gained 19.1 per cent.
83 Reviewers were favourably impressed by *The Seventh Veil*'s 'filmcraft'; for example, see *Spectator*, 26 October 1945.
84 *KW*, 1 March 1945, 37.
85 *Daily Mirror*, 19 October 1945.
86 *Observer*, 21 October 1945.
87 Kit Porlock, *The Seventh Veil: The Book of The Film* (London: World Film Publications, 1946), p. 80.
88 *Film Music Notes*, 5:7 (March 1946), 20.
89 *KW*, 18 October 1945, 9.

90 *Spectator*, 5 April 1946.
91 Joan Lester, *Reynold's News*, 21 October 1945.
92 Frederick Mullally, 'Whither Rank?' in Noble (ed.), *British Film Yearbook, 1947–48*, pp. 92–5.
93 Sir Stafford Cripps, 'A Good Reputation for British Films', speech delivered to Rank executives, 16 January 1947; on BFI microfiche for *The Seventh Veil*.
94 Simon Harcourt-Smith, 'A British Producer Gets a New Deal', *Picture Post*, 13 April 1946, pp. 26–7.
95 Sydney Box, 'My Plan for Finding Film Talent', *KW*, 20 December 1945, 203.
96 See *Daily Film Renter*, 20 December 1945, 3.
97 Box, 'My Plan for Finding New Talent', p. 211.
98 'I became, thanks to the Boxes, a piece of merchandise distinctly worth bidding for in Hollywood' (Mason, *Before I Forget*, p. 201).
99 Muriel Box, interview in Aspinall and Murphy (eds), *Gainsborough Melodrama*, p. 65.
100 Muriel Box, quoted in Martyn Shallcross, *The Private World of Daphne Du Maurier* (London: Robson Books, 1991), pp. 112–13.
101 In all, twenty-five minutes appear to have been cut; see Diaries, 6 March 1946; 21 March 1946.
102 Diaries, 27 March 1946.
103 *Ibid.*
104 *Daily Mail*, 24 May 1946.
105 Details from press book.
106 Richard Winnington, *News Chronicle*, 25 April 1946.
107 *Monthly Film Bulletin*, 13:184 (April 1946), 46.
108 *Film Industry*, 1:1 (July 1946), 34–5.
109 See *KW*'s yearly round-up, 20 December 1945, p. 245; and Julian Poole, 'British Cinema Attendance in Wartime: Audience preference at the Majestic, Macclesfield, 1939–46', *Historical Journal of Film, Radio and Television*, 7:1 (1987), 15–34, p. 28.
110 Diaries, 6 March 1946. Muriel Box was brought in as dialogue director.
111 *Monthly Film Bulletin*, 13:150 (June 1946), 79.
112 *Daily Mirror*, 8 October 1946. *The Times*'s reviewer (8 October 1946) thought it was an anecdote spun out to fill ninety minutes.
113 E. Arnot Robertson, *The Listener*, 10 October 1946.
114 Diaries, 1 August 1944. Greene had no contact with the production, became annoyed by the Boxes' treatment, and inserted a clause in every future film contract forbidding its resale to Box; see Quentin Falk, *Travels in Greeneland: The Cinema of Graham Greene* (London: Quartet Books, 1984), p. 51.
115 See Muriel Box's comments in Falk, *Travels in Greeneland*, pp. 48–9.
116 Diaries, 30 June 1944; 14 May 1944.
117 Diaries, 27 March 1946.
118 Box, memo to John Davis, 17 May 1946, SBP.
119 Diaries, 2 May 1946.
120 Diaries, 22 December 1945; 18 June 1946.
121 Diaries, 14 February 1948. Unfortunately no details are given.
122 The Boxes' second screenplay (dated 1946) makes this homoeroticism more explicit throughout. See *The Man Within* (S17411), BFI library.
123 *The Man Within*, press book, BFI library.
124 *Daily Worker*, 6 April 1947.
125 Dilys Powell, *Films Since 1939* (London: British Council/Longmans Green, 1947), pp. 4–5.
126 Diaries, 28 March 1947.
127 Jympson Harman, *Evening News*, 7 April 1947.

128 Arthur Vesselo, 'Films of the Quarter', *Sight and Sound* (Summer 1947), 76.
129 Basil Wright, *Spectator*, 18 April 1947.
130 Joan Lester, *Reynold's News*, 6 April 1946; Angela Milne, *Observer*, 8 April 1946.
131 Diaries, 11 July 1945. I have been unable to locate a copy of Hoffe's story.
132 See Ginette Vincendeau, 'Noir Is Also a French Word: The French Antecedents of Film Noir', in Ian Cameron (ed.), *The Movie Book of Film Noir* (London: Studio Vista, 1992), p. 54.
133 *Ibid.*, p. 55.
134 Arnold Meredith, *Daybreak: The Book of the Film* (London: World Film Publications, 1948), p. 80.
135 Diaries, 2 July 1946.
136 Diaries, 1 January 1947.
137 Diaries, 17 May 1948.
138 *Ibid.*
139 Joan Lester, *Reynold's News*, 23 May 1948.
140 Included on the BFI microfiche for *Daybreak*.
141 *Ibid.*
142 MSBC, box 2, item 2, 'Minute of Exception', dated 23 April 1948.
143 Meredith's *Book of the Film* was clearly produced before these cuts had been made and contains an interesting description: 'The film was able to trace the last moments of a condemned man more frankly than any previous one. When the door of his cell slides open to reveal the gallows, however, the camera has to turn away [the Home Office had refused to allow gallows to be photographed], and it is the prisoner's reaction to his first sight of the execution that is seen, not the chamber itself' (p. 80). This book also contains two stills that do not appear in the film as released.
144 *Daily Star*, 21 May 1948.
145 *Daily Mirror*, 21 May 1948.
146 *Daily Mail*, 21 May 1948.
147 *Evening News*, 20 May 1948.
148 See Rupert Hart-Davis, *Hugh Walpole* (Stroud: Sutton Publishing, 1997), pp. 425, 432–8.
149 Diaries, 17 May 1947.
150 Sheridan Morley, *Odd Man Out* (London: Coronet, 1990), pp. 77–8.
151 Betty Box, *Lifting the Lid*, p. 35.
152 L. A. G. Strong, *The Brothers*, unabridged film edition, ed. William R. T. Rodger (London: Methuen/Triton Films, n.d.), p. i.
153 See the interview with David Macdonald, 4654/3, Imperial War Museum.
154 KW, 19 December 1946, 187.
155 Strong, *The Brothers*, p. i.
156 Details from press book for *The Brothers*, BFI Library.
157 Diaries, 2 July 1946.
158 *Tribune*, 16 May 1947.
159 Reg Whiteley, *Daily Mirror*, 9 May 1947.
160 *Sunday Times*, 11 May 1947.
161 '*The Brothers*: Sydney Box replies to Harman', *Evening News*, 16 May 1947.

'The apple of Mr Rank's mercatorial eye': managing director of Gainsborough Pictures (1946–49)

5

Cometh the hour

The Seventh Veil's combination of modest cost and huge popularity was a powerful demonstration of Box's ability as a producer and was highly attractive to the Rank Organisation, which had ambitious plans to increase production now that wartime restrictions on plant and film stock had been lifted.[1] However, volume production was precisely not what was forthcoming from Rank's existing producers. In particular, the output of under three films a year from Gainsborough Pictures was considered inadequate.[2] Rank himself, who had been content to pursue a hands-off policy since acquiring the company in 1941, was now determined that its output should rise significantly, and Maurice Ostrer, in charge of production at Gainsborough, came under growing pressure.[3] Ostrer, who was opposed in particular to Rank's moves to centralise production, became ever more frustrated about his increasingly marginal status and his inability to influence production policy, resigning in April 1946.[4]

Box had been invited to join the Gainsborough board in May 1946, and was appointed as Ostrer's successor as managing director on 1 August 1946.[5] Box had been making strenuous efforts to buy both Twickenham and Riverside studios as a base from which to continue independent production, and taking control of Gainsborough meant giving up his hard-won independence.[6] But it was a tremendous opportunity to gain control of a powerful, well-established production company with a staff of nearly 1,000, and to become a real force within the British film industry. His appointment attracted considerable attention in film journals and the trade press. As one noted: 'To become Britain's premier producer in four years from his first feature film is good going'.[7] As Box later remarked with characteristic deadpan humour: 'To have two studios as my personal playthings, with all the money I needed to make pictures in them – who could possibly refuse that?'[8]

Box's films would now be fully financed and distributed by Rank, thereby ending all the tribulations he had experienced over the past three years, including fitting his films into the 'immovable' schedules at Riverside. Rank's offer also came, as Betty Box recalled, 'with a large down payment, a sum of money that it was very difficult to refuse'.[9]

Box was appointed on the understanding that he would increase production at Gainsborough to twelve films annually as part of Rank's expanded programme.[10] In a statement issued immediately after he took up the post, Box declared that his 'principal aim will be to step up the quantity of good British pictures. It is more than ever necessary that British producers should provide enough British pictures to occupy a substantial portion of the screen-time in our own cinema – and in addition as much of the world market as our pictures merit.'[11] He judged that although the figure of 200 domestic feature films per year, for which the Association of Cine-Technicians (ACT) had been lobbying, was optimistic, if his own commitment to produce twelve films per annum was matched by the rest of the industry, 100 'real full-length features' was a realisable target. Such a total would require 'careful and ingenious use of studio space' and the full co-operation of 'all branches of studio labour', but this should be possible, as technicians would gain most from such an expansion. As John Barber commented in the *Leader Magazine*, Box's willingness 'to discipline himself to forward planning, strict schedules, tight budgets, and interlocking inter-studio facilities' made him 'the apple of Mr Rank's mercatorial eye'.[12] Box seems to have genuinely admired efficiency in film production, writing approvingly of the Hollywood system where production units were better supervised and worked longer than in Britain, thereby reducing the shooting schedule for a first feature from the British norm of seventy days to forty.[13] He also wrote of the 'thrill' of finishing a film on time and under budget.[14]

Box was acutely conscious that in order to meet his target of twelve films a year he needed to ensure that both Gainsborough studios, Islington and Shepherd's Bush were continuously occupied. He also came to understand that it was only by making twelve films a year that he could make a profit, because of the crippling overheads he had to work with as part of the Rank Organisation.[15] Notwithstanding these constraints, his appointment afforded Box the opportunity to put into practice his already formulated strategy of creating a sustainable British film industry. Box argued that he was now in a position where he could 'afford to experiment with writers and to work out a balanced production programme'.[16] Such a programme could be more progressive than that of an independent producer who was forced to follow trends. Box judged that he now had a real opportunity to 'look ahead and try not merely to acquiesce in box-office trends but to lead public opinion and gauge future audience requirements'.[17] However, he understood that this opportunity to influence taste and attitudes would have to be taken within the context of producing entertaining films that could be enjoyed by the broad cinema-going public. As he told *Picturegoer*: 'I do not want to see propaganda in a feature film. People go to the cinema for enjoyment and relaxation.'[18]

Production policy

Box's overall production policy had three interrelated dimensions: the maximum use of the physical resources at his disposal; a 'balanced programme of films' that extended over a wide variety of genres; and a three-tier system of film-making. Box had seven stages at his disposal – five at Lime Grove in Shepherd's Bush and two at Poole Street in Islington – which generated '300 floor-weeks' for building sets and shooting. As the average film took twenty-four weeks, twelve films a year meant 288 weeks were committed, leaving very little margin for retakes, over-runs and essential repairs and maintenance.[19] Box was determined to reduce shooting schedules to under eleven weeks and to institute the practice of using his sound stages in pairs so that shooting and building could progress simultaneously. Even so, he was careful to maintain that: 'Production economy is linked with careful planning and does not imply a cheaper production.'[20] Any productions that could reduce pressure on studio space were encouraged, including 'open air' films (ones made almost entirely on location) such as *A Boy, a Girl and a Bike* (1949), shot along Wharfedale Valley in the Yorkshire Dales.[21] Even so, there was a constant struggle to keep to schedule, because the studio facilities were cramped and difficult. Both Shepherd's Bush and Islington, 'had been built upwards rather than outwards, so that each had studios one above the other, which meant that sets, props, furniture, actors and such occasional extras as horses or camels or tanks, had to be transported in a rickety elevator from the ground floor to the studios above'.[22] Lime Grove, rebuilt by the Ostrers in 1929, was reasonably salubrious, with accommodation for 600 artists, star dressing rooms, laboratories, three private theatres, an orchestration room, plasterers' and carpenters' workshops, property rooms and monitor and recording rooms.[23] Its five sound stages, all with large soundproofed doors, gave a total area of 31,000 square feet, with the capacity to shoot two or three films simultaneously.[24] At Islington, a converted power station, conditions were considerable worse. Betty Box recalled that it 'was a filthy place, next door to a glue factory which stank'.[25] Although there were two sound stages, with a total of 10,220 square feet, only one production could be handled at a time because there was inadequate soundproofing, which also made the dubbing of music a real problem and held up production. The lift between the two stages was so small that sets with large props (such as a vehicle) had to be shot on the ground floor.[26]

In his report 'Production and Future Planning', submitted to the Rank board in July 1947, Box complained that much of the equipment at both studios was 'obsolete or obsolescent', including cameras, lamps and projectors, but especially the British Acoustic sound equipment, installed because the company was an Ostrer subsidiary.[27] He argued that both studios should be equipped with Western Electric sound channels which would offer better quality, encourage some 'artists who are loath to appear in pictures using British Acoustic' to work at Gainsborough and create a flexible interchangeability with Rank's flagship studios at Denham and Pinewood. If such a capital investment was not forthcoming, Box argued that production should be scaled down to eight films a year. He also suggested splitting Shepherd's Bush from Islington creating separate organisations that could be better managed individually. The report fell on deaf ears, partly because of its inopportune timing. Stafford Cripps had made a special appeal to Rank to step up production to bridge the gap created by the American embargo on film exports to Britain, made in retaliation to the imposition of the 'Dalton Duty', a 75 per cent *ad valorem* tax on luxury imports (including films) imposed in August 1947.[28] Box's twelve films a year were therefore even more vital to Rank's plans.

Box introduced significant changes in the subject matter of Gainsborough films. From 1943 onwards, Ostrer had concentrated on one genre, costume drama, to the virtual exclusion of all others.[29] Box was forced to continue this policy by making *Jassy* (1947), because it was the only script that was in any state of preparedness when he arrived and it would have been more expensive to keep the stages idle.[30] But he swiftly began to concentrate on topical social realism. As *Kinematograph Weekly* reported, Box was consistently looking for 'subjects dealing with live people and things which will lend themselves to production on the actual spot'.[31] However, the necessity to have a 'balanced production programme' meant that this tendency was not exclusive and Box made a wide range of different types of films at Gainsborough, not only social issue films and 'topicals' based on actual incidents that had caught the public's attention, but thrillers, comedies, portmanteau films in which a number of different stories were grafted together, and even further costume dramas.

In his 'Production and Future Planning' report, Box emphasised that under his leadership Gainsborough was committed to making a 'series of middle-budget pictures at an average cost of well below £200,000 and not a series of super-productions at £350,000 and upwards'.[32] Although the large majority of Box's Gainsborough films cost between £150,000 and £200,000, closer inspection of his output reveals there were two other categories of production: a bottom tier of films costing between £100,000 and £120,000 and a top tier, referred to variously as 'super-productions', 'prestige films' or 'specials', which cost well over £200,000. The bottom tier, as exemplified by *My Brother's Keeper* (1948), had short shooting schedules of around six to ten weeks, relative unknowns in the leading roles, untried or inexperienced production teams and relatively little in the way of costumes or sets. Other examples include the 'Huggett' series, which had well-known leads in Jack Warner and Kathleen Harrison, but were quickly assembled and made for around £100,000;[33] the portmanteau films *Marry Me!* (1949; £117,900), which used a largely unknown cast, and *Easy Money* (1948; £116,000). Costs were controlled by using the more expensive stars (Jack Warner, Dennis Price and Greta Gynt) in a single episode.[34] The preponderant middle tier – including *Holiday Camp* (1947; £150,400), *Miranda* (1948; £170,400), *Broken Journey* (1948; £197,000) and *Quartet* (1948; £168,000) – had a twenty-week shooting schedule, a quite experienced production team and reasonably well-known stars. The 'specials' were the costume films, which included *Jassy* (1947), the first Technicolor film shot at Gainsborough; *The Bad Lord Byron* (1949), which cost £223,900; and *Christopher Columbus* (1949), whose costs soared to over £500,000.[35] The 'specials' had far longer shooting schedules which could include a second unit on location abroad. Although these specials were highly disruptive of Box's schedules – and, as I shall discuss in the next chapter, were made reluctantly – it was not planning schedules that constituted the main difficulty Box faced at Gainsborough, it was lack of experienced personnel.

Personnel

When Maurice Ostrer left to found Premier Productions, he took with him two of the principal figures responsible for Gainsborough's highly successful cycle of costume dramas: writer-producer R. J. Minney and director Leslie Arliss. Another significant figure, producer-director

Harold Huth, had also departed to form Burnham Productions with John Corfield. Although Box was careful to retain some key personnel, including directors Arthur Crabtree and Bernard Knowles, production designer Maurice Carter, costumier Elizabeth Haffenden and editor Alfred Roome, whose experience was invaluable, he was keen to bring in his own people to stamp his identity on Gainsborough Pictures.[36] As Val Guest recalled ruefully: 'it soon became obvious that there weren't enough offices for all of them and all of us. So, as contracts expired, off into the wide blue yonder went the old Gainsborough alumni.'[37] Box encountered a certain amount of hostility and opposition from the 'old alumni' who resented his arrival and felt a sense of loyalty to the previous regime.[38] Although Box was an affable, approachable figure, both Roome and Carter recalled that he was also tough, and expert, through a variety of stratagems, at getting his own way. Roome experienced the Box charm: 'Whilst you were with him, you almost couldn't resist him. It was extraordinary, and yet as you went up the corridor, it wore off, you see.'[39] However, whether or not they agreed with his policies, the Gainsborough staff were in no doubt who was in charge. Box presided over weekly meetings with his senior staff on Friday afternoon, at which the following week's business was discussed, in which he could be forceful and quite ruthless.[40] However, although he wanted things done his way, Roome also recalled that he valued a 'team' approach: 'I found he was very receptive and liked listening to people. He would take their ideas and digest them, possibly turn them around a different way, but he'd often use them.'[41]

Box brought to his new post all the tireless energy that had characterised his career so far. All the press profiles of Box at Gainsborough attest to his amazing capacity for hard work: 'Now in control of Gainsborough, his brain is crammed with a mass of detail and he does not delegate much work – even the detail side – to others. Behind the innocent, almost childish face, the quiet, unexcitable voice, is a photographic memory and a brain capable of working eighteen hours a day.'[42] The same article noted that Box viewed seven films a week and 'all notable plays'. Brenda Cross in *Picturegoer* noted that Box was: 'Almost continually on the telephone, with calls to look in at the films in production. He is sometimes compelled to hold inter-office conferences when journeying in the lift from one floor to another.'[43] Box planned the overall production strategy of both studios, allocating each film's budget and ensuring that the stages were in continuous use, and saved studio time by transferring as much business as possible to workshops and rehearsal rooms.[44] His ability to plan ahead and to juggle schedules and personnel to ensure that productions were completed on time was much admired. Box was ultimately responsible for all decisions regarding which personnel were assigned to each production and on what terms, including the often delicate problem of how much a star should be paid. He also viewed all the daily rushes and would have to settle any differences between star and director or director and producer, and had to dismiss anyone whose work was not adequate. This could include the director, as happened on *The Lost People* and *Miranda*. Box was also responsible for arranging distribution of the finished product, and overseeing publicity.

The range of Box's duties can be appreciated less abstractly through examining his role in the production of *Broken Journey*, for which extensive contemporaneous documentation exists.[45] *Broken Journey* was a 'topical': Box had sensed the screen potential of the dramatic and ultimately successful rescue of the crew and passengers of a US Army Dakota plane – one of many that were used by commercial airlines after the war – that crashed in the Alps in November 1946 and made front-page news for several days. Michael Balcon had registered an exactly similar idea with the British Film Producers' Association, but 'when he heard that we were already well advanced in our production, he very sportingly withdrew his registration, leaving the field clear for us'.[46] In order to work quickly, Box chose an experienced writer, Robert Westerby, with an established reputation for topical thrillers, who was able to produce an initial treatment in six days. Once this had been completed Box, with a clear idea of who he was going to cast in the film and with the practised eye of the professional writer, suggested alterations and encouraged Westerby to write the full screenplay with specific actors in mind. In particular, Westerby had to create a suitable role for one of Gainsborough's most popular stars, Phyllis Calvert, who was under contract to play one more role before departing for America. It took all Box's charm, and a certain amount of low cunning, to cajole Calvert into accepting a role she was reluctant to take. After Calvert had been sent the completed script, Box pretended that he was going to ask Westerby to enhance her role. She declined the offer, insisting that the film worked as an ensemble piece. Box had got his way: 'The part I offered Phyllis was exactly her weight and it would have been fatal to build it up. But if I had said so to her, she'd have thought there was a catch in it somewhere. So I helped her ever so gently to find it out for herself.'[47] The final key decision was to assign direction to Ken Annakin, a Box protégé known to be reliable, efficient and used, as an ex-documentarist, to working on location. Box already had a Gainsborough unit working in the Alps on *Snowbound* (1947), and part of the attraction of the project was that Annakin would be able to draw upon their expertise, equipment and knowledge of the best locations.

Once Box had made the key decisions, he left the details of the production to his subordinates. Arthur Alcott, Gainsborough's production manager and another Box 'discovery', was responsible for working out the precise shooting schedule to ensure that sets and floor space were used as economically as possible, and to make sure that Calvert, who was only available for half of the fourteen weeks that Box had allocated to the film, could be present when her scenes were filmed.[48] The problems of filming on location, shooting in a cramped space in the mock-up cockpit at Shepherd's Bush and matching studio and exterior shots were all worked out by the chief technicians – art director Richard Yarrow, cinematographer Jack Cox, sound recordist Brian Sewell and editor Esmond Seal – in conjunction with Annakin. However, Box was always on hand, if not on the studio floor, to cope with 'the daily worries of production – not the least of which is keeping up the morale of the unit and smoothing out temperamental difficulties'.[49] He also viewed each day's rushes to ensure their quality was adequate and to spot any faults. In addition, all the time that *Broken Journey* was in progress, Box had to 'keep a fatherly eye' on the two other films which were being shot at the same time, the five in post-production and the four being scripted. When *Broken Journey* came off the floor, Box was 'immediately plunged into conferences on music, editing and dubbing – and long arguments on delivery dates, titles, censorship and cuts'. Finally, after the first screening he became enmeshed in 'a welter of advertising, billing, exploitation, press shows and trade shows'.[50] Unfortunately, when the film was released in April 1948, some 18 months after the incident had made the news, critics judged that it was no longer topical.[51]

Box has exacting responsibilities, but one of his most important achievements at Gainsborough was to continue his existing policy of encouraging and training new talent and giving opportunities to new entrants to the industry, especially those who were recently demobbed. Although Box's 'Company of Youth' had been subsumed into Rank's 'Charm School' as part of the policy of centralisation, Box was very conscientious, unlike many other of Rank's producers, in giving Charm School alumni, such as Diana Dors and Anthony Steel, opportunities in Gainsborough films. Box's commitment to new blood extended to other creative personnel. In an article, 'Gainsborough: A Nursery for New Names', he identifies eleven new people he had taken on, including Ken Annakin, Terence Fisher, Ralph Thomas, Alfred Roome, Roy Rich, Ralph Smart, Ralph Keene, Peter Rogers and Jan Read, who are characterised as 'youthful, imaginative and believe in and enjoy what they are doing'.[52] His trust in untested personnel was exemplified at its most radical by the thriller *Double Pursuit*, released as *My Brother's Keeper* (1948), in which the whole unit was new to feature films. The original tale was bought from Maurice Wiltshire, a *Daily Mail* reporter writing his first story, and was adapted by Frank Harvey as his inaugural screenplay. It was Antony Darnborough's first film as full producer, and editor Alfred Roome's debut as a director, assisted by Roy Rich, who had previously worked as a production manager for Moss Empires, as dialogue director. Esmond Seal, one of Roome's deputies in the cutting rooms, was given his head as editor, and camera operator Gordon Lang was promoted to cinematographer. Company of Youth graduate Jane Hylton and George Cole were given their biggest roles to date, and Jack Warner was cast against type as an anti-hero. *My Brother's Keeper* was completed in only forty-five days, nine days ahead of schedule and £20,000 under budget, and all those mentioned were awarded long-term contracts. Box argued that *My Brother's Keeper* was notable for 'the proof it has afforded that British studios are full of young people who can make pictures every bit as good as those from Hollywood, if they are given a reasonable break'.[53]

Producers

Broken Journey was one of six films on which Box acted directly as the producer. In order to cope with the volume of work, he used several other producers working under his overall control and direction, all of whom were Box appointees, trusted to operate within the cost-conscious, rationalising framework he had devised for Gainsborough. The most important was Betty Box, who had proved her efficiency and reliability at Verity, as associate producer on several Riverside films and on *The Upturned Glass*, which she co-produced with James Mason. Betty Box was given the onerous task of running Islington studios, where she was responsible for ensuring continuous production, juggling the stages and equipment to fit the exacting shooting schedules, and bringing in all her films on time and preferably under budget. Box allocated her an overall budget of £500,000 to maintain the studios and produce four films a year at an average cost of £120,000.[54] However, Betty Box did not choose the subjects, or the principal cast or crew, nor did she decide on the overall budget for the production: all those decisions were taken by Box himself. Islington was generally used for the lower-tier productions, including the 'Huggett' series, for which Betty Box was also responsible for the promotion and publicity, running readers' competitions in the *Daily Mail* and *Picturegoer*. However, if

Shepherd's Bush was full, Islington could also be used for middle-tier productions, including *The Blind Goddess* (1948) and *Miranda*, or for 'overspill' work such as 'The Colonel's Lady' episode of *Quartet*. When the pressures on Box increased in 1949 and 1950, Betty Box gradually assumed more autonomy, notably with *So Long at the Fair* (1950), but always within the parameters that Box had set. Betty Box was entirely in accord with her brother's policy, priding herself on her 'good housekeeping' and her ability to smooth over the wrinkles in a production, rather than creativity or artistic flair.[55]

The other key producer was Antony Darnborough who, like Betty Box, was responsible for ten films. Darnborough had been introduced to Box in 1945 by his brother-in-law, the music director Muir Mathieson.[56] Darnborough worked on several Riverside productions before moving with Box to Gainsborough, initially as studio manager at Islington, then at Shepherd's Bush. When Alcott took over this role, Darnborough became an associate producer, then a full producer, starting with *My Brother's Keeper*, where his training as a journalist was a valuable asset to a production which featured a reporter covering the pursuit of a criminal. Darnborough was an important part of Box's rationalising ethos, asserting that the pace of production at Gainsborough would not compromise quality because 'it all depends how quickly one can think'.[57] His ability to think quickly and strategically was used to the full with the very tight filming schedules of the bottom-tier comedies, including *Helter Skelter*, *Once upon a Dream* and *Traveller's Joy*. Darnborough also embraced Box's drive for authenticity wherever possible. With *Portrait from Life* (1949), the story of a girl missing in a refugee camp, his initial plan to take the entire unit to Germany and film on the spot proved unworkable because it could not be fed and housed in the devastated country. Darnborough sent production manager Douglas Pierce, with art director Cedric Dawe and Charles Hale, the stills photographer, on a research tour of the Detained Persons camps in Germany, and 'they took enough pictures to ensure complete accuracy in the construction of the studio sets for the film'.[58] In order to obtain authentic types for the mixture of Europeans who were to appear in the crowd scenes, Darnborough advertised widely and hand-picked his 120 extras from over 2,000 applicants.[59] A mark of Box's growing confidence in Darnborough was that he assigned him to the important Somerset Maugham adaptation, *Quartet* (1948), then *Trio* (1950); he was instrumental in persuading Maugham to introduce both collections. As a friend of Noël Coward, Darnborough was called upon to co-direct *The Astonished Heart* (1949) with Terence Fisher.

Aubrey Baring joined Gainsborough after he had been demobbed.

He produced two films directed by David Macdonald, *Snowbound* (1948) and *The Bad Lord Byron*; they had worked together before the war at British National. According to one report it was a complementary partnership, as Baring's easy-going manner was a good foil to Macdonald's robust temperament, but he too could be relied upon to keep costs low.[60] When Baring left to form Mayflower Pictures with Maxwell Setton in 1949, A. Frank Bundy, who had worked with Box as an associate producer on *Daybreak* and had moved with him to Gainsborough where he functioned as Box's personal assistant, took Baring's place.[61] He worked with Macdonald on *Christopher Columbus* and *Diamond City*, travelling 70,000 miles in 1948 gathering background scenes for both films.[62] Two other producers were used for one film each: Ralph Keene, who had worked for Box during the war as managing director of Greenpark Films, was appointed to take charge of the documentary-drama *A Boy, a Girl and a Bike*; and Gordon Wellesley, a screenwriter who had directed films for Verity, was offered the ill-starred *Lost People* (1949), Box's second film about the fate of displaced persons after the war.

Writers

Box and his producers used the screenplay as the key instrument to ensure cost-effective film-making at Gainsborough, working closely with the writer(s) at the planning stage. As a writer himself, Box thought the script was the key to the entire production process and that it was vital for the film industry to attract the best writers and ensure that they had 'an opportunity to learn the technique of scenario writing'.[63] In 'A New Deal for Film Writers', Box argued that the subordination of the writer to the technicians, actors and the director in the film industry must be reversed, and that the writer should assume the same status he or she enjoyed in the theatre, where the script was regarded as sacrosanct, to be altered only with the writer's consent.[64]

Unsurprisingly therefore, Box made his most significant changes at Gainsborough in reorganising scripting. Having persuaded Muriel Box to delay her ambitions to direct, he placed her in charge of a significantly enlarged scenario department, where she was expected 'to find new writers and stories, and with those authors develop them into scripts suitable for the talents of the stars under contract at that time', and also to train new writers 'with film potential'.[65] This was a huge task as, in order to achieve the target of twelve films a year, over forty scripts were required; for each screenplay in production at least three others had to be ready to meet unexpected circumstances such as the star falling ill, contractual difficulties or defaulting. Many projects had to be abandoned at various stages during Box's time at Gainsborough because of the numerous such problems that arose.[66] When the studios were closed in 1949, forty-two scripts were in various stages of preparation, only just enough to keep the stages filled.[67]

Muriel Box was assisted by Peter Rogers, whose job was to sift through the scripts that had been submitted and to work on those that seemed promising. Rogers had been appointed by Box after they had met when Rogers was covering the press reception for *The Seventh Veil*. He was invited to submit his ideas about *Holiday Camp* and, on the strength of these, was asked to join the team of writers and offered a full-time contract.[68] Rogers wrote three further screenplays for Box during this period. Box also gave an opening to another newcomer, Jan Read, who, after a spell in Hollywood training as a screenwriter under Louis de Rochemont and Fritz Lang, had been introduced to Box by Colonel 'Jock' Lawrence, Rank's American representative.[69] When Rogers was made associate producer and became a more established scenarist, Read, who was joined by Alan MacKinnon and Roger MacDougall, became increasingly involved in rewriting and working on scripts under Muriel Box's direction, supervising freelancers and negotiating their contracts; he also wrote the original screenplay for *Helter Skelter*. Read recalled that there were always 'some couple of dozen [scripts] in the works' to cover any contingency, all mapped out on a chart in Muriel Box's office.[70] Read also seems to have worked directly for Box as 'novels in proof, scripts, ideas written in longhand from people who thought they would make a wonderful film began arriving from his office down the corridor with terse requests for précis and opinions on them'.[71] Read was also clear that, although Muriel Box was in charge of the Scenario Department, the ultimate decision rested with him: 'The final responsibility for buying or not buying books or plays and for approving prices and scripting fees was Sydney's'.[72]

This voracious appetite for scripts also meant a constant struggle to find suitable writers, and over forty were used during Box's period of office. Box wrote an article for the *Sunday Despatch* asking for new writers to come forward, part of his wider scheme to seek out and nurture fledgling talent.[73] Those who did emerge were handled according to a well worked-out system:

> we like a short draft and from this we can tell the writer if his yarn has screen possibilities or if they should be torn up and forgotten. If promising, we ask for a full shooting script, telling the author what aspects to play up and what to expand. We like dialogue and action,

> nothing else. We got *Hildegard* [the working title of *Portrait from Life*] in this fashion. David Evans wrote a synopsis, and was asked for a shooting script. Frank Harvey revised it and then Sydney and I took over.[74]

In addition to encouraging new writers, Box also used experienced ones who were affordable, but not those, like Terence Rattigan, whose standard fees went well beyond Box's budget; the exceptions were Coward and Maugham, discussed below. Following the success of *29 Acacia Avenue*, Box used Mabel and Denis Constanduros to help write the first Gainsborough film, *Holiday Camp* (1948). The Constanduros's major contribution was the creation of the Huggett family, based on their sagas of a working-class family, the Bugginses, begun in 1928, which had gained increasing currency as a highly successful wartime radio series. After the reception of *Holiday Camp* established that the Huggetts were the most appealing ingredient in the film, the Constanduroses went on to co-write the three 'sequels', *Here Come the Huggetts* (1948), *Vote for Huggett* (1949) and *The Huggetts Abroad* (1949), which were also popular and cheap to produce.

Ted Willis, who had collaborated on *Holiday Camp*, first met Box when he offered to buy the film rights of his successful play *Buster*, which was performed at the Unity Theatre in 1943 and transferred to the West End for a short run. Unfortunately, Willis's agent tried to hold out for a sum that was not forthcoming.[75] Because of his reputation as someone who could write sympathetically about the aspirations of ordinary people, Willis was drafted in to help script *Holiday Camp* and also worked on *The Huggetts Abroad*. He wrote the entire script for the cycling drama *Wheels within Wheels* (released as *A Boy, a Girl and a Bike*), based on an idea that had come to Box whilst he was on a Sunday afternoon drive.[76] Willis collaborated with the Boxes on *Good Time Girl*, an adaptation of Arthur la Bern's *Night Darkens the Street*, which again shows a sympathetic understanding of the plight of a working-class character.

Despite prodigious efforts, the struggle to find suitable writers was one of Box's most serious problems at Gainsborough – a problem that affected the industry as a whole.[77] Box complained in his 1947 report of

> the difficulty of obtaining twelve first-class scripts each year (we have now used some twenty-four different writers, with mixed results), but we have been forced to work on the majority of the scripts ourselves in order to obtain the standard we require. A reduction of four pictures in the year would enable us to give fifty per cent more time to each script.[78]

No such reduction was forthcoming, and the Boxes had to continue as Gainsborough's main writers, collaborating on the screenplays of eight films – over a quarter of the total – and frequently acting as script 'doctors'. The Diaries record numerous instances when Box rose at 5.00 a.m. in order to rewrite a scene, cut superfluous sections or polish dialogue ready for shooting that day. Ken Annakin recalled that Box could rewrite a scene while he was on the telephone and still make an expert job of it.[79]

However, although Box developed fifteen original screenplays during his tenure at Gainsborough, he was never able to find the time to develop with Muriel one of their own scripts, which had been the basis of *The Seventh Veil*'s success. Instead they worked on adaptations of properties, not necessarily those they would have most liked to film, but ones for which Box could afford to bid in a highly competitive marketplace. In all he commissioned seventeen adaptations, nine from plays and eight from novels or short stories. When the rights had been obtained, 'a really practised script writer was set to work on them to make sure the storyline was kept intact and the theme not twisted or distorted when translated into film'.[80] This was very difficult to achieve in every case. Peter Blackmore made a superb adaptation of his West End hit, *Miranda*, but the pedestrian adaptation of *Traveller's Joy* by Allan Mackinnon and Bernard Quayle only made Arthur Macrae's one-note play more leaden. The Boxes' own invention occasionally flagged, as with *Christopher Columbus*.

Despite all these difficulties and limited resources, Box was determined to secure the services of talented writers, including two, W. Somerset Maugham and Noël Coward, whom he 'admired only just on this side of idolatry'.[81] His work with Maugham was highly successful and is discussed in detail in the next chapter. But with Coward, Box learned a hard lesson about the power of an established literary figure. Box had spent £10,000 in July 1948 to obtain Coward's agreement to script four plays from his 1935 one-act play collection *Tonight at Eight-Thirty*, and a revue, *Nothing New*.[82] Although Box was very pleased with the package he thought he had obtained, only one film was actually made, *The Astonished Heart*, for which the script was virtually ready. Box thought Coward's screenplay excellent and was also highly satisfied with the first week's rushes. But when 'The Master' returned from Jamaica and viewed them, to Box's consternation he demanded that the male lead, Michael Redgrave, be sacked, despite having agreed to all the principal casting before production began.[83] Box was powerless because he had relinquished creative control to Coward, whose contract said that his judgement on any matter was absolute. With an appalled admiration, Box watched as Coward persuaded Rank that Coward himself should play the lead vacated by Redgrave's departure, and be paid £15,000 to do it – money Coward badly needed at the time.[84] Although Box considered Coward's 'rigid' and 'unappealing' performance was the film's main weakness, he was unable to intervene.[85]

Jan Read also recalled that Box 'was always on the lookout for new and inventive writers, and at one time or another I explored projects with Dylan Thomas, Christopher Fry, and James Forsyth'.[86] Unfortunately, these explorations came to nothing, with the partial exception of the collaboration with Dylan Thomas. Box was able to secure Thomas's services by offering him far better terms than Ealing had offered. With typical decisiveness, once Box had heard of Ealing's offer, he drove down to Brighton, where Thomas was staying, to make sure an agreement was reached.[87] Thomas began work for Gainsborough in August 1948, his contract assuring him of £1,000 as advance against three feature scripts which he was to write within the year: *The Beach of Falesá*, based on Stevenson's story of murder and romance in a South Sea island setting; *Rebecca's Daughters*, about the protests against tollgate taxes in rural Wales in the 1840s; and an original script entitled *Me and My Bike*, a fantasy film operetta. He also did a first treatment of a Technicolor version of *Vanity Fair* as a vehicle for Margaret Lockwood in 1949, although no script has been traced, and one of Winston Graham's *The Forgotten Story*, though this did not proceed partly because of Thomas's enthusiasm to start work on *Me and My Bike*.

Thomas was a quick, but highly erratic, worker, constantly struggling with domestic and financial worries, and only *The Beach of Falesá* was completed before Gainsborough was wound up. Jan Read, who had special responsibility for Thomas, considered the adaptation outstanding – 'vivid, poetic and marvellously eloquent' – as did the producer, Ralph Keene, and the director, Ralph Smart, who had been assigned to the project. But it was strongly disliked by Muriel Box, with Box himself noncommittal, aware that by February 1949, when the script was finished, he was no longer in a position to fund an expensive Technicolor production.[88]

Rebecca's Daughters, completed after Gainsborough had been closed, was eventually published in 1965 as one of the launch titles for Box's company Triton Books. As Box comments in his foreword, it was written in fulfilment of Thomas's ambition, disclosed to his friend J. Maclaren Ross, to write a complete screenplay 'ready for shooting, which would give the ordinary reader an absolute visual impression of the film in words and could be published as a new form of literature ... The script had to be an original, specially written in this form and not any kind of adaptation, and that actual film production must be possible.' Box concludes that the script 'is the nearest Thomas came to realising his ambition ... it is technically capable of being filmed without the slightest alteration ... Anyone reading *Rebecca's Daughters* in its present form should be able to imagine the film, as Dylan conceived it, unrolling on the screen before him.'[89]

The final script, *Me and My Bike*, was not completed, but it illustrates how far Box was prepared to encourage unconventional work. Thomas commented: 'For me, as a supposedly imaginative writer, it's got wonderful possibilities, and I feel very enthusiastic about it. Sydney's *carte blanche* as to freedom of fancy, non-naturalistic dialogue, song, music, etc. is enormously encouraging.'[90] The completed fragment was also published by Triton in 1965 and Box wrote about its composition with characteristic warmth:

> *Me and My Bike* was never finished. It was scarcely even begun. As always with Dylan, it started with high hopes. His head appeared around the door, like a dissolute cherub's, his eyes shining with excitement. I want to write the first original film operetta, he told me. It will be all about a man who loves a bicycle ... It covers the whole span of a man's life. He rides penny-farthings, tandems, tricycles, racing bikes – and when he dies at the end, he rides on his bike up a sunbeam straight to heaven, where he's greeted by a heavenly chorus of bicycle bells. Naturally I commissioned Dylan to write it.[91]

It must be a matter of regret that unpropitious circumstances, Thomas's dilatory progress and Gainsborough's increasingly precarious independence, did not allow these scripts to become films.[92]

Directors

In the Gainsborough hierarchy under Box, directors were less important than producers or, in some cases, screenwriters, because they were rarely present at the initial planning stage. In Box's view, the director was the person who realised the finished shooting script. It was a crucial role – requiring someone with 'creative energy, [the] ability to recreate a story in the fire of his imagination and to clothe it with the reality of voices and gestures, movement and setting' – but a subordinate one.[93] Michael Chorlton was swiftly replaced on *Miranda* because his direction, which used the wide-angle, deep focus style of *Citizen Kane*, was judged inappropriate for a light comedy where the dialogue was paramount.[94] Box believed that a good director should have 'a thorough apprenticeship, practical experience in the studios is essential for one whose main task is to co-ordinate the efforts of others and produce an artistic unity'.[95] Ideally, this experience needed to be both in fiction films, in order to understand the art of narrative and to become used to working with actors, and in documentaries, to inculcate a sense of actuality that avoided staginess. It is notable that all the directors that Box brought in from outside – Ken Annakin, David Macdonald, Ralph Smart and Montgomery Tully – had extensive experience in documentaries. These four, who may be described as the 'new boys', formed one category; another was experienced directors – Arthur Crabtree, Harold French, Lawrence Huntington, and Bernard Knowles; and a third the Gainsborough 'nursery' of first-time directors promoted by Box – Terence Fisher, Alfred Roome and Ralph Thomas.

Unsurprisingly the experienced directors were used frequently in the first year of Box's tenure. Knowles, for instance was given the film Box inherited from Ostrer, *Jassy*; while Crabtree directed the first Islington film, *Dear Murderer*; and Lawrence Huntington, who had directed *The Upturned Glass*, was assigned to *When the Bough Breaks*. After that they tended to be given routine films – Crabtree directed *The Calendar* and *Don't Ever Leave Me* – or were dropped altogether as in the case of Huntington. Knowles directed a Box 'topical', *Easy Money*, but was dropped after Box became dissatisfied with his work on *The Lost People* and Muriel took over and reshot most of the film. Harold French was more favoured because of his ability to handle actors and to direct unobtrusively; he was given the solid courtroom drama *The Blind Goddess* and episodes of *Quartet* and *Trio*.

In his profile of the Gainsborough 'nursery', Box called Terence Fisher a 'Highbury graduate', in reference to his training on the 'B' features produced in Rank's low-budget studio. By way of an apprenticeship, Box used Fisher on the low-budget *Marry Me!*, then the middle-tier *Portrait from Life*, before he was given the more prestigious assignments *The Astonished Heart* and *So Long at the Fair*, albeit in collaboration with Darnborough. Ralph Thomas had joined Gainsborough after demobilisation and caught Box's eye because he was 'doing a brilliant job of supervising trailers at Denham Studios'.[96] He was transferred to Islington, where his work on *Miranda* impressed Betty Box, which led to his promotion to director. However, he was obliged to cut his teeth on three bottom-tier comedies: *Helter Skelter*, *Once upon a Dream* and *Traveller's Joy*. Box also encouraged the experienced editor Alfred Roome to direct (in partnership with Roy Rich) *My Brother's Keeper*, as has been mentioned, and also *It's Not Cricket*, an unpretentious comedy-thriller.

Box encouraged the documentarists to try their hand at feature-film direction, usually with 'topicals' and social issue films where their sense of 'actuality' would be beneficial. Ralph Smart, who had directed a number of propaganda shorts for the Australian government during the war and had worked on Ealing's *The Overlanders* (1946), shot almost entirely on location, was given the 'open air' film, *A Boy, a Girl and a Bike*, working with another documentarist, Ralph Keene, as producer. Montgomery Tully, who had directed several propaganda shorts, was given the social issue drama about borstal, *Boys in Brown*, which he also adapted. The other two documentarists, Annakin and Macdonald, were the Box directors whose work was crucial in defining Box's oeuvre.

Annakin had been closely associated with Box since he started at Verity in 1942 and was highly valued as 'quiet, perceptive and unobtrusive' – qualities which lent themselves to the rationalising Box regime under which directors were expected to be efficient rather than artistic. Box's confidence in Annakin was shown by the unprecedented ten-picture contract he was given.[97] His eight films made Annakin the most prolific Box director, showing the confidence placed in him. Annakin proved to be adaptable, skilful and immensely hard-working, prepared to churn out the 'Huggett' films as well as take over projects such as *Miranda* at short notice. Here Annakin realised that the strength of the film lay in the tight, witty script and the excellent cast, and his unobtrusive direction did full justice to those qualities. He was highly adaptable and able to cope with difficult location and studio conditions, as on *Broken Journey*, where he also showed the ability to handle an occasionally temperamental cast. Annakin's first film was the quintessential Box picture, *Holiday Camp*, on which his background in documentaries helped to bring the requisite authenticity to the six interwoven stories. With typical shrewdness, Box surrounded his fledgling director with the best technical support available, to ensure that he learned the ropes of feature-film making quickly.[98] Annakin was also used to direct episodes of both the Somerset Maugham compilations, *Quartet* and *Trio*, and he had his pick of which Maugham stories to direct.

If Annakin was the journeyman director, Macdonald was the 'star', and within the strict limits of the studio's overall economy, he was given the high-status assignments. Macdonald was a more experienced director than Annakin, having directed pre-war thrillers as well as prestigious wartime documentaries including *Desert Victory* (1943) and *Burma Victory* (1945). As a Lieutenant Colonel and ex-head of the Army Kinematograph Unit, Macdonald's appointment to Gainsborough represented something of a coup for Box, who had been highly impressed by his work on *The Brothers*, already discussed. A contemporary profile characterised Macdonald as 'quick-thinking, dynamic and decisive in action, a fast worker who knows exactly what he wants and gets it in the shortest possible time'.[99] His elevated status may also have been the result of Compton Bennett's departure for Hollywood, on the strength of directing *The Seventh Veil*, which left Box without his key director.

Macdonald's first Gainsborough assignment was *Snowbound*, adapted from a Hammond Innes thriller, *The Lonely Skier*, which required extensive location shooting in the Alps. Reviewers thought the skill of the location work was not matched by the rather ham-fisted studio scenes and what one described as a 'messy' denouement.[100] *Good Time Girl* was judged to be much stronger, but it had an excellent screenplay by the Boxes and Ted Willis. Where the scripts were weaker, as was the case with *The Bad Lord Byron* and *Christopher Columbus*, Macdonald seems to have floundered, and, according to Alfred Roome, showed his limitations in handling actors and in his inability to shape a scene so that it was well focused and built to an effective climax.[101] Perhaps in the wake of the critical drubbing of these two films, Macdonald became demoralised and he began to suffer from poor health; his final film for Gainsborough, *Diamond City*, the story of the formation of a 'digger's republic' in South Africa in 1870 when diamonds were first being mined, was his worst. Critics judged it dull, derivative and cliché-ridden, neither illuminating a moment of imperial history nor effective as an adventure story, with a lacklustre visual style and leaden direction.[102]

Cinematographers, set-designers, costumiers and musical directors

The department where Box could draw upon the greatest expertise, and consequently where he made the fewest changes, was cinematography. Jack Asher, Jack Cox, Stephen Dade and Gordon Lang were all established Gainsborough technicians, and between them were responsible for eighteen of Box's films. However, Box brought in two men with whom he had worked at Verity: Ray Elton and Reginald Wyer. Elton shot five films, but Wyer, who had shot the bulk of the Riverside output, was the most prolific of all Box's cinematographers, photographing eight films in total, though mainly routine productions including the 'Huggett' series. It was the relative newcomer Dade, whose work on *The Brothers*, *Snowbound* and *Good Time Girl* had been consistently impressive both in studio scenes and on location, who became the favoured cinematographer, used on both *The Bad Lord Byron* and *Christopher Columbus*. The latter was a particularly significant as Dade was preferred to Geoffrey Unsworth, who had photographed Box's other two Technicolor films, *The Man Within* and *Jassy*. However, neither film gave Dade much scope for the rich tonal contrasts that characterised his earlier films, and in both cases the location work was by other hands, Cyril Knowles and Gordon Lang respectively.

Although James Carter, who had designed Box's Riverside films, did not make the move to Gainsborough, preferring to remain at Riverside as an executive producer for Alliance, Box initiated several far-reaching changes in design policy and the role of the art director. As Laurie Ede has discussed, after the expressionist design that had characterised the Ostrer costume dramas, Box's preference for documentary aesthetics and the emphasis on topicality, authenticity and location work, tended to attenuate the input of the designer.[103] The majority of Box's films used workmanlike sets and gave priority to the script. The key figure was George Provis, an art director on 'quota quickies' in the 1930s who had joined Box on *Daybreak*, and who was promoted to take charge of the art department over the heads of existing incumbents Maurice Carter and Andrew Mazzei. In general, as on *Broken Journey*, Provis worked with the art director, in this case Richard Yarrow, to create sets that complemented the mode of the film.[104] Provis's main concern was to speed up set construction, producing functional sets with the minimum of fuss that would help Box meet his production targets.[105] Occasionally, as with *Easy Money*, on which the sets were criticised as mediocre, the drive to streamline was detrimental to the quality of the production.[106] The exceptions to Box's overall policy on set design, as in so much else, were the historical films, which placed major emphasis on sets and décor. Here Maurice Carter was given more autonomy and a generous budget which afforded him ample scope. On *Jassy*, where Box appears to have wished to outshine the previous regime, Carter's sumptuously detailed sets are the high point of the production, for which he received an Oscar nomination. Chief scenic artist Albert Jullion's resplendent tapestries complemented Carter's designs. Blicking Hall in Norfolk, used for exteriors, was enhanced with imported yew trees.[107] Although Carter's sets for *Christopher Columbus* required the most elaborate sets he had ever built, he was highly critical of the film, as discussed in the next chapter.

Under Box, Elizabeth Haffenden continued her role as chief costume designer, specialising in historical melodrama. Her work on *Jassy*, essentially a continuation of her work under the Ostrers, was often praised, benefitting from a generous budget and the added lustre of colour; it was only outdone by her costumes for *Christopher Columbus*, the most lavish she ever designed. But, as Sue Harper has noted,

Haffenden's 'expressionist' style was rather at odds with Box's penchant for realism, which hamstrung her work, to a degree, on *The Bad Lord Byron*.[108] Haffenden's specialised work had to be supplemented by that of others, notably Yvonne Caffin, Joan Ellacott and Julie Harris, who were competent in modern and contemporary designs and could work effectively within a realist aesthetic. Ellacott's work, for instance, was utilitarian on such films as *Snowbound* and *Portrait from Life*, but she took what opportunities there were, as with Greta Gynt's split-skirt dress, in which she sings the 'Lady Spiv' number in *Easy Money*, which one commentator called an 'eye-opener which could well be entitled the "new look and look again" gown'.[109]

Box's Riverside films, notably *The Seventh Veil*, had demonstrated a knowledgeable concern with orchestration and the use of music. When Box took over at Gainsborough, he no longer used Louis Levy, who had been head of the music department since the coming of sound in 1929; he too moved to Premier Productions.[110] In his place Box used Levy's rival Muir Mathieson, the principal musical director for all Rank's productions, working with particular composers assigned to specific films including Sir Arthur Bliss, who wrote the swelling music for *Christopher Columbus*, and Francis Chagrin, an experienced composer in prewar French cinema, who wrote the distinctive score for *Easy Money*.[111] Benjamin Frankel, who had scored a number of Riverside films, was used for several at Gainsborough, including *Dear Murderer* and *So Long at the Fair*, but no one composer was dominant.

Stars

Box was well aware of the importance of stars, especially for the marketing of a film and for its chances of success outside London: 'As long as the average run of a film in the provinces (where the real money is made) lasts only six days, there is no time to nurse a film into success. The impact has got to be made quickly – and the star is the battering ram.'[112] Box was clearly determined to secure the services of Phyllis Calvert for *Broken Journey* for precisely this reason, but the decisive difference between Box's and the previous regime was that he no longer had the *exclusive* services of the roster of stars who had been the mainstay of Ostrer's costume dramas: Calvert, Stewart Granger, Jean Kent, Margaret Lockwood, James Mason, Dennis Price and Patricia Roc. They were now part of the new central casting system and therefore under contract to Rank rather than to Box. Mason had already departed for Hollywood on the strength of his success in *The Seventh Veil* and was therefore unavailable, but Box found himself competing for the others' services with Michael Balcon and other Rank producers, not always on favourable terms. Despite several announcements of films in which he was to star, Granger never made a Gainsborough film under Box, preferring to work for Cineguild, Two Cities and Ealing, after which he left for Hollywood.[113] Box only secured Margaret Lockwood for the title role that had been specifically prepared for her in *Jassy*, another of the spirited, upwardly mobile outsider heroines that had made her a star, because Rank insisted that it was part of the new seven-year contract which she had signed in July 1946 and she agreed to help Box over his initial difficulties.[114] After this point, Lockwood was not so amenable and turned down the starring role in *Roses for Her Pillow* (released as *Once upon a Dream*) because she considered the script to be inadequate. Box suspended her, which cost Lockwood £13,000 and put the production back eight months, before a replacement was found in Googie Withers.[115] Box also had to accept that his Company of Youth alumni, including the most successful, Joan Greenwood, would appear in other Rank films, because the Company had been absorbed into Rank's Contract Artists Department, a branch of Production Facilities (films) Ltd, the central servicing agency for all Rank films.[116]

Box had already released one of the stars he had under personal contract, Ann Todd. This was detrimental to his films – notably *The Brothers* – but not to Box's bank balance, as he loaned her to David O. Selznick for *The Paradine Case* (1947) for a handsome fee and then sold her contract to Rank so she could make films with David Lean.[117] Eric Portman, a notoriously difficult actor who had also refused to appear in *The Brothers*, gave a mesmerising performance as the jealous husband in *Dear Murderer*, and a more routine one as the eminent lawyer in *The Blind Goddess*. It may have been Portman's irascible temperament that made Box reluctant to cast him in other films, which might explain why Box chose to cast the more equable Dennis Price as Lord Byron, a role that had been Portman's when the film had been announced by Two Cities in 1944.[118] Box had professed himself in favour of loaning stars to American studios as it would raise their profiles and help sell British films in the American market, but he argued that the process must be reciprocal.[119] However, his experience of using an American star, Fredric March, in *Christopher Columbus*, which was always planned as an 'international' production, involved a number of problems. March agreed to David Macdonald directing only if the Boxes were on the floor the whole time, and it seemed to Box that he wanted to take over the running of the film as well as, in Box's opinion, over-acting. There were further problems about March's payment and his reluctance to do the commentary.[120]

As Muriel Box's comments quoted earlier indicate, Box's films were expected to provide roles for Rank's stars, both established and up-and-coming. Claire Bloom was given her first important screen role in *The Blind Goddess*, while the young Dirk Bogarde was cast in the 'Alien Corn' episode of *Quartet*, Jean Simmons in the 'Sanatorium' episode of *Trio* and both together in *So Long at the Fair*, on which Simmons exploited her star power to make sure that Muriel Box did not direct the film.[121] There were ample roles for Rank's personable young men: David Tomlinson in comedy, Derek Bond in melodrama and John MacCallum and Guy Rolfe in both. Glamorous parts were provided for Greta Gynt and Linden Travers, while Anne Crawford, Sonia Holm (a Company of Youth alumna) and Googie Withers could play variations on the attractive, capable middle-class woman, with Nora Swinburne as an older version. Mai Zetterling, on the strength of her success in Ealing's *Frieda* (1947), played similar winsome, pitiable, displaced women in *Portrait from Life* (1948) and *The Lost People* (1949) but had the opportunity to play a more louchely romantic role in the 'Facts of Life' episode of *Quartet*. Her touching performance as Teresa Guiccioli was the only element in *The Bad Lord Byron* that garnered praise. Flora Robson was a friend of Muriel Box's from the latter's early acting days in Welwyn Garden City and also knew Sydney Box well. She was placed under a contract by Box which stipulated that she would be given a starring part after three supporting roles and would also be free to work in the theatre.[122] Robson did play, selflessly, supporting roles in *Holiday Camp* and *Good Time Girl* in addition to playing the nanny in *The Years Between*, another saintly mediator. But she refused the starring role of Queen Isabella in *Christopher Columbus* once she had read the script – an early nail in its well-upholstered coffin.[123]

However, if the need to provide roles for Rank contract players was an important determinant of Box's choice of films, his preference for social realism was another. Ideally, established stars – Patricia Roc as the hapless single parent in *When the Bough Breaks* and Jean Kent as the 'delinquent' in *Good Time Girl* – could sink themselves into these roles and create a convincing portrayal of ordinariness. However, these social realist films also required actors, such as Jack Warner and Kathleen Harrison, who could look ordinary rather than exceptional, as did films such as *Holiday Camp* that needed convincing ensemble performances. These provided opportunities for actors who were not big stars to shine: Jimmy Hanley as the eternal boy-next-door, and Company of Youth graduates Jane Hylton and Susan Shaw. The Huggett films also promoted the screen career of Petula Clark, the child star who was later given her own vehicle with *Don't Ever Leave Me*. The portmanteau films provided unusually good opportunities for character actors whose specialism was playing the average man: James Hayter in the 'Verger' episode of *Trio* and Mervyn Johns in *Quartet*'s 'The Kite' and in the second episode of *Easy Money*. Indeed, several reviewers objected to the third episode of *Easy Money* because they felt it had been used inappropriately as a star vehicle for Dennis Price and Greta Gynt, playing an ex-RAF type and a nightclub singer respectively, compromising the film's quasi-documentary mode. In *When the Bough Breaks*, another Company of Youth graduate, Bill Owen, was given a rare starring and romantic role as the decent shopkeeper who befriends the heroine, placed by Patricia Roc.

Overall, Box managed to impose his individual stamp on Gainsborough Pictures and his tenure marked a decisive break with the Ostrer regime. Though he experienced problems with stars, directors and the lack of good scripts, Box was a strong leader who managed to turn Gainsborough into a genuine 'nursery' for new talent and put into practice his programme for achieving a stable and sustainable domestic film industry. Box showed himself ready to submit to the rigorous conditions necessary to increase substantially the number of films produced at Gainsborough and, despite protesting about the facilities at his disposal, his ability to plan ahead and juggle schedules where necessary meant that he was remarkably successful in sustaining high production levels: thirty-six films were made during his two-and-a-half-year tenure. The next chapter examines Box's varied and undervalued output in some detail, and also discusses the reasons for the closure of Gainsborough in March 1949.

Notes

1 Political and Economic Planning, *The British Film Industry*, p. 95.
2 Geoffrey Macnab, *J. Arthur Rank and the British Film Industry* (London: Routledge, 1993), p. 118.
3 Murphy, 'Gainsborough after Balcon', pp. 144–6.
4 'Sydney Box to Succeed Maurice Ostrer', *KW*, 2 May 1946, 3.
5 *Daily Film Renter*, 8 May 1946, 3.
6 Diaries, 6 March 1946; 27 March 1946; 'Box to Buy Twickenham Studios', *Today's Cinema*, 5 March 1946, 3. Twickenham and Riverside, together with Southall studios were acquired by Box's erstwhile backer, Alfred Shipman, in July 1946 to form Alliance Studios; see *KW*, 22 August 1946, 3.
7 'The Mass Producer', *Cinema and Theatre Construction*, 13:6 (May 1947), 18.
8 Box, *The Lion That Lost Its Way*, p. 52.
9 Betty Box, *Lifting the Lid*, p. 35.
10 'Box Controls Gainsborough's Two Studios at Full Steam', *The Cinema*, 7 August 1946, 5.

11 Quoted in Noble (ed.), *The British Film Yearbook 1947–48*, pp. 137–8.
12 John Barber, 'Sydney Box: How He Got to the Top', *Leader Magazine*, 1 May 1948, 14.
13 Sydney Box, 'Hollywood Has Tightened Its Belt – But is Still a Power to be Reckoned With', *KW*, 11 September 1947, 6, 23.
14 Sydney Box, 'I Challenge the Critics', *Picturegoer*, 1 January 1949, 7.
15 A point also made by one of his predecessors, R. J. Minney, see *KW*, 6 February 1947, p. 20. Minney asserted that overheads could add as much as £40,000 to a film that would otherwise have cost £100,000.
16 Sydney Box, 'Sadism: It Will Only Bring Us Disrepute', *KW*, 27 May 1948, 18.
17 *Ibid.*
18 Quoted in Brenda Cross, 'Sydney Box Producer', *Picturegoer*, 12 April 1947, 7.
19 Sydney Box, quoted in 'The Evolution of a Feature Film', in John Cross and Arnold Rattenbury (eds), *Screen and Audience* (London: Saturn Press, 1947), p. 11.
20 Sydney Box, 'Our Average for 8 Pictures: Under 11 Weeks', *Cinema and Theatre Construction*, 14:1 (June 1947), 4–5.
21 Box had ambitious plans to set up a special exterior unit which would shoot location scenes on four films each year; see *Cinema and Theatre Construction*, 13:3 (February 1947), 11–12.
22 Box, *The Lion That Lost Its Way*, pp. 52–3.
23 Patricia Warren, *British Film Studios* (London: B. T. Batsford, 1995), p. 139.
24 Peter Noble (ed.), *British Film Yearbook 1949–50* (London: Skelton Robinson, n.d.), p. 294.
25 Betty Box, interviewed by Robert Murphy, in Aspinall and Murphy (eds), *Gainsborough Melodrama*, p. 62. See also the interview with Googie Withers in Brian McFarlane, *An Autobiography of British Cinema* (London: Methuen, 1997), p. 610.
26 BECTU, tape 174, Maurice Carter.
27 MSBC, box 4, item 12.1.
28 Wood, *Mr Rank*, p. 227.
29 See Sue Harper, 'Historical Pleasures: Gainsborough Costume Melodrama', in Christine Gledhill (ed.), *Home Is Where the Heart Is* (London: BFI, 1987), pp. 167–96.
30 Muriel Box, *Odd Woman Out*, p. 185.
31 *KW*, 25 September 1947, 11.
32 MSBC, box 4, item 12.1.
33 Figure given in The British Film Academy, *The Film Industry in Great Britain* (London: BFA/Frederick Kahn, n.d.), p. 9.
34 All figures in this paragraph taken from PRO, BT 64/4490, 'Data on Production Costs for Rank Films up to December 1949'. See Appendix.
35 The figure for *Jassy* is not available, but must have been well in excess of £200,000.
36 A full list of the principal staff with whom Box started out at Gainsborough is given in *Film Industry*, 2:7 (January 1947), 19.
37 Val Guest, *So You Want To Be In Pictures* (London: Reynolds and Hearn, 2001), p. 77.
38 See the recollections of Joe Mendoza, a staff writer promoted by Box, in Drazin, *The Finest Years*, p. 211; Ken Annakin, interview with author, 15 May 2001.
39 BECTU, tape 14, Alfred Roome (interview transcript), p. 150.
40 BECTU, tape 174, Maurice Carter.
41 BECTU, tape 14, Alfred Roome, transcript, p. 222.
42 'The Mass Producer', 18–20.
43 Cross, 'Sydney Box', 6–7.

44 Barber, 'Sydney Box', p. 14.
45 'Evolution of a Feature Film', pp. 8–17.
46 *Ibid.*, p. 9.
47 *Ibid.*, pp. 10–11.
48 Ken Annakin thought Alcott an 'outstanding' organiser; interview with author, 15 May 2001. Alcott went on to be general production manager at Pinewood.
49 'Evolution of a Feature Film', p. 17.
50 *Ibid.*
51 There was also some carping about the characterisation. The *Daily Express*'s reviewer (19 April 1948) dubbed *Broken Journey* '*Grand Hotel* in the Snow' and opined: 'it is a curious cinematic convention that whenever you want to show how ordinary people behave in such circumstances you do it by making your characters as extraordinary as possible'.
52 Sydney Box, 'Gainsborough: A Nursery for New Names', *Film Industry*, 4:23 (May 1948), 4–5.
53 'Box's £125,000 Gamble', *Film Industry*, 5:26 (July 1948), 5.
54 See Hubert Cole, 'The Lady in Charge', *Picturegoer*, 7 December 1946, 8; *Cinema and Theatre Construction*, 14:1 (June 1947), 5.
55 See the interview in McFarlane, *An Autobiography of British Cinema*, p. 85.
56 Obituary, *Daily Telegraph*, 24 September 2000.
57 'Men at Work: Andrew Gray and Hutson Visit Shepherd's Bush', *Film Industry*, 4:22 (April 1948), 10–12.
58 '*Portrait from Life*: Photo-Preview', in Warwick Mannon, *Here Come the Huggetts: Book of the Film* (London: World Film Publications, 1948), p. 79.
59 *Ibid.*
60 *Film Industry*, 6:41 (10 February 1949), 8.
61 'New Appointments at Shepherd's Bush', *Daily Film Renter*, 13 December 1945, 10.
62 Gainsborough press release, included in the microfiche for *Diamond City*, BFI Library.
63 Sydney Box, 'More British Films', *Cinema and Theatre Construction*, 12:1 (June 1946), 13.
64 Box, 'A New Deal for Film Writers', pp. 49–52.
65 Muriel Box, *Odd Woman Out*, p. 186.
66 Drazin, *The Finest Years*, p. 211.
67 Muriel Box, *Odd Woman Out*, p. 186.
68 Morris Bright and Robert Ross, *Mr Carry On: The Life and Work of Peter Rogers* (London: BBC Worldwide, 2000), p. 61.
69 Jan Read, *Young Man in Movieland* (Lanham, Maryland and Oxford: Scarecrow Press, 2004), p. 70.
70 *Ibid.*, p. 71.
71 *Ibid.*, p. 73.
72 *Ibid.*, p. 74.
73 See Diaries, 2 July 1947.
74 Muriel Box, quoted in Box, 'More British Films', 13.
75 Ted Willis, *Evening All: 50 Years Over a Hot Typewriter* (London: Macmillan, 1991), pp. 11, 23.
76 *Ibid.*, p. 66.
77 John Sullivan, 'Scripts Not Studios', *Film Industry*, 2:8 (February 1947), 3, 7.
78 MSBC, box 4, item 12.1.
79 Annakin, *So You Wanna Be a Director?*, p. 26.
80 Muriel Box, interview in Aspinall and Murphy (eds), *Gainsborough Melodrama*, p. 64.

81 Box, *The Lion That Lost Its Way*, p. 70.
82 Diaries, 8 July 1948.
83 Box, *The Lion That Lost Its Way*, p. 198.
84 See also Michael Redgrave's account: Redgrave, *In My Mind's Eye: An Autobiography* (London: Weidenfeld and Nicolson, 1983), pp. 186–7.
85 Diaries, 21 July 1949; *The Lion That Lost Its Way*, pp. 82–6.
86 Read, *Young Man in Movieland*, p. 70.
87 *Ibid.*, p. 80.
88 *Ibid.*, pp. 71, 81. Box helped Read persuade Rank to adopt the project in 1958, but an American partner could not be found and the script was again shelved (Read, *Young Man in Movieland*, 83). It was published as a novel by Cape in 1964.
89 Sydney Box, 'Foreword', *Rebecca's Daughters* (London: Triton, 1965).
90 Dylan Thomas, letter to Ralph Keene, 27 July 1948, in Paul Ferris (ed.), *The Collected Letters of Dylan Thomas* (London: Dent, 1985), p. 680.
91 Sydney Box, 'Foreword', *Me and My Bike* (London: Triton, 1965). This edition contained illustrations by Box's daughter Leonora.
92 For an overview of Thomas as screenwriter see John Ackerman, 'Introduction', *Dylan Thomas: The filmscripts* (London: Dent, 1995), pp. vii–xxvii.
93 Sydney Box, 'Puzzle – Find the Director', in Noble (ed.), *British Film Yearbook 1948–49*, p. 90.
94 Annakin, *So You Wanna Be a Director?*, p. 33.
95 Box, 'Puzzle – Find the Director', p. 91
96 Box, 'Gainsborough: A Nursery for New Names', p. 5.
97 Annakin, *So You Wanna Be a Director?*, p. 24.
98 *Ibid.*, p. 25.
99 Leonard Wallace, 'Backroom Boys at the Bush', *Picturegoer*, 14 February 1948, 5.
100 See the *Manchester Guardian*'s review of *Snowbound*, 27 March 1948.
101 BECTU, tape 14, Alfred Roome, transcript, p. 159.
102 See the reviews of *Diamond City* on the BFI microfiche. The *Daily Express*'s reviewer 'winced with shame through most of it' (23 September 1949). The film was another Ostrer legacy, as *Digger's Republic* (the working title) had been announced for the 1946 programme; see *KW*, 20 December 1945, 173.
103 Laurie Ede, 'The Role of the Art Director in British Films 1939–1951', unpublished Ph.D. thesis, School of Social and Historical Studies, University of Portsmouth, 1999, pp. 129–30.
104 Box inherited a highly experienced model maker and special effects designer in Filippe Guidolbaldi whose work on numerous films, including *Columbus*, was excellent. See the profile in *Cinema and Theatre Construction*, 15:3 (February 1948), 22–6.
105 *Film Industry*, 4:22 (April 1948), 11.
106 *Film Industry*, 4:20 (February 1948), 25.
107 Details from the press book, BFI library.
108 Harper, *Women in British Cinema*, p. 215.
109 'Men at Work', p. 12.
110 K. J. Donnelly, 'Wicked Sounds and Magic Melodies: Music in 1940s Gainsborough Melodrama', in Cook (ed.), *Gainsborough Pictures*, p. 167.
111 Mathieson had worked on Box's Riverside films.
112 Quoted in 'The Evolution of a Feature Film', p. 9.
113 Box had wanted Granger to star in an adaptation of his play *Self-Made Man*, but this had to be dropped when Granger was unavailable, as did an historical epic, *The Rocket*. Diaries, 22 December 1946.
114 Hilton Tims, *Once a Wicked Lady: A Biography of Margaret Lockwood* (London: Virgin Books, 1989), p. 137.

115 Margaret Lockwood, *Lucky Star* (London: Odhams Press, 1955), p. 136.
116 See Dennis Vance, 'The Company of Youth', *Film Industry*, 4:19 (January 1948), 6–7.
117 Box, *The Lion That Lost Its Way*, p. 51.
118 *KW*, 5 July 1944, 9.
119 Sydney Box, 'The Value of Lease-Lend', *Film Industry*, 1:5 (November 1946), 2–3.
120 Diaries, 15 February 1949.
121 Muriel Box, *Odd Woman Out*, p. 201.
122 Janet Dunbar, *Flora Robson* (London: Harrap, 1960), p. 235.
123 Derek Bond's observation, quoted in Eric Braun, 'A Decade of Gainsborough Melodrama 1942–1950', *Films* (April 1984), 24.

'One a month': the Gainsborough films

6

Box's overall output of thirty-six films during his tenure at Gainsborough was an impressive achievement, but led to the charge of commodification: churning out films irrespective of their aesthetic or cultural value. Richard Winnington, always Box's sternest critic, talked scathingly about 'the mills of Gainsborough [which] has endured, like any other sausage machine of the British film world, by producing goods no less tasty and digestible than those from the factories of Hollywood'.[1] A more disinterested commentator, Patrick Gibbs, observed: 'For Mr Rank the Independent Producers provide the handmade goods; to Sydney Box he looks, and does not look in vain, for the hardly inferior mass-produced article. On Gainsborough we can depend for one good English film – one a month.'[2] However if, as Box himself conceded, his films rarely aspire to the status of great art, as Gibbs indicates, they did more than simply provide a high British production quota. As this chapter seeks to demonstrate, Box's films were not uniformly successful, far from it, but they were more aesthetically varied than has been usually been conceded, and more culturally ambitious.

There is not room in a study of this length to provide a comprehensive analysis of all the Gainsborough films. Rather, the aim is to define what was distinctive about the films produced during Box's tenure and, while characterising his output as a whole, to provide more detailed analysis of those films that best exemplify that individuality, even if, as was the case with *The Bad Lord Byron* and *Christopher Columbus*, they were notorious critical and box-office failures.[3] Indeed, failures are important in understanding Box's aspirations, the pressures he was under and what may have been a misjudgement of public taste. Overall, Box's Gainsborough films may be divided into four broad categories: topical social issue films, the Somerset Maugham adaptations, comedies and thrillers, and costume dramas. It is appropriate to begin with the 'topicals', what Box referred to as 'sociological studies', as they formed the backbone of Box's output and in some respects are his most distinctive achievement.

Topical/social issue films

Box was proud of his achievement at Verity: 'the documentary method of social reporting with a fictional story' that had evolved during the war, he argued, 'I regard as a real contribution to cinema, and we shall develop the method'.[4] It also made good box-office sense, after the war, as Box was convinced that 'the public wants a few films about the people who live as they do'.[5] His development of this 'method' at Gainsborough covered a varied range of post-war concerns: child adoption (*When the Bough Breaks*); the delinquent, both female (*Good Time Girl*) and male (*Boys in Brown*); displaced persons (*Portrait from Life* and *The Lost People*); and new or rapidly expanding forms of leisure such as cycling (*A Boy, a Girl and a Bike*), gambling (*Easy Money*) and seaside recreation (*Holiday Camp*).

Holiday Camp (August 1947) was Box's first Shepherd's Bush picture, and the first film to focus on family life being restored to normality after the war, rather than the returning combatant. The original idea and the basic storyline came from the newspaper columnist Godfrey Winn, a friend of Billy Butlin, the man chiefly responsible for popularising the idea of the holiday camp, which had started to transform traditional conceptions of the seaside holiday.[6] Winn persuaded Butlin to give permission for location filming to take place at his camp in Filey on the North Yorkshire coast.[7] The screenplay itself was written by the Boxes, Peter Rogers and Ted Willis, assisted by the Constanduroses, as Box felt Winn's ideas needed 'pepping up'.[8] It was probably the Boxes who wrote the passage in which the camp's announcer articulates the guiding spirit of the film: the individual in the mass. Watching from his control tower he has come to understand that the apparent noisy, frantic and desperate search for collective pleasure masks a deeper reality: 'Then I saw it wasn't a crowd at all – just separate individuals, each one of them with a different set of problems and worries, hopes and fears; each one of them tired and dispirited, eager for peace and yet frightened to be alone.' This continues the key concern – the difficulties of the transition from war to peacetime – that characterised Box's Riverside films.

Box assigned Ken Annakin as the director, knowing that his documentary background would help to ensure the necessary verisimilitude. *Holiday Camp* contains extensive location footage which emphasises the cheery communality of camp life – morning exercises, eating together in the vast restaurant, beauty competitions, doing the 'Hokey-Cokey' – forming the backdrop to the six deftly interwoven fictional stories. Only on one occasion does the style depart from an overriding naturalism: a short expressionist sequence when Esther Harman (Flora Robson) approaches the control tower and glimpses the blurred image of a young soldier, framed by the outline of a loudspeaker, which seems to be drawing her back into the past. The scene's economy and concern with disturbed psychology suggest a Box invention.

Esther, the central character of Winn's original story, is one of a number of characters who are marked by the depredations of war. In her case this is the First World War, from which the man she loved never returned, leaving her a disillusioned spinster, her life blighted by the ceaseless demands of her wheelchair-bound mother. The camp's announcer (Esmond Knight), whose voice seems hauntingly familiar to her, but whose memory has been obliterated by the shell blast that also destroyed his sight, turns out to be her lost love. He is happily married with no recollection of his engagement to Esther, who departs without revealing her story. The Huggetts' daughter Joan (Hazel Court) is a war widow, while the man she befriends, demobbed sailor Jimmy Gardner (Jimmy Hanley), has been jilted by his fiancée even though he had saved up four months' chocolate rations to give her – 'even bought some off a chap with bad teeth'. 'Binkie' Hardwicke (Dennis Price) embodies the unacceptable aftermath of the war, cashing in on a fraudulent glamour and status as a bogus Wing Commander. He represents a restless, criminal-type – shown in a milder form by the pair of spivs who cheat Harry Huggett (Peter Hammond) of his money – addicted to the excitement and social confusion the war had created.[9] After his attentions are finally rebuffed by the hedonistic but streetwise Angela Kirby (Yvonne Owen), Hardwicke murders the hapless Elsie Dawson (Esma Cannon), whom he lures into an ill-advised moonlight walk along the cliffs. Price gives a fine performance as a man who is charming and psychopathic, unable to control the violent impulses that have dominated his life.

However, if *Holiday Camp* acknowledges the dislocation and suffering that the war has caused, it also looks forward to a brighter future. Esther, freed by her mother's death, has broken with the hallowed promenades of Torquay to embrace the new, becoming the protector and patroness of Michael Halliday (Emrys Jones) and his pregnant girlfriend Valerie Thompson (Jeannette Tregarthen), who are considering suicide. In contradistinction to Valerie's vindictive aunt (Beatrice Varley), who condemns her 'disgrace', Esther embodies the spirit of acceptance and forgiveness, representing the modern tolerant and caring society that should evolve from the war. That tolerance extends to Jimmy and Joan, who eventually learn to trust each other, free themselves from the past and find romance.

The spirit of tolerance is also embodied in paterfamilias Joe Huggett (Jack Warner) and his wife Ethel (Kathleen Harrison), who 'rub along', grumbling over trivialities, but fundamentally content with their lot. Joe might ogle the bathing beauties through his binoculars, or give the woman next to him on the dance floor a passionate kiss – 'I was only doing what the bandleader told me' – but he is happy with Ethel, 'something plain round the home', and a reliable and caring father. Their scene together on the cliff top, where they muse about their honeymoon but also about the exigencies of their working lives, is a key moment, blending a sentimental, melodramatic pathos with sober, quotidian realism, and placing respectable upper-working-class ordinariness at the centre of the film.

One or two critics cavilled at the introduction of a serial killer – the *Manchester Guardian* called it 'the caterpillar in the salad' – but for the most part the film drew lavish praise.[10] Elspeth Grant in the *Daily Graphic* was typically fulsome in her praise of 'the warmly human though shrewd observation that went to the film's making, and the completely British air of good humour and grousing which invests it'.[11] Ewart Hodgson in the *News of the World* thought the film over-episodic, but admired its 'authenticity', an adjective frequently invoked.[12] Felix Barker in the *Evening News* placed it in the tradition of *Bank Holiday*, *Quiet Wedding* and *Millions Like Us* which 'give a real picture of an aspect of English life'.[13] Even if the quality press could not resist sniping at 'joy factories' with their 'totalitarian gaiety', it praised the film's command of realistic detail, which created 'a social document illustrative of the tastes and manners of the age'.[14]

Holiday Camp, as Box hoped, seemed to capture the mood of the times, going into profit less than three months after its release and generating revenues of £184,300 in the UK alone, an excellent return.[15] Box had shrewdly trailed the film by promoting a nationwide search for a 'holiday princess', which generated a lot of good publicity, and the film's poster featured four bikini-clad women leaning forward towards the viewer with the slogan 'They all have fun at *Holiday Camp*', which lent an air of sauciness to the film.

In several ways *Holiday Camp* is the quintessential Box picture, combining topicality, comedy and realism in a quasi-portmanteau format. Although it convinced Box that films about ordinary people were viable at the box office, its most obvious legacy was three further

Huggett films, made in response to public demand: 'Sydney Box has been inundated with requests for further glimpses into their family life'.[16] The first was *Here Come the Huggetts* (November 1948), accompanied by an advertisement which boasted: 'The Lively, Laughing, Lovable Huggetts are Britain's very own family'. This first film concentrates on establishing the family's domestic mores, and it is augmented by Amy Veness as Grandma and Petula Clark as the youngest daughter. The temporary disruption caused by the arrival of Joe's niece Di Hopkins (Diana Dors), 'fast', Americanised and overtly sexual, is occluded by the marriage of the eldest daughter Jane (Jane Hylton) to Jimmy (Jimmy Hanley), playing, as in *Holiday Camp*, the ordinary sailor and decent boy-next-door. This marriage echoes the royal wedding of Princess Elizabeth, which, despite the tribulations involved in turning out for the procession, rouses Joe and Ethel to a sentimental patriotism, underlining the Huggetts' status as the national family.

In *Vote for Huggett* (February 1949) Joe even tries his hand at local politics, saving the community of Strutham (which is 'like a family') from corrupt developers. However, in *The Huggetts Abroad* (May 1949), in which the family has decided to emigrate to South Africa, the earlier social-democratic progressiveness has collapsed into a conservative Little Englandism: all foreigners are odd and there is no place like home, despite the queues and the rationing. The meandering storyline collapses into a series of episodes, which presaged the franchise's transformation into a radio 'soap', running from 1953–1962.

The other Gainsborough films about ordinary people struggled harder to make their characters representative, straying into facetiousness or straining after significance. The two portmanteau films – *Easy Money*, which focused on the rapidly expanding football pools industry, and *Marry Me!* which looked at the growth of marriage bureaux – were split into four separate episodes. *Easy Money* was 'told in a semi-documentary style with an explanatory preamble and a linking commentary between the four fictional episodes', as *Film Industry* explained, while *Marry Me!* dispensed with the commentary.[17] Neither was very successful, partly because insufficient time was spent on their script development. In *A Boy, a Girl and a Bike*, Ted Willis's original screenplay hovers uneasily between depicting a love triangle among the cycling community at the picturesque Yorkshire dales, and tackling the topical social problems of the delinquent in embryo (Anthony Newley), who has been difficult 'ever since he's been moved from London when his dad was killed', and the sympathetic deserter (Cyril Chamberlain).

When the Bough Breaks (November 1947), with a screenplay by the Boxes and Peter Rogers, was more overtly issue-based. It is the story of a young woman, Lily Bates (Patricia Roc), who discovers after giving birth to her son that the father is married to someone else. She allows her child, Jimmy, to be adopted by an affluent middle-class couple (the Normans), who will give him the opportunities she cannot offer, but wants him back after she has met and married a respectable suburban tobacconist, Bill (Bill Owen). The adoptive mother (Rosamund John) is distraught and believes that Jimmy, torn away from the life to which he has become accustomed, will be unhappy. The film handles the struggle over the child even-handedly, and presents a genuine dilemma sympathetically, but it is let down, rather like *The Years Between*, by too neat a resolution, in which Jimmy is restored to the Normans and Lily and Bill have their own child.

Box made two films about the problem of displaced persons in Europe, *Portrait from Life* (December 1948) and *The Lost People* (July 1949), underlining his determination to tackle some of the more intractable problems that the war had created. In the former, the Boxes' screenplay adopts the basic conventions of the romantic investigative thriller to illuminate the plight of refugees. Major David Lawrence (Guy Rolfe), cooling his heels in post-war London after having been jilted by his fiancée, finds his attention arrested by the enigmatic features of the beautiful Hildegard (Mai Zetterling), whose portrait he sees in a gallery. He is intrigued by the story he hears from the old man standing next to him, Professor Menzel (Arnold Marle), an Austrian Jew, who claims the portrait is Lydia, the daughter he had to abandon when he fled from Nazi persecution. They attempt to discover her whereabouts by tracing the painter, Duncan Reid (Robert Beatty), but he dies in an advanced state of alcoholism, before he can reveal what he knows. Lawrence, who puzzles about his own ambiguous motivations in his voice-over narration, pulls strings as an officer in the British Army of Occupation to track her down in a displaced persons' camp in Germany. She is living as the supposed daughter of Hendlmann (Herbert Lom), a high-ranking SS-officer who has forcibly adopted her in his attempts to cover up his true identity.

In a motif that recalls *The Seventh Veil*, Lydia's memory has been wiped out by the trauma of the events that have overtaken her. A lengthy flashback, a favourite Box device, explores her earlier relationship with Reid, who appears to have had deep-rooted psychological problems, seemingly unable to adjust to the transition to civilian life. When Lydia tells him 'There is no war now', he replies: 'No, and there's no peace either for some of us'. Reid seems to have lost the desire for a peacetime future, burdened by his desire for Lydia, who is much younger than he is, by his illness and alcoholism, and by his inability to free her from the influence of Hendlmann, another disturbing Svengali figure. Reid's place is taken by Lawrence, whose own post-war *ennui* and shallow rootlessness (skilfully conveyed in Rolfe's subtle performance) have been overcome by his determination to help Lydia. In a rather contrived conclusion, he plays the lay psychoanalyst, restoring Lydia's memory by confronting her with objects from her childhood. In the process, Hendlmann is exposed and Lydia and Lawrence can now happily contemplate marriage.

The Lost People, Bridget Boland's adaptation of her play *Cockpit*, depicts the efforts of Captain Ridley (Dennis Price) to impose order on a group of displaced persons of various nationalities in a derelict German theatre commandeered as a dispersal centre. Its concern with a pressing social issue and attempt to give voice to the unheard become, in the film version, a rather hackneyed triumph of British fair play over the unruliness of foreigners. Although part of its attraction for Box was that it could be filmed on one set, which could reduce the shooting schedule to 10–15 days, he and Muriel became increasingly concerned about the film during shooting, finding its screenplay problematic and at one point describing the production as a 'huge mess'.[18] Rank executives suggested that the film be shelved, but Box obtained permission to rewrite the script with Muriel, and she reshot over half the footage.[19] Despite their efforts, critics found *The Lost People* lacking in atmosphere, sympathetic characters or filmcraft. *Film Industry*'s reviewer opined that it 'gives the impression that the editor has tried manfully to cope with the demands of an uneven script and various production changes and a good deal of the lighting does not match from scene to scene'.[20] Whereas critics had found Mai Zetterling expressive and convincing in *Portrait from Life*, here, in her tight blonde curls, they thought she looked like Harpo Marx.[21] More significantly, Paul Dehn in the *News Chronicle* observed that Boland's epic drama –which could not but involve its audience in the theatre as it took up the whole auditorium – was unsuited to translation into film, at least in literal terms: 'The play's strength lay in the fact that its theatrical setting would readily be identified with the actual theatre of performance. On the screen, however closely a director may observe the unity of place, such realism is bound to be a little weakened.'[22]

Portrait from Life was much more successful at the box office than *The Lost People*, exemplifying the public's preference for cinematic narrative over theatrical artifice, and for an implied message over an overtly didactic and declamatory one. These differences resurfaced in Box's two 'delinquency' films, *Good Time Girl* (May 1948) and *Boys in Brown* (December 1949). In post-war Britain, delinquency had become a major preoccupation; as the war receded, the delinquent replaced the maladjusted veteran as a 'concealed metaphor' for fears about rapid social change, the lack of community cohesion and the breakdown of traditional values, particularly among the working classes, all of which had been exacerbated by wartime disruption. The delinquent became a convenient folk devil around which to mobilise these concerns, and its lineaments were constructed by official and quasi-official discourses – psychiatric, legal and social scientific – corroborated by a tide of media attention.[23]

A wide range of films about the delinquent were produced up until the early 1960s. What makes Box's two studies distinctive within this broader spectrum is their sympathy towards the disruptive protagonists rather than the systems of control and punishment. In addition, *Good Time Girl* is the only such film to centre on a female protagonist, exploring the phenomenon of the 'good time girls', who were conventionally viewed as undesirable leftovers from the sexual licence of wartime and a serious threat to the nation's moral fibre.[24] The Boxes, assisted by Willis, adapted Arthur la Bern's 1947 novel, *Night Darkens the Street*, itself loosely based on the life of Elizabeth Jones, the eighteen-year-old girl involved in the 'cleft chin' murder case of 1944, in which she and two American soldiers murdered a taxi-driver.

The screenplay differs from la Bern's novel in emphasising the social deprivation that Gwen (Jean Kent) experiences – her home is sordid and mean, rather than respectable – and her exploitation by the men she encounters. Whereas in the novel Gwen leaves her job at the pawnbroker's because she feels it is beneath her, she is forced out in the film by the unwelcome attentions of her boss, Pottinger (Elwyn Brook-Jones), who emerges from the shadows, leering, lascivious and repulsive, expecting sexual favours in return for not informing the police that she borrowed a brooch to wear at a dance. When she rejects him, Pottinger makes it his business to tell her father why she has been sacked, knowing full well what the consequences will be. The scene where Gwen's father beats her is darkly disturbing, made all the more so by the restraint with which director David Macdonald handles the brutal violence. Nearly all the men that Gwen meets after leaving home – the waiter Jimmy Rosso (Peter Glenville), his boss at a Soho nightclub, Max (Herbert Lom), and even a passing motorist (Garry Marsh) who offers her a lift – are lecherous and selfish. The one man who is different, Red Farrell (Dennis Price), is powerless to prevent her unjust and severe sentencing to three years at reform school (the maximum permitted). She becomes the victim of Rosso's spite rather than her own actions.

More subversively, the film questions the effectiveness of the reform school to which Gwen is sent. Although the matron (Nora Swinburne) is a conventionally virtuous figure who intones the standard pieties, she presides over a repressive institution. Gwen's letters from Red are deliberately withheld without her knowledge and she learns of this deception only through a fellow inmate, Roberta (Jill Balcon), who acts as her true guide and mentor, inculcating the pretence of conformity that will win official approval. It is difficult not to feel that her escape is desirable, just as it is impossible not to feel outraged at the injustice and severity of her sentence. This bid for freedom carries with it an implicit rejection of hypocritical middle-class philanthropy, and of the conformist femininity it requires. It is clear that Gwen has been brutalised by her time at the school, losing her essential good-heartedness and learning to survive in a callous and indifferent world, first with a Brighton gangster, Danny Martin (Griffith Jones), who assaults her when she tries to leave him, and then with two American deserters, Mickey (Bonar Colleano) and Al (Hugh McDermott). She becomes part of their world of vicious petty villainy and, in a grim irony not in la Bern, is sentenced to fifteen years imprisonment as an accomplice when Red is killed by Al. Gwen's descent into a netherworld of crime and vice is effectively rendered by Stephen Dade's expert *noir* cinematography, which creates an unstable and oppressive world where glamour and violence are intertwined. Maurice Carter's imaginative designs are equally potent, particularly the main Soho set with its twisting cobbled road and claustrophobic alleyways.

Good Time Girl was an accomplished thriller, which also contained a social critique and was very successful at the box office.[25] This was achieved despite its actually being banned by some local authorities,[26] which were not appeased by the moralising framework on which the censors had insisted, whereby Gwen's story becomes a moral lesson ensuring that the wayward Lyla Lawrence (Diana Dors) returns to her family.[27] The public's appetite for the film was unaffected by its generally disparaging reviews, including one in the *Daily Mirror* which called *Good Time Girl* 'another of those unsatisfactory, unsavoury pictures which depend on sordid brutality for box-office appeal ... A story which should never have been filmed.'[28] Box defended the film, saying that it was based on official records.[29] In a more considered piece, the *Monthly Film Bulletin* judged *Good Time Girl* to be well made and intelligent – 'tensely gripping in its seamiest situations' – and also detected its subversiveness: 'It is difficult not to sympathise with Gwen; upbringing, wrongful accusation, misunderstanding, lack of supervision in the approved school, bad companions, combine to ruin what might have been a decent young woman. Is this an indictment against Juvenile Courts and the way in which approved schools are run?'[30]

Boys in Brown, the first film to concentrate exclusively on delinquency rather than under-age criminality, was based on Reginald Beckwith's play, first performed in June 1940. Beckwith took a documentary approach, basing his drama on his own research in and around Trafalgar Square, to get the real views of ex-Borstal inmates, including those on the run.[31] Box had seen the revival in July 1947, and invited Montgomery Tully to both direct and write the screenplay. The adaptation, under pressure from the censors, draws some of the play's teeth, but it too takes a sympathetic look at delinquency. The central characters, Jackie Knowles (Richard Attenborough) and Bill Foster (Jimmy Hanley), are the objects of compassion rather than condemnation. Jackie has a devoted mother, but no father, and has drifted into petty crime through boredom and restlessness. Bill is illegitimate and his poor home background has pushed him into crime. In the film's most telling scene, Bill's mother rejects the Borstal governor's pleas for her to take Bill back; she has remarried and does not want Bill to intrude into her detached, stockbroker-Tudor home in the leafy suburbs. As in *Good Time Girl*, the middle class does not escape censure. Although the wise paternalism of the Borstal governor (Jack Warner) is instrumental in redeeming the protagonists, the film makes it clear that many inmates are unreachable. The truculent Casey (Andrew Crawford) will have none of the Governor's blandishments, while Rawlins (Dirk Bogarde) is a disturbingly intelligent figure whose rebelliousness is given considerable narrative space, even if his motivations remain unfathomable.

Boys in Brown suffered from its low budget, Tully's unimaginative direction and straightjacketing by the notorious Independent Frame technique, which Box did not endorse.[32] Released after Rank had decided to close Gainsborough (*Boys in Brown* was filmed at Pinewood), it received little active promotion. *Kinematograph Weekly*, reporting that a release date had not been fixed, did the film few favours by describing *Boys in Brown* as a 'Slow, uneven British dead end kids romantic melodrama ... [which] fails to get anywhere'.[33] Although the *Monthly Film Bulletin* judged that the film was not sensationalised and had an excellent cast, it expressed the reservation that *Boys in Brown* failed to provide 'a true picture of life in a Borstal Institution' because there was so little depiction of the boys' actual day-to-day lives, the routines and tasks they were required to perform. It never escaped its theatrical origins and the melodramatic contrast of stock types.[34]

The Maugham adaptations

The other most distinctive group of films was the three Somerset Maugham adaptations: *Quartet* (1948), *Trio* (1950) and *Encore* (November 1951) – the latter two of which were completed at Pinewood.[35] It was one of Box's most successful initiatives to persuade Maugham to sign over the rights to his short stories, which numbered over 100, representing a potentially almost inexhaustible source. Box was well aware that Maugham's stories are excellent sources for screen adaptation, because they are economical, show a mastery of colloquial expression and dramatic conflict with a careful attention to plot and narrative structure, and let the characters' external appearances, words and actions illuminate their feelings and attitudes. Maugham's sceptical, ironic view of human nature (which Box shared), and his sense of the troubled impermanence of relationships, resulted in stories which did not date markedly, or which could be given a contemporary gloss without losing their essential form and focus. As portmanteau films, the Maugham adaptations offered Box the potential to juggle schedules by using a variety of directors and stars for short periods only. But they also offered him the opportunity to celebrate the status of the writer within film-making; as he commented at the time: 'I have thought for a long time that writers do not get sufficient prominence on the screen ... This series is aimed at putting writers in their proper perspective as the most important single element in picture-making.'[36] This perspective was achieved by presenting the adaptations as a mark of respect to Maugham and having each introduced by the author himself.[37] *Quartet* opens with Maugham perusing books in the study of his villa in Cap Ferrat, meticulously reproduced at the Shepherd's Bush studios, while the anonymous narrator intones: 'The star of this film is not an actor or an actress, but a writer, and those of us who helped to make it take pleasure in paying tribute to him'.

In having the author as the unifying element, these adaptations broke new ground. The screenwriter, R. C. Sheriff, argued: 'There is nothing new about grouping a number of short stories into one picture, but as far as I know they have always been linked by a common theme. In *Quartet* they are entirely independent of each other and played by different actors. Each is a short entertainment in itself.'[38] Sheriff also acknowledged that he was working to a very open brief, as Box had 'asked me not to concern myself with time, but to let each screenplay run its natural course. As a result they are of unequal length, but in every case the screenplay ends when the story is finished.'[39] This flexibility was designed to break the stranglehold of the conventional presentation of short stories whereby each was padded or cut to fit the rigid mould of the ninety-minute feature film. Sheriff admited that cuts had been made and scenes added, but insisted that these were the result of the 'normal business of adapting for the screen', which required a more intense focus on a single narrative thread. This necessary pruning of the 'side shoots ... is not the same as mutilating the main stem to squeeze the story into the picture'.[40]

The stories that make up both *Quartet* and *Trio* are of unequal length, and have deliberately contrasting styles and moods to provide interest and variation. *Quartet* begins with the facetious, ironic comedy of 'The Facts of Life', followed by the sombrely tragic 'The Alien Corn', and 'The Kite', a quirky tale of obsession; it concludes with 'The Colonel's Lady', a tragi-comedy of marriage. There is an underlying thematic unity, as each deals with young men and their aspirations, even if, as in 'The Colonel's Lady', those aspirations are buried in the past. Each story, albeit in very different ways, is about defying convention.

The four stories are not uniformly successful. 'The Facts of Life' is a rather whimsical narrative about a young man, Nicky (Jack Watling), playing in a tennis tournament in Monte Carlo. He defies his father's advice not to gamble, lend money or become involved with women and inadvertently triumphs over the seductive adventuress Jeanne (Mai Zetterling); the story is neat and deftly handled. But Sheriff's adaptation of 'The Alien Corn' rips out the heart of Maugham's story by excluding its focus on race. In the original, George, the young heir of an affluent family, flouts his father's expectations by rediscovering and then flaunting his German-Jewish origins at Munich where he is training to be a concert pianist. His family has been at pains to conceal this background in its attempt to gain acceptance in British society. Sheriff's adaptation makes the rebellion of George (Dirk Bogarde) solely a clash of art against convention, and he trains in Paris rather than Munich. The episode's director, Harold French, thought the characters should have been played by Jewish actors, but Box's casting is a conventional use of Rank's contract players.[41]

'The Kite' shifts the focus to the lower-middle class, and deals with the attempt of Herbert (George Cole) to break free from the control of his domineering mother (Hermione Badderley) and avoid becoming emasculated like his father (Mervyn Johns). However, his defiant marriage to Betty (Susan Shaw), whom he defends against his mother's withering accusation that she is common, becomes compromised by his passion for kite flying, which his parents have always encouraged and which Betty despises. In Maugham's story the anonymous narrator suggests that the kite is a sublimated escape from the monotony of

Herbert's life: 'It may be that in some dim, confused way it represents an ideal of freedom and adventure' (p. 149). Encouraged by his parents, Herbert secretly flies the kite on Saturdays. When Betty finds out, she destroys the new model on which he had worked for many months. Herbert returns home and, refusing to continue Betty's maintenance, is imprisoned. Maugham leaves the tale there, allowing the reader to reflect on the meaning and nature of the choices that Herbert faced, but the adaptation concocts a sentimental ending in which all parties are reconciled and fly the kite together.

'The Colonel's Wife' is one of Maugham's most celebrated stories, and in this case the adaptation is deft and arguably augments the original. A series of economical scenes capture the embarrassment, bewilderment and finally the anger and anguish of bluff, Blimpish Colonel George Peregrine (Cecil Parker), who is good-natured but emotionally shallow and insensitive. His apparently dowdy and devoted wife Evie (Nora Swinburne) has published a best-selling book of poetry, *Though Pyramids Decay*, in which she writes movingly of a passionate affair with a much younger man. George has, over time, become estranged from Evie and has a mistress in London (Linden Travers), who goads him about the content of his wife's verses. Maugham's story ends with Peregrine's male-chauvinist bewilderment as he tells his friend, the lawyer Harry Blane, 'there's one thing I shall never understand till my dying day: What in the name of heaven did the fellow ever see in her?' Box rewrote parts of Sheriff's adaptation adding a final scene because he felt that Maugham's ending was too cynical for film audiences.[42] In the added scene the Colonel finally confronts his wife, demanding to know who the man was, only to be given the answer that it was the Colonel's own youthful self: 'It was you – as you were – all those years ago – in those happy days when we first met, and you loved me.' Groping for understanding and consolation, he takes her in his arms and she comforts him. It is a moving and compassionate scene, which credibly offers the possibility of a reconciliation and allows Cecil Parker to round off what was his finest screen performance.

Quartet was moderately successful at the British box office, popular in London and a few major cities rather than in the suburbs and the provinces, but its high standing with critics provided Box with some badly needed prestige.[43] Joan Lester judged *Quartet* the film of the week, arguing that its episodic construction had been overcome because 'the flavour of Maugham's pungent and sophisticated wit has been nicely preserved throughout'.[44] Retrospectively, the *Saturday Review* suggested that it set new standards for adaptations by treating its source with genuine respect, reflecting both Maugham's artistic limitations and strengths and therefore preserving his distinctiveness.[45] Audiences apparently responded very favourably to Maugham's introduction, in which he appeared both modest and candid.[46] What was even more important for Box was *Quartet*'s success in Europe and, especially, America, where it ran for two years at the Sutton Cinema in New York.[47] This ensured that further adaptations would be attempted and, by the time of *Trio*'s release, *Quartet*, like *The Seventh Veil*, had become a byword for intelligent filmcraft in both the home and the overseas markets, and critics who had largely ignored *Quartet* on its initial release were fulsome in their praise.[48] Box negotiated a deal with Columbia which ensured that *Trio* had a wider American release from the beginning than *Quartet*.[49] The film also benefited from the presence of the 'Old Party' himself at the premieres in London and New York, and from Maugham's willingness to be interviewed about the adaptations now that they had proved to be successful.[50]

Trio followed the same format of varied lengths and contrasting moods. 'The Verger', adapted by Maugham himself, is a classic study of the unsung qualities of the 'little man' and a neatly ironic attack on middle-class double standards. 'Mr Know-All' has a similar target, the hypocrisies and pretensions of British society, where outsiders are shunned, distrusted or actively repulsed, but its treatment is more comic. 'Sanatorium', by far the longest of the three, is a faithful adaptation of one of Maugham's most compassionate and optimistic stories, therefore a good choice for cinema audiences. Harold French's smooth, unobtrusive and precise direction, in which not a frame is wasted – Alfred Roome observed that it was the easiest film he ever had to edit – allows the various relationships that the inmates of a Scottish sanatorium form to develop in an unforced and convincing way. The decision of Major Templeton (Michael Rennie) and Evie Bishop (Jean Simmons) to marry, made despite the warning from Dr Lennox (André Morell) that this will shorten their lives, acts as a spur to others to accept their situation. The most moving moment occurs when, watching the happy couple depart, the irascible and selfish Henry Chester (Raymond Huntley) takes the hand of his long-suffering wife (Betty Ann Davies) and tells her to be happy because he has now become reconciled to the inevitability of his own death. The adaptation did not strive for strict authenticity. As its director, Harold French, observed, the cast were uniformly too healthy to be really convincing sufferers from tuberculosis, but he was reluctant, prompted by the censors, to make them show the obvious signs of consumption by frequently coughing and spitting.[51]

In a perceptive review of *Trio*, the *Manchester Guardian* thought it represented the triumph of a writer's cinema in which the screen itself had been adapted 'to the role of plain reporter, trying simply to repeat three well-written tales with as little interference as possible'.[52] The virtues of this style consisted in its self-abnegation, with the minimum of wastage in the adaptation, and a quality of unfussy urbanity. In pioneering this approach, Box was striking a blow for the status of the writer in the film industry, and also attempting to provide intelligent entertainment for audiences which, within the parameters set by the censors that ruled out the development of some of Maugham's more controversial stories, could be both thought-provoking and emotionally satisfying.[53]

Comedies and crime thrillers

In his pursuit of a 'balanced programme' of films, Box was naturally drawn to the two most prolific British genres, comedies and crime thrillers, as these were relatively cheap to produce and popular with audiences. They are less distinctive than the social issue films, but Box's comedies did constitute a break with the Gainsborough tradition of 'comedian comedy' in which the films were vehicles for established stars such as Arthur Askey, Will Hay and Tommy Handley. Box's comedies were principally adaptations of West End stage successes that had at least a veneer of topicality. By far the most accomplished and successful was *Miranda* (April 1948), Peter Blackmore's excellent adaptation of his West End hit, which appears to have commanded a substantially higher budget, at £170,400, than subsequent comedies. This was partly occasioned by directorial problems, which extended its shooting schedule, but also by its closeness to the sophisticated, satirical comedy of manners of *On Approval*, which Box admired. Annakin's unobtrusive direction places the emphasis where it should be – on the expert playing of the talented cast, including Margaret Rutherford, who does wonders with the potentially dull role of the nurse. If not overtly topical, *Miranda* is sharply contemporary, a study of the chaos inflicted on English middle-class respectability by the arrival of an uninhibitedly sexy mermaid, Miranda Trewella (Glynis Johns), who has ensnared Harley Street surgeon Paul Marten (Griffith Jones) while he was on a bachelor fishing holiday in Cornwall. In order to be released from her cave beneath the sea he has to accede to her demand that he show her London. Martin takes her back to his elegant Chelsea flat, where her presence creates endless suspicions in the active mind of his wife Clare (Googie Withers). Her rampant flirtatiousness also drives a wedge between two other couples – Marten's servants Charles (David Tomlinson) and Betty (Yvonne Owen), and Clare's friends Isobel (Sonia Holm) and Nigel (John McCallum).

In one of the funniest scenes, both Charles and Nigel wait nervously for Miranda's return in order to propose, only to have their hopes dashed when each reveals he possesses a locket of her hair as a 'token of love that might have been'. When Clare finds a similar pendant round Paul's neck, and exclaims 'My dear, it's a wonder you have any hair left!', Miranda replies, with a typical mixture of innocence and guile, 'They're only made from combings.' This sharp, incisive and witty dialogue is complemented by more visual comedy associated with her identity – hiding her tail and excusing her penchant for drinking salt water and eating raw fish – and comic set pieces, including the delightful scene in which she sings an aria during the interval of a performance of *Tristram and Isolde* at Covent Garden. Miranda's relationship with Paul has a depth which provides several moments of real tenderness between them, contrasting satisfyingly with the general mode of light comedy, and preparing the audience for the risqué final shot of Miranda cradling her mer-baby in the warmth of the Mediterranean. This provoked some comment from the censor, but the scene remained.[54]

Miranda's enthusiastic critical response – one reviewer judged it 'unquestionably the best British light comedy that has emerged since the war'[55] – was mirrored at the box office, but proved to be exceptional: Box's other comedies were markedly unsuccessful. The three directed by Ralph Thomas, *Once upon a Dream* (February 1949), *Helter Skelter* (July 1949) and *Traveller's Joy* (December 1949), all performed dismally, though this was the fault of the scripts rather than the direction. Patrick Kirwan's and Victor Katona's original screenplay for *Once upon a Dream* was a topical romantic comedy, in which affable but ineffectual Major Gilbert (Guy Middleton) brings his ultra-efficient batman, Jackson (Griffith Jones), back home with him as his domestic servant after demobilisation. This causes a series of misunderstandings with his wife, Carol (Googie Withers), who dreams of having a romantic affair with Jackson and wakes believing it to be true. The censors were dubious about even implied adulterous desires, but the scene remained.[56] Even if mildly risqué, the film had a slender premise which was resolved rather tediously. *Helter Skelter* was another original screenplay, by Patrick Campbell, Jan Read and Gerard Bryant, which afforded a starring role to Rank hopeful Carol Marsh as a young woman who suffers an attack of violent hiccups during a quarrel, which she cannot shake off. This remarkably thin storyline is padded out by the efforts of various parties, including a psychiatrist, to cure her. One commentator pointed out rather acidly that Box needed a 'pre-fabricated comedy' in which various acts – including Terry-Thomas performing his famous 'technical hitch' routine – could be thrust into the free-wheeling plot, filmed 'wherever he can snatch space from other productions', so as to save time and money.[57] Box had bought the rights to Arthur Macrae's *Traveller's Joy*, first performed at the Criterion on 2 June 1948, an extended joke about the impecunious British abroad, hamstrung by the government's draconian currency restrictions. It provided roles for John McCallum, as Reggie Pelham, and for Googie Withers, as his estranged wife Bumble, stranded in an elegant Stockholm hotel because they cannot pay their bills. Their increasingly desperate attempts to get money bring the couple back together. Unfortunately *Traveller's Joy* could not be shown until 1951, when the play had finished its theatrical run, by which time all its topicality had evaporated.[58]

Don't Ever Leave Me (April 1949), with a screenplay by Robert Westerby from Anthony Armstrong's novel, was designed as a vehicle for the child star Petula Clark, who had been successful in the Huggett series. Its storyline, in which she befriends her kidnappers because they give her more attention than her self-regarding thespian father, was another example of a Box picture in which the idea could not support a full-length film. There were complaints about lack of punch in Crabtree's direction, which had 'the light witty touch of an elephant on roller-skates, heavy-handed, dull and devoid of fun'.[59] *It's Not Cricket* (April 1949), another original screenplay (by Bernard McNab and Lyn Lockwood), was also a star vehicle, an opportunity for Basil Radford and Naunton Wayne to play another variation on their double act as asinine Englishmen unequal to any situation. Captain Early (Wayne) and Major Bright (Radford), demobilised from gloriously ineffectual careers in Intelligence, set up as private detectives, but their fortunes continue to be dogged by a dangerous Nazi – a role that allowed Maurice Denham to mug furiously – whom they eventually capture by sheer fluke at a cricket match. Again it was a slight, rather tiresome affair which betrayed traces of haste and lack of invention.

Box's crime thrillers display a similar tendency to fall back on rather hackneyed conventions, but they too started brightly, with *Dear Murderer* (June 1947), in which the Boxes and Peter Rogers adapted St John Legh Clowes's West End success. Box seemed to have been determined that Islington's launch film would be a quality production. The period furniture used in the main set consisted of genuine collector's pieces; Yvonne Caffin, the dress supervisor, spent £2,000 creating 'one of the most choicely sophisticated wardrobes in any recent film', and the female lead, Greta Gynt, wore a loaned mink worth £3,000; the portrait of her that hung over the mantelpiece on set was painted by a well-known artist, Anthony Mendelson; and the commissioned score, by Benjamin Frankel, was played by the London Philharmonic Orchestra.[60] Crabtree's direction highlights the expensive décor, but is chiefly concerned to allow his talented cast to construct their roles. The star is Eric Portman as Lee Warren, a successful businessman, blindly in love with his beautiful wife Vivien (Gynt), who contrives to kill her lovers when he discovers her infidelity. Portman's performance is a masterpiece of subtlety coupled with superb control, which allows him to alternate suavity and menace, nonchalance and a barely suppressed brutality. Gynt is also highly effective as the shallow and coldly calculating Vivien, the most ruthless *femme fatale* in British cinema. *Dear Murderer* also benefits from Reginald Wyer's accomplished *noir* cinematography, including the virtually wordless opening scene, in which Warren returns to his empty flat, where the ominous atmosphere is economically conveyed by the oppressive darkness and occasional pools of light, with Warren's shadowy figure framed in the doorway by back lighting.

Dear Murderer also explores the complex psychological terrain that characterised Box's Riverside films, and uses an extended flashback, typical of Box. As Martha Wolfenstein and Nathan Leites argue, at the centre of the film is the strangely intimate bond, both physical and emotional, forged between the murderer (Warren) and his victim, Vivien's lover Richard Fenton (Dennis Price).[61] As in *The Man Within*, this masculine relationship is a powerful mixture of guilt, paranoia and betrayal in which, even as Warren coldly describes to Fenton the manner of his death and its undetectability, he cannot refrain from confiding to Fenton the suffering he has undergone at the destruction of his marriage. Warren is a typically English murderer, a man of distinction, an artist, who needs to ensure that his victim understands that he is dying at the hands of someone altogether finer, more intelligent, and with greater depth of feeling than himself. The emotional complexity extends to the denouement, in which Warren himself is the victim, poisoned by Vivien, whose love he thought he had reclaimed. Their moment of greatest intimacy is achieved as he gradually acknowledges, for the first time, the true nature of their relationship, and she reveals the depths of her cunning and cruelty as she tells him, with chilling equanimity: 'You've got to die so that I may go on living as I want to live'.

Dear Murderer's psychological depth and subtlety, its accomplished acting and polished screenplay, were not reproduced in Box's subsequent crime thrillers. *The Blind Goddess* (September 1948) also had a Box screenplay and a strong cast – particularly Anne Crawford as the ambivalent fiture of Lady Brasted, the upwardly mobile woman who seems prepared to go to any lengths to protect her husband's reputation and her own position – but both failed to animate Sir Patrick Hastings's old-fashioned courtroom drama from which the film was adapted. The *Daily Telegraph* thought that it 'takes us back to Victorian morality, Sardou, and the "well-made" play', while the *Sunday Graphic*'s reviewer remarked tartly that *The Blind Goddess* was 'as artificial as a set of Victorian dentures'.[62] *The Calendar*, released slightly earlier, in June 1948, was altogether shabbier, a tedious revival of Edgar Wallace's racing drama, which had been made into a film by Gainsborough (under Michael Balcon) back in 1931. *My Brother's Keeper* (July 1948) was fresher and much more topical with a central protagonist, the escaped convict George Martin (Jack Warner), who is psychologically disturbed and another unstable mixture of the intelligent artist and the cold-blooded murderer. In the final scene, which the *Monthly Film Bulletin*'s reviewer thought was 'mesmerising', Martin is blown up, defiantly scrambling across a minefield and screaming: 'I can tackle [this]. Did it in the war fighting for you, you.'[63] It is a powerful, shocking scene, which lingers in the mind, disturbingly suggesting that Martin is a product of the anarchic forces which the war has liberated, an unassimilable man who has no role in peacetime.[64] The film might have achieved greater recognition had its release not coincided with that of Ealing's *It Always Rains on Sunday*, which critics preferred.[65]

Costume films

The costume films were the most problematic group, partly because Box was fighting on ground not of his own choosing. As already discussed, *Jassy* (August 1947), was an Ostrer left-over, and *Christopher Columbus* (July 1949) was also forced onto Box despite his serious misgivings. *Columbus*'s origins can be traced back at least ten years. In August 1939 British National announced a proposed biography of Columbus, and arrangements were being made in late 1941 to shoot some location scenes in Spain.[66] A further announcement in 1944 stated that shooting had been delayed because of the shortage of Technicolor cameramen, but Brian Desmond Hurst is named as the director, with producer John Corfield undertaking to assemble 'well-known stars' for what was to be an Anglo-American release.[67] The project seems to have gone cold at this point, but *Columbus* formed part of Box's first announcement about Gainsborough's forthcoming releases in December 1946.[68] Dallas Bower, working with Sam Goldwyn Jnr, was reported to be preparing a film 'which Sydney Box intends to make with the world markets in mind ... an international star is to be selected for the role of Columbus'.[69] It was to be based on a Raphael Sabatini script.

There are obvious reasons why Rank, which owned British National, would wish to resurrect a project that could form part of its 'prestige experiment', expensive productions designed to conquer the world market, as the subject would have an obvious attraction for American audiences. Sabatini had an excellent track record as the author of several novels from which successful action adventure films had been adapted, including *Captain Blood* (1935), *The Sea Hawk* (1940) and *The Black Swan* (1942). However, despite the announcement, Box was reluctant to take on a project for which he knew the Gainsborough studios were ill-equipped, and which would have a disruptive effect on his schedules and his attempts to keep the company profitable. Box asked to be excused making the film, but was overruled by Rank, which had paid a large sum of money to secure Sabatini's script and was anxious to recoup its outlay.[70] Preparations therefore continued, and in April 1948 the *Daily Mirror* reported that 'what is hoped will be the British picture of the year' was in production, based on Sabatini's script.[71] In May the *Star* reported that there would be 'plenty of romance', with Sonia Holm cast as Columbus's wife Philippa.[72]

Unfortunately Sabatini's original screenplay has not survived, but the novel he wrote based on his screenplay, *Columbus*, has a highly romantic conception of Columbus, animated by love above everything. The culmination of his quest is not the triumphal entry to the Spanish court, but his embrace of Beatriz, the low-born woman with whom he had his second child but whom he could not marry: 'The lover is greater than the discoverer'.[73] A third draft script exists, dated April 1948, which contains several scenes deleted from the final film, including a prologue in which Columbus, living at Porto Santo, listens to the tales of ship-wrecked seamen, which encourage him that his concept of a spherical earth is sound and that he should continue his efforts at circum-navigation; his rejection by the King of Portugal; the death of his wife Philippa; and his marriage to Beatriz Enríquez de Arana, all of which derive from Sabatini.[74] Production stills exist showing that these scenes were filmed.[75]

However, it seems that Box became increasingly dissatisfied with Sabatini's work, having been advised by Muriel that, 'after extensive research', she had 'found this long script to be both inaccurate and inferior in quality'. Maurice Carter, who considered the Sabatini script 'pretty good', recalled: 'one weekend I went up to their house to help where I could. They divided the script into four parts and they each wrote a part in separate rooms, shouting between two terrace doors to each other. It was all rewritten that way.'[76] The Boxes' final screenplay not only considerably shortens the film, but also, by excising Philippa and Columbus's marriage to Beatriz, moves decisively away from Sabatini's romantic figure.

One further important change occurred after the press screenings in mid-June 1949. The version the reviewers saw ended with Columbus's closest associates telling him: 'It wasn't all in vain. A great nation will one day rise in the New World ... Listen, Admiral, listen to the voices of the New World', whereupon part of the Declaration of Independence is read out, followed by a short excerpt from Lincoln's Gettysburg address and finally the voice of Roosevelt declaiming the Three Freedoms (speech, expression and worship) of the Atlantic Charter. Unsurprisingly, British critics mercilessly ridiculed this American triumphalism – what Richard Winnington, ever Box's scourge, described as his 'final elephantine grab for the US Market'. A later script, dated 1 July 1949, removes this ending, leaving a much more downbeat conclusion.[77] This was the version that went on release in Britain, shortened from 104 to 95 minutes. In fact three versions were prepared, the third a compromise between the first two, with some earlier scenes shortened but the deathbed scene retained. This was the version used for export.[78] Unfortunately the press book was produced before these decisions were made, so it gives a running time of 104 minutes and refers to the deathbed scene.

In addition to the extensive script changes, *Columbus* suffered from severe, and much publicised, production difficulties.[79] As with Box's other historical projects, great pains were taken to achieve authenticity. The 400 remaining descendents of the original Carib Indians were taken from their native reserve on Dominica for the crowd scenes. Unfortunately, on the first day of shooting a cable bridge collapsed injuring sixteen of them, including the beautiful Juliana Tisa, who was earmarked to play a prominent role.[80] Enormous sums were spent on making exact replicas of the *Nina* and the *Santa Maria*, accurate down to the 'intricate medieval rigging, the colour of the crosses on her sails, the height of the poop and mainmast, every small detail', which were constructed on the beach at Holetown in Barbados.[81] But ill fortune dogged Box's production. The *Santa Maria* was rammed amidships by the *Valena*, a large steam-yacht used to house the sixty-strong film unit and its equipment, manoeuvring for close-ups. Lying in dry-dock awaiting repairs, she was burnt to the waterline and thus became a complete write-off. To cut costs, half the sailors and most of the film crew were sent home and the production continued using the *Nina* alone, though it was lost at sea, twice, which, as Lady Bracknell might have said, smacks of carelessness.

At this point location work was suspended and the director, David Macdonald, returned to London with virtually no usable footage of the ships at sea. This not only robbed the film of much potentially exciting cinematography, but also added £100,000 to an already huge budget, which now topped £500,000.[82] Box purchased Frank Launder and Sidney Gilliat's tropical island set from *The Blue Lagoon* and the studio New World scenes were filmed at Pinewood.[83] But even back on dry land problems continued, when a huge replica of the *Santa Maria* crashed to the studio floor because the elaborate (and expensive) cantilever rocking system made to reproduce the motion of a ship proved to be too frail to support the weight of the model.[84]

These production problems have tended to obscure Box's challenging conception of Columbus, which was decidedly modern. No longer the romantic lover, or God's instrument, or even a conventional hero, Box's Columbus is a complex, multifaceted figure whose motivations are often ambiguous, a mixture of ambition, rational calculation and idealism. Columbus's sense of himself as a man of destiny who was 'elected, preordained' for a special purpose, means that he fights shy of romantic intrigue (the stuff of Sabatini) and explicitly rejects the need for a wife. Rather the emphasis falls on the nature of his enterprise – hence the need for the extended scenes in which he tries to persuade the Royal Commission that his voyage is based on knowledge, mathematical deduction and scriptural allusion – and on the forces that try to prevent him realising his dream. However, although his purposes may be noble, Columbus's attitude to others is basically exploitative. In the first scene, at the monastery in Rabida, Father Perez (Felix Aylmer) recognises his combination of vision and calculation, as a humble traveller who knows full well that Perez is Isabella's confessor and therefore can provide his entrée to the Spanish court. Columbus is quite capable of low cunning as he falsifies the ship's position to intimidate his crew into sailing further and further west despite their misgivings. In his dealings with the native people we see little attempt to convert them to Christianity, the other ostensible purpose of his mission. A revealing moment occurs when the arch-sceptic Pedro (Edward Rigby), who fomented an aborted mutiny, is trying to barter a broken plate for a gold pendant. Columbus sees this, reproves him for trying to exploit the natives, and then takes a falcon's bell from Pedro's purse: 'It's worth at least this'. But, taking a closer look at the pendant, Columbus then pockets it for himself.

In Box's conception, the defining moment is not the voyage itself, nor even the 'discovery' of America, but Columbus's triumphal return to the Spanish court, complete with dancing girl, talking parrots, subjugated natives and the trappings of wealth. This is at once a legitimate celebration of his achievement and a demonstration of his egotistical desire for power and pre-eminence as the man who wants to be recognised as a 'conqueror' as well as an explorer. In the midst of this scene there is a telling exchange between Talavera, the head of the Commission (Ronald Adam), and the Chancellor, Luis de Santangel (Abraham Sofaer). Talavera remarks, 'In everyone's life there is a moment when he reaches the climax of his achievement', to which the Chancellor replies, 'I agree with my Lord Bishop, but the great thing, of course, is to have the wit to know it and to make the most of it'. Columbus's fatal flaw, but also his greatness, is that he lacks that 'wit' and therefore must continue his quest, never satisfied.

It is crucial to Box's conception of Columbus's character that the film encompasses the ignominious aftermath of his career as an explorer, which sees, in the words of the anonymous narrator, 'an old man, old before his time, worn out by intrigue and rebellion', He suffers the supreme indignity of being supplanted and overruled by his old adversary Francisco de Bobadilla (Francis L. Sullivan), who is appointed as the king's commissioner in the New World. His return to the court in chains, where he throws himself in mute suppliance on the steps of the throne, is handled with great dignity and effectiveness by March. Despite Box's misgivings, March's declamatory style is well suited to conveying an implacable character now burning with a sense of ingratitude. He protests to his old friend Juana de Torres (Nora Swinburne): 'Don't they realise who I am? ... It's time they did. People will remember me long after they're dead and forgotten.' At this point, he shambles off along the palace colonnade and, metaphorically, into history. It is an effective ending, far more so than the hymn to American values – which was, in all probability, forced on Box – because it preserves Columbus's duality, the egotism and the idealism that are inextricable.

If the characterisation of *Columbus* is consistent, the Boxes' script bears the marks of its rather hasty rewriting. Columbus's flirtation with the femme fatale Beatriz de Peraza (Linden Travers) goes nowhere, and Kathleen Ryan as the other, virtuous Beatriz is completely wasted, the part clearly having been pared back and back until it has become virtually non-existent. As the *Evening News* commented: 'Kathleen Ryan, cast as the pretty little thing who becomes the explorer's mistress, hastily leaves the screen before the American censor gets a chance to dislike her.'[85] Her presence is distracting because it seems to be a remnant of the earlier and much more romantic version. But it may also have been the case that Box chose to forestall any problems with the Hays Office by pretending that Columbus did not have a mistress, or a second son.

The other besetting weakness is the film's leaden pace, which makes the early scenes at court seem interminable. David Macdonald seems to have been unable to inject a brisk tempo – Carter thought he was not a strong enough character to handle a production of this size or cope with an overweening American star, and recalled that his health was poor at this point, partly as a result of his alcoholism.[86] Sir Arthur Bliss's score is highly effective; its majestically swelling chords lending an appropriately epic mood to the film, but the lack of location footage means that the visual style struggles to match the music. However, Maurice Carter's sets are excellent: the beautifully subtle décor of the chamber in which the Commission sits to listen to Columbus's explanations and the grandeur and scale of the resplendent throne room are notable. Columbus's first return used the most elaborate sets that Carter had ever built in his long career, with a scale and splendour rare in British cinema, clearly designed to outdo Hollywood. These sets are complemented by Elizabeth Haffenden's costumes, which are her finest work for Gainsborough.

There was some admiration for the sets and the music, but *Columbus* was assailed mercilessly from all quarters, excoriated for being dull, lacklustre, slow and pedantic, with an 'inept script, flat dialogue, and feeble humour'.[87] There was some grudging awareness that Box had attempted to be realistic and avoid conventional 'hooey', but this was usually seen as a fault: 'Hollywood might have fiddled the history, but it would at least have jollied things up a little with battles with pirates and perhaps an earthquake or two', producing something more lively.[88] Rather more sympathetically, some reviewers thought the subject, not the treatment, might be the at the root of the problem. The *Evening News*'s reviewer opined that Hollywood had never made a film about Columbus because his life was a failure.[89] In the most considered piece, the *Daily Telegraph*'s critic observed:

> In every life there are contradictions and obscure motives, loose ends and tiresome delays; and often the whole thing ends in anti-climax ... If the whole is less exciting and moving than its producers must have hoped it would be, the fault, in the main, is history's. Columbus was a great man who changed the history of the world; but that doesn't necessarily make him a good subject for a film ... Dramatically, his life was the wrong shape.[90]

Box's determination to accept, indeed emphasise, this 'wrong shape', caused him to lose contact with his public. The meagre box-office returns of *Columbus* indicate that British cinema-goers would have liked more action, romance and an upbeat ending. Strenuous efforts were made to sell the film in America: 150 copies were made in order to have an unprecedented pre-release at 115 US and 25 Latin American cinemas on Columbus Day, 12 October.[91] But a poor initial performance in America, and another dismal set of notices – several American reviewers likened the film to a series of dull tableaux – led to a limited circuit release that did little to recoup the huge outlay.[92]

The Bad Lord Byron also seems to have been a partially existing Rank property that was passed on to Box. In December 1945, Two Cities had announced a film about Byron, written, produced and directed by Terence Young and starring Eric Portman.[93] In his book about the production, Box states that he had been contemplating a life of Shelley when 'it was proposed' that Byron should be the subject, based on Terence Young's existing screenplay, which derived from Peter Quennell's two books *The Years of Fame* and *Byron in Italy*.[94] Box assigned Aubrey Baring and director David Macdonald to the project as both, according to Dennis Price, 'had long cherished the idea of a film about Byron'.[95] However, Box was very actively involved in the production at every level, especially scripting, where his was the dominant voice.[96] Box was motivated by an enormous enthusiasm for the subject, describing Byron as 'one of the most fascinating Englishmen who ever breathed', a man whom fate had singled out, physically and emotionally.[97] It may be that Box felt an emotional pull to explore the life of someone with a similar affliction to himself, but he was also clearly attracted by Byron's complexity, the paradoxical and contradictory product of four ages: the passionate Elizabethan man of action, obsessed with freedom; the controlled and classical Augustan satirist; the morbid, melancholic Gothic 'lost soul'; and the Romantic rebel, in revolt against convention.[98]

Byron's life therefore provided an *embarras de richesse*, reflected in Young's script, which Box felt was an 'imaginative and very full survey', but without any guiding perspective and far too long.[99] Macdonald and Baring reduced its length by half, but it still lacked a satisfactory approach. Working with the *Daily Express* journalist Paul Holt, who had joined Gainsborough as script adviser, Box began to reconceive the film as a debate about Byron's qualities and also a psychological exploration of his motivations. Beginning with Byron's death at Missolonghi and his plangent utterance 'I am perfectly fit – to die', the intention was to use the women in Byron's life to unlock his innermost feelings through a series of flashbacks, which would 'make the film a subtle kind of documentary, the camera choosing out each contrasting figure moving into a close-up of each face and then dissolving through the face as the film becomes a memory of each individual'.[100]

Unfortunately, this radical conception was abandoned because Box felt it was too derivative of *Citizen Kane* and would make Byron's own presence too insubstantial.[101] A second possibility – to reorder Byron's life from the perspective of his liaison with Teresa Guiccioli, with whom he finally achieved 'spiritual and emotional purgation' – had to be abandoned because Mai Zetterling, who was to play Guiccioli, was not available for long enough to make this approach possible.[102] The eventual 'solution' was inspired by Laurence Kitchin's radio play *The Trial of Lord Byron*, in which Byron appeared as a prisoner before a celestial court 'being weighed in the balance for the judgement of history' with the radio listeners as the audience.[103]

In keeping with his analytical, documentary approach to Byron's life, Box strove for absolute authenticity of detail. Exhaustive research was carried out in order that Carter and Haffenden could makes the sets and costumes, including borrowing Byron's footwear from Sir John Murray in order to be make sure that Byron's limp was correct.[104] *Byron* was an expensive production, costing £223,900.[105] The set for Lady Melbourne's ballroom boasted over £11,000 worth of gilt Louis XIV furniture, was lit by four eighteen-light crystal chandeliers and was large enough to accommodate 200 guests.[106] A full eight weeks were spent on location in Venice in order to ensure that Byron's study, and the hall where he kept his famous menagerie at the Mocenigo Palace, could be faithfully reproduced. However, when *Film Industry*'s correspondent visited the studio and judged Mocenigo Palace 'was without doubt the most beautifully decorated set we have yet seen in a British studio', he expressed surprise that the production was not in colour.[107] Box himself thought Haffenden's 'brilliant costume designs made us sometimes sigh for Technicolor'. Although the decision to film in black and white may have been taken on the ground of cost – shooting in Technicolor added a third to a film's budget – the crucial factor could have been lack of technical resources. Box had to abandon his plans to film *Melba* in colour because of Rank's decision to send Technicolor cameras to Fiji for Launder and Gilliat's *The Blue Lagoon*.[108] He also had to abandon plans to film *Mantilla* and *So Long at the Fair* in colour at the same time.[109] *Byron* may have been another victim of scarce resources being deployed elsewhere.

The absence of colour was not *Byron*'s only flaw. Box's decision to have the trial as the focus stifles the film. As the *Evening News*'s reviewer judged, it is as an essentially lazy script device.[110] More crucially, it reduces Box's conception of Byron as a multifaceted and paradoxical character down to a series of binary oppositions: 'poet and liberator or a seducer and a libertine'. As with *Columbus*, the problems of the script were exacerbated by David Macdonald's direction, which tends to be slow-paced and rather literal. Box was clearly unhappy with his handling of the film and asked Alfred Roome to re-edit it. Although Box was pleased with the results, in Roome's own judgement he could not rescue a film in which the director had not imposed sufficient control on the material: '[he] had just let it run, pages of stuff without any cuts. I did all sorts of tricks with it – bits of Byron's poetry, travel shots – but it was an unsaveable film.'[111]

The other crucial weakness was to cast Dennis Price as Byron. As Linden Travers, who played Augusta Leigh, recalled: 'I think it needed a wilder type than Dennis Price for Byron'.[112] The *Monthly Film Bulletin* was unequivocal: 'The film's real weakness, however, is that Dennis Price is not convincing as Byron; he does not show the fascination that would make his supposed power over women credible, and so the whole fabric of the film is weakened.'[113] Although Price was keen on the role and stated that his performance strove to be realistic, he did confide in one interview that Eric Portman, earmarked by Two Cities, should have had the part.[114] At forty-five, Portman might not have reproduced the fire and passion that had made his performance as Byron in the 1936 production of Catherine Turney's *Bitter Harvest* so memorable, but he would have given the role far greater range and shading. The other obvious choice, though he was unavailable, was James Mason. Price's interpretation is mannered and monotonous, too corseted in a one-dimensional sceptical world-weariness to be convincing as a lover or a poet. He is certainly unable to convey a man who was the product of four ages, and hence the film as a whole fails to ignite, despite fine performances from Joan Greenwood as the quixotic Lady Caroline Lamb and Zetterling as Teresa Guiccioli.

The provocative title *The Bad Lord Byron,* which had helped Box generate huge interest in the film, was a gift to the critics, who were merciless about the film's shortcomings. The *Evening Standard* considered that if this 'glossy vulgarisation' was 'sent abroad it will, with one fell blow, destroy whatever reputation British pictures have built up for integrity and maturity'.[115] The *Sunday Pictorial* fumed about this 'woefully weak film ... One lacking any element of good taste, imagination or excitement'; while the *Star* thought *Byron* to be 'an inept piece of work that reduces a notable figure to the most commonplace proportions and misses nearly every suggestion of greatness in his career'.[116] Richard Winnington's review, in which he described *The Bad Lord Byron* as 'a nasty back-alley joke of a film', a 'monstrosity' that 'titters and sniggers as it degrades a story that commands the fullest of artistic reverence', bordered on the hysterical.[117] Perhaps the most wounding review was Harold Nicolson's in the *Spectator,* which took Box to task for numerous inaccuracies: 'Byron did not limp in the way that is represented, he slithered; he did not talk with the voice of a BBC announcer, he talked with a Devonshire drawl with an undertone of Scotch.'[118] Box could not seek solace in the public's reactions as the box-office returns were little short of disastrous, netting a revenue of only £45,000, which meant a huge loss.[119]

The end of the nodding lady: the closure of Gainsborough Studios and the move to Pinewood

During his first eighteen months in charge at Gainsborough, Box was highly successful. In December 1947, *Kinematograph Weekly* reported that he had exceeded his one film a month target, and 'Josh' Billings commented: 'The Gainsborough Studios are Number One again this year. Sydney Box has successfully stepped into 'Bill' Ostrer's shoes and proved that the reputation he gained with *The Seventh Veil* was no fluke. He, like Herbert Wilcox, has keen box-office sense.'[120] In January 1948, *Film Industry* reported that according to Rank's figures, Box had three of the six most profitable films playing on its circuits in 1947: *Jassy, Holiday Camp* and *The Upturned Glass*. It estimated that they took £850,000 for an outlay of £600,000.[121] In addition to those three films, *Good Time Girl* was highly successful – also rated 'excellent' by John Davis, Rank's managing director, in his comments on the box-office grosses.[122] He rated the returns from the three 'Huggett' films, the two Maugham adaptations *Quartet* and *Trio, Miranda* and *Portrait from Life* as 'good'. However, 1948 and certainly 1949 showed a marked falling off at the box office, *The Lost People, A Boy, a Girl and a Bike, Marry Me!,* and *The Astonished Heart* were all rated 'poor'. In particular, the returns from the two historical biographies were dire: *Byron* lost £179,200 and *Columbus* around £279,000.[123]

There has been a tendency to see the failure of *Byron* and *Columbus* as the reason why Gainsborough Studios were closed. This is a misconception. Their poor performance weakened Box's position within the Rank Organisation, but they were certainly not responsible for the decision to shut Gainsborough Studios. The reasons were more complex and more deep-seated. It was very difficult for any producer, however astute, to make money during this period. Box claimed that, taken as a whole, his Gainsborough films had been profitable, making £30,000,000 at the box office against an outlay of £6,500,000.[124] But they made little money in real terms because of the crippling effects of the British government's entertainment tax. This had been raised to 38 per cent in 1944, twice as high as anywhere else in the world. Rank's biographer Alan Wood paints a bleak picture of the situation that faced British producers once the huge expansion in audiences, which the war had stimulated, began to decline. From the total box-office receipts of £109,000,000 in 1948, £39,000,000 went to the government in entertainment tax, £42,500,000 to exhibitors and '[b]y the time distributors and Hollywood producers had taken their share of the remainder, British producers were left with about £7,500,000 from the British market for films which had cost them about £14,000,000 to make. That gap could not be bridged from overseas sales.'[125]

The difficulties facing producers were exacerbated by government pressure, particularly during the US embargo, to step up production. Rank, by his own admission, had overstretched his organisation's resources: 'Our plans to meet an unexpected and critical situation were too ambitious ... We made demands on the creative talent in the industry that were beyond its resources ... As a result we spread our production capacity, in which I have unshaken faith, too thinly over the films we made.'[126] Once the embargo on US films was lifted in May 1948, a backlog of films was immediately released which then competed with the products of a native film industry stretched beyond its capabilities. The Rank Organisation announced an overdraft of £13,589,858 in October 1948, which had worsened to £16,286.581 a year later.[127] Rank had lost £6,000,000 on production in four-and-a-half years since the war. All of Rank's producers lost money, including Balcon; Del Giudice's losses at Two Cities were particularly heavy.[128]

To combat these huge losses, Rank decided to cut back on the number of films made and to centralise production at Pinewood. In December 1948, Rank announced that the Independent Producers organisation was to be disbanded and a new company created, Pinewood Films.[129] It was also announced that arrangements were being discussed by which Box would leave Shepherd's Bush at the end of 1948 to produce at Pinewood and Denham, making five films a year divided between the two studios. Betty Box was to be left in charge of production at Shepherd's Bush 'assisted by a group of young producers and directors trained by Sydney Box'.[130] However, at the end of February 1949, Box was told by Rank and Davis that they had decided to shut Shepherd's Bush down by mid-March and Islington with immediate effect following the conclusion of work on *Marry Me!*[131] Certain productions, including *Trio, Diamond City, The Astonished Heart* and *So Long at the Fair*, were completed at either Denham or Pinewood.

At an emotional meeting with his staff, Box, 'with tears in his eyes', explained that Rank's decision to cut back production had rendered Shepherd's Bush unnecessary. Pinewood and Denham between them had the requisite capacity to make the target of twenty-five films a year, and they had extra capacity should the economic situation improve.[132] As has been discussed, both Islington and Shepherd's Bush were antiquated, ill-equipped and unsuited to efficient production. In particular, neither was suitable for colour film-making, which was rapidly becoming more important. When Rank visited Shepherd's Bush during the filming of *Columbus*, he witnessed how the studio doors had to be opened every two hours in order to let out some of the intense heat that the lamps had generated.[133] As Box was moving to Pinewood, the real casualty of the closure, as Box knew full well, was the wastage of 'a great number of experienced and talented technicians' who would be lost to the industry.[134]

The closure of Gainsborough was therefore based on problems within the Rank Organisation as a whole and the decision to cut back production, which meant shedding unnecessary and inconvenient plant. It was not made to remove, demote or even 'discipline' Sydney Box, who was expected to continue producing at Pinewood. It is inconceivable that Box would have been allowed to remain as head of a separate and unwanted studio, whatever his profitability. The decision to close Gainsborough was thus made well before the films that performed poorly at the box office, including *Byron* and *Columbus*, had even been released.

Even before the closure of Gainsborough Studios, there was an announcement in the trade press that Box would produce a batch of seven films at Pinewood.[135] After the closure, Box took his place as one of the new company directors of Pinewood Films, along with John Davis, Michael Balcon, Earl St John, George Archibald (the managing director of Independent Producers), and Spencer Reis (the managing director of Denham). However, the move to Pinewood was far from smooth or straightforward for Box. There were two interrelated problems. The first was the difficult and often acrimonious attempt to merge three separate groups of people – the existing Pinewood staff, Gainsborough staff who had been retained, and a further cohort transferred from Denham when that closed in 1950. St John, Archibald and Box were jointly responsible for turning these three staffs into one workforce. Box commented: 'I never hated a job so much in my life. It was heart-breaking to be faced with three production managers, three editors or three cameramen and know that two of them would be out of work within a week.'[136] Even after this culling had taken place, the personnel retained old loyalties and tended to remain in separate groups, jockeying for position in the new hierarchy. Peter Rogers recalls that Box was regarded as an interloper, a view exacerbated by his characteristic determination to guarantee the employment of his family – Rogers, Betty Box, and also Muriel Box, although she had to resign her position as head of the scenario department and became freelance.[137] He was also protective of the ex-Gainsborough staff as a whole, including Alfred Roome, Maurice Carter and Antony Darnborough. There was a sense, therefore, that the former Gainsborough staff did not become Pinewood staff, but remained a relatively autonomous unit which gravitated around Box. Maurice Carter recalled that 'Those already there hated our guts – that awful lot from Shepherd's Bush coming in'.[138]

The second and more formidable problem was the ascendancy of John Davis as the controlling figure within the Rank Organisation. In Alan Wood's account, Davis was engaged in a 'knockout competition', in which anyone with power and influence within the Rank Organisation was manoeuvred out.[139] This process had begun in 1947, when the 'profligate' Del Giudice was removed as managing director of Two Cities.[140] This was followed by the sacking of his successor, Josef Somlo, in 1949 when the company was terminated. Shortly after, Archibald and Reis were also shed, followed by the removal of General Film Distributors' joint managing directors, John Woolf and Edward Carr, and also Stanley Bates, who had been joint managing director of Odeon Theatres along with Davis. Many other staff at lower levels were also dismissed or encouraged to resign. These changes enabled Davis to exercise an increasingly autocratic control, especially as the biddable Earl St John had been installed as head of production at Pinewood, who could be cut out of the decision-making process when it suited Davis to do so.[141] It was Davis who set the ceiling for film budgets at £200,000 and who had, along with Rank himself, the most powerful voice on the board in giving or withholding approval for a project.

According to Alfred Roome, Box gradually lost ascendancy to Earl St John in the Pinewood hierarchy and was engaged in a 'sort of armed neutrality' with Davis.[142] Davis seems to have objected to the personal profit that Box was making on his films, which Box regarded as legitimate gain from risking his own private capital on several projects.[143] Even this uneasy state of affairs worsened as Box experienced increasing difficulties in developing any of his projects. In a diary entry Muriel noted that the 'political manoeuvrings' made it impossible to predict the rapid changes in production policy that Davis and St John decided upon: 'Pictures are set and then cancelled from day to day and nobody knows what he is doing next, which is all terribly unsettling and bad for planning ahead'.[144] Increasingly frustrated, Box asked for a year's leave of absence, but not before he made sure that his current projects were in safe hands: Darnborough took over *Trio* and *Highly Dangerous*, and

Betty Box *The Clouded Yellow*. These were projects that were very likely to be successful and so would help to secure the Boxes's position within the reconstituted Rank structure.

Box's future within the Rank Organisation had become the object of press speculation since the closure of Gainsborough, and his departure was reported as being on medical grounds.[145] Box was quoted as stating: 'Mr Rank and I made this arrangement very comfortably. He would not hear of my contract being torn up, and for my part I am very glad to be able to come back.'[146] However in a journal entry dated 3 April 1950, Box disclosed: 'Today Muriel and I begin what is officially known as "one year's leave of absence on doctor's orders". The fact that I gave the orders to the doctor and not he to me is tacitly understood by most of our intimates, but the polite convention that I am ill and must rest is preserved between JAR, JD, the other directors of the Rank Group and me.'[147]

Box's achievement at Gainsborough

On one obvious level, Box's tenure at Gainsborough was remarkably successful: he fulfilled his commitment to produce a film every month and kept the studios fully occupied and, overall, his films were profitable for Rank's shareholders. He also made a clear break with the Ostrer regime and stamped his own identity on Gainsborough Pictures. His topical, social issue films, if not uniformly good, were distinctive and demonstrated his commitment to continuing the drama-documentary format that had evolved during the war. *The Lost People, Boys in Brown* and *When the Bough Breaks* may be flawed, but they are prepared to tackle difficult issues and to challenge orthodoxies. This is also demonstrated by the number of run-ins that Box had with the censor, extending beyond the changes required in the films that were released to several films which were aborted at the scenario stage because of a very hostile reaction, including an adaptation of J. B. Priestley's unpublished story 'Tober and the Tulpa'.[148] Box forestalled Rank's possible disapproval of the notorious *No Orchids for Miss Blandish*, which he had submitted to the BBFC in July 1944, by selling it on to Alfred Shipman at Renown, but he has unable, as discussed in Chapter 3, to prevent Rank from cancelling another challenging thriller, *The Killer and the Slain*.

Box's continued commitment to presenting topical problems and the experiences of working-class people is also demonstrated by two films that were never released. *Flowers for the Living*, based on the play by Toni Block, was the story of an ATS girl returning after the war to her slum home. The production was reported on in some detail in April 1948, but did not proceed for reasons which are now obscure.[149] *Street Paved with Water* was announced in December 1948, and in the trade press it was reported as the 'story of canal life ... About the common people of Britain [set] against one of the most British of all possible backgrounds.' It was to be another 'open air' film, directed by Ralph Keene, with another very young and inexperienced crew, and a screenplay by Ted Willis. Willis attributes its cancellation to the increasing 'financial problems gathering around Gainsborough', which also claimed the police thriller, *The Blue Lamp*, scripted by Willis with Jan Read, which went to Ealing.[150] It was one of a number of projects which were cancelled in 1949, or which did not survive the move to Pinewood, including the fully scripted *The Huggetts' Christmas Party*.[151]

The increasing financial and logistical pressures on Box – as noted, the costume films were hugely disruptive of his tight schedules – partly explain the marked falling-off in the vigour and invention of Box's later Gainsborough films, which were produced when he was less directly involved either in screenplays or as producer (the Maugham adaptations are the striking exceptions). This was reflected in their poor or indifferent performance at the box office. Had Rank listened to the cogent arguments in Box's July 1947 report on production and future planning and allowed him to cut production from twelve films a year to eight, then this situation might have been avoided, or its worst excesses averted. But Rank, then under pressure from the government, felt he had no option but to produce as many films as possible.

The weaknesses of the later Gainsborough films occasioned justifiable criticism, and it is noticeable how much the obvious warmth that had greeted Box's appointment had cooled by 1948–49. But, in retrospect, what is striking is the severity of the critical onslaught that greeted the later films, notably *Byron* and *Columbus*, which seems out of proportion to their obvious flaws. In 'I Challenge the Critics', published in January 1949, Box criticises reviewers for being out of touch with the public they serve, and for failing to recognise that his films are designed as entertainment, not works of art, and that they subsidise the 'prestige epics'. Box was so exasperated by reviews of his films that he was considering bypassing the critics by eschewing a West End premiere or a trade show.[152] This is somewhat disingenuous – Box himself seemed to have lost touch with his public to a marked extent, and *Columbus*, released after this point, was a prestige epic – but it is difficult not to conclude that many critics would have been dissatisfied whatever Box had done, and seemed to want to see British films fail.

There were more measured and discerning judgements. Patrick

Gibbs, quoted at the beginning of this chapter, argued: 'Films of the highest class are not, I think, to be expected from Sydney Box, however long he might be given to make them. He is a naturally quick worker, getting a story written, cast and on the floor in the minimum of time; but he is not, I should say, a very finished artist, or indeed an artist at all, except in the commercial sense.'[153] A similar critique came from John Barber, who dubbed Box 'The Film Journalist', and judged his strengths to be speed, efficiency and economy, arguing that 'his best work is fresh, contemporary, journalistic', as exemplified by original scripts such as *Holiday Camp*, 'derived from everyday realities'. Barber considered that Box's films lacked staying power, the expected shortcoming of a one-act playwright.[154] There is much truth in these judgements, but, as I hope this chapter has demonstrated, they fail to acknowledge the genuine artistic, cultural and educative aspirations that mark Box's Gainsborough films, even the failures. Box's best films – *Dear Murderer, Holiday Camp, Miranda, Good Time Girl* and *Portrait from Life* – were accomplished, entertaining and engaged cinema-goers. The also demonstrated clear aesthetic and thematic continuities with Box's Riverside films, notably a concern with the legacy of the war and the difficulties of the transition to peacetime. Perhaps the most important films were the Maugham adaptations, which were something genuinely new, pioneering a 'writer's cinema' that would elevate the status of the creative author within the film industry, a subject close to Box's heart.

Notes

1 Richard Winnington, 'Box is Back – with his Happy Family', *Picturegoer*, 26 April 1952, 7.
2 Patrick Gibbs, 'Sydney Box and the Problem of Production', *World Review* (January 1948), 59.
3 The Appendix gives the production costs and box-office returns, where available.
4 Sydney Box, 'Puzzle – Find the Director', in Noble (ed.), *The British Film Yearbook 1949–50*, p. 91.
5 Box, 'More British Films', 14.
6 See Kenneth Adam, 'Anatomy of Butlin', *Pilot Papers*, 2 (April 1946).
7 See Godfrey Winn's postscript in Kit Porlock, *Holiday Camp: The Book of the Film* (London: World Film Publications, 1947), pp. 80–7.
8 Annakin, *So You Wanna Be a Director?*, p. 24.
9 In Winn's conception, Hardwicke was merely a 'show-off and small-time crook', but Muriel Box deepened the characterisation, based on the sadistic serial killer Neville Heath, whose trial and conviction had caused a sensation in 1946.
10 *Manchester Guardian*, 9 August 1947.
11 Elspeth Grant, *Daily Graphic*, 8 August 1947.
12 Ewart Hodgson, *News of the World*, 10 August 1947.
13 Felix Barker, *Evening News*, 8 August 1947.

14 Campbell Dixon, 'Islanders At Play', *Daily Telegraph*, 4 August 1947; see also *Reynold's News*, 10 August 1947.
15 See appendix.
16 Mannon, *Here Come the Huggetts*, p. 2.
17 *Film Industry*, 4:20 (February 1948), 25.
18 Diaries, 21 December 1948.
19 Muriel Box, *Odd Woman Out*, pp. 199–200.
20 *Film Industry*, 7:55 (25 August 1949), 5.
21 *Daily Express*, 26 August 1949.
22 Paul Dehn, *News Chronicle*, 28 August 1949.
23 See Bill Osgersby, *Youth in Britain Since 1945* (Oxford: Basil Blackwell, 1998).
24 Robert Murphy, *Realism and Tinsel: Cinema and Society in Britain 1939–49* (London: Routledge, 1989), p. 90.
25 See appendix.
26 See *Evening Standard*, 30 April 1948.
27 Muriel Box recalled that the censor 'was an absolute bastard!' demanding several scenes, including the fight between Gwen and Roberta, be toned down: 'It was dreadful to have cut it about as they did'. Interview in McFarlane, *An Autobiography of British Cinema*, p. 91.
28 *Daily Mirror*, 30 April 1948.
29 See the review by Campbell Dixon, *Daily Telegraph*, 3 May 1948.
30 *Monthly Film Bulletin*, 15:173 (May 1948), 59.
31 Reginald Beckwith, 'Preface', *Boys in Brown* (London: Percival Marshall, 1948), pp. v–x.
32 See Muriel Box's comments, *Odd Woman Out*, pp. 201–2.
33 *KW*, 15 December 1949, 184. See also Philip Gillett, *The British Working Class in Postwar Film* (Manchester: Manchester University Press, 2003), p. 132.
34 *Monthly Film Bulletin*, 16:192 (December 1949), 211.
35 Box's involvement in *Encore* was minimal, as he had gone on sabbatical – see p. 182. He left the film in the hands of Antony Darnborough.
36 *KW*, 4 December 1947, 19.
37 Box, *The Lion That Lost Its Way*, p. 70.
38 R. C. Sheriff, 'Foreword', *Quartet* (London: Heinemann, 1948), p. v.
39 *Ibid.*, p. vi.
40 *Ibid.*
41 BECTU, tape 179, Harold French.
42 Diaries, 14 February 1948.
43 Diaries, 21 December 1948.
44 *Reynold's News*, 8 October 1948.
45 'SRL', *Saturday Review*, 7 October 1950.
46 Bryan Connon, *Somerset Maugham and the Maugham Dynasty* (London: Sinclair-Stevenson, 1997), p. 227.
47 Annakin, *So You Wanna Be a Director?*, p. 42.
48 See especially the reviews in *Daily Mail*, *Daily Mirror* and *Daily Graphic*, all 4 August 1950; and the review in *Sunday Pictorial*, 6 August 1950.
49 Diaries, 7 October 1950.
50 Robert Calder, *Willie: The Life of W. Somerset Maugham* (London: Heinemann, 1989), p. 316.
51 BECTU, tape 179, French.
52 *Manchester Guardian*, 5 August 1950.
53 In October 1947, Box submitted ten Maugham stories for possible adaptation. Two, 'The Force of Circumstance', about a mixed-race couple, and 'Unconquered', about rape, abortion and prostitution in Occupied France, were deemed 'difficult'

and 'unsuitable' by the BBFC. See the Scenario Reports, 93, 94, 95 , 97 and 101 in the BFI Library. For *Trio* Box had to replace his choice of 'Daisy', the story of a 'fallen' woman who enjoys success, with 'Mr Know-All', because the censors deemed 'Daisy' unsuitable; Diaries, 22 November 1949. Box also wanted to make a series of films based on Maupassant's short stories, using George Bernard Shaw as the link, but plans had to be aborted because of copyright problems. See Betty Box, *Lifting the Lid*, pp. 38–39.

54 'The mer-baby is unexplained. We have seen no mer-man. Are we to conclude it had a landsman father, or is this being too fastidious?', BBFC Scenario Report, 70a, 2 June 1947.

55 *Sunday Chronicle*, 11 April 1948.

56 BBFC Scenario Reports, 90 and 90a, 30 September 1947.

57 *Cinema and Theatre Construction*, 15:5 (April 1948), 14.

58 David Quinlan, *British Sound Films: The Studio Years 1928–1959* (London: Batsford, 1984), p. 254.

59 *Observer*, 24 July 1949.

60 Robert Parry-Ellis, *Dear Murderer: The Story of the Film* (London: Axtell Publications, 1947), p. 65.

61 Martha Wolfenstein and Nathan Leites, *Movies: A Psychological Study* (Glencoe, Illinois: Free Press, 1950), pp. 212–13.

62 Campbell Dixon, *Daily Telegraph*, 20 September 1948, *Sunday Graphic*, 23 September 1948.

63 *Monthly Film Bulletin*, 15:176 (August 1948), 108.

64 The censors disliked the film (whose scenario was submitted under its working title, *Double Pursuit*), and insisted that Martin could not be an ex-major as this would bring the army into disrepute; Scenario Reports 108 and 108a, 6 November 1947.

65 A point made by Alfred Roome, in McFarlane (ed.), *An Autobiographyof British Cinema*, p. 499.

66 *KW*, 17 August 1939; 16 October 1941.

67 *KW*, 5 July 1944, p. 7.

68 *KW*, 19 December 1946, pp. 186–7.

69 *Ibid.*

70 Muriel Box, *Odd Woman Out*, pp. 196–7.

71 *Daily Mirror*, 28 April 1948.

72 *Star*, 14 May 1948.

73 Raphael Sabatini, *Columbus – A romance* (London: Hutchinson, n.d.), p. 304.

74 'Christopher Columbus', S901, pre-production script, dated April 1948, BFI.

75 Stills held by the BFI, Stills, Posters and Designs.

76 Maurice Carter, interview in McFarlane, *An Autobiography of British Cinema*, p. 118.

77 'Christopher Columbus', S13986, post-production script, dated 1 July 1949, BFI.

78 See also 'Christopher Columbus', S19247, post-production script, dated 1 July 1949, BFI.

79 The most detailed account is given in 'Columbus Sails Again', *Picture Post*, 6 November 1948, 16–19.

80 See *Film Industry*, 4:24 (June 1948), 20.

81 Diaries, 20 September 1948; *Star*, 22 July 1948. The boats were made by Robert Clark, a well-known designer of racing yachts and personal friend of Box.

82 Diaries, 8 July 1948; *Daily Mail*, 24 July 1948.

83 B. H. Petlock, *Film Industry*, 5:28 (12 August 1948), 12.

84 See BECTU, tape 174, Maurice Carter. The decision to have a large replica made was taken by George Provis.

85 *Evening News*, 16 June 1949.
86 BECTU, tape 174, Maurice Carter.
87 *The Times*, 20 June 1949. The notable exception was Ewart Hodgson in *News of the World*, 19 June 1949, who thought Columbus 'a towering, unforgettable motion picture miraculously matching in drama and dignity the events it set out to portray. It's lovely to look at. It has sweep and majesty. But most of all, it's splendid entertainment.'
88 Fred Majdalany, *Daily Mail*, 17 June 1949.
89 *Evening News*, 16 June 1949. Typically, the reviewer concluded that Box should have cheated and ended with Columbus's triumph.
90 *Daily Telegraph*, 20 June 1949.
91 'U.S. Pre-Release for Columbus', *Film Industry*, 7:54 (11 August 1949), 3.
92 Street, *Transatlantic Crossings*, p. 147. Its box-office performance was unfortunately not boosted by the enthusiasm of Peter Rodino Jnr in the House of Representatives, who considered Columbus timely and inspirational, a film that should be seen by every American child. See *KW*, 17 November 1949, p. 14.
93 *KW*, 20 December 1945, 174.
94 Sydney Box and Vivian Cox, *The Bad Lord Byron* (London: Convoy Publications, 1949), p. 12. Box, as mentioned in chapter 3, had contemplated a film about Byron and Shelley in 1943.
95 Dennis Price, 'Bringing a Character to Life', *Picturegoer*, 28 February 1948, 10.
96 A diary entry, 12 February 1948, apportions scripting credit as follows: Box 50 per cent, Terence Young 22 per cent, Paul Holt 16 per cent, Anthony Thane, 8 per cent.
97 Box and Cox, *The Bad Lord Byron*, pp. 11, 26.
98 *Ibid.*, pp. 99–109.
99 *Ibid.*, pp. 44–5.
100 *Ibid.*, p. 49.
101 *Ibid.*, p. 55.
102 *Ibid.*, pp. 99–109, 57–8.
103 Kitchin's play was broadcast on the BBC's Third Programme in 1947 and published in the collection *Three on Trial* (London: Pall Mall Press, 1959).
104 Box and Cox, *The Bad Lord Byron*, pp. 87–92.
105 See appendix.
106 *Cinema and Theatre Construction*, 15:4 (March 1948), 17.
107 'Can Price Make Byron Box-Office?', *Film Illustrated Monthly*, 3:3 (March 1948), 6–7.
108 *KW*, 4 December 1947, 19.
109 *KW*, 18 December 1947, 43.
110 *Evening News*, 17 March 1949.
111 Alfred Roome, interviewed in McFarlane, *An Autobiography of British Cinema*, p. 499.
112 *Ibid.*, p. 572.
113 *Monthly Film Bulletin*, 16:186 (June 1949), 9.
114 *Daily Express*, 18 March 1949. For his conception of the role see 'Bringing a Character to Life'.
115 *Evening Standard*, 17 March 1949.
116 *Sunday Pictorial*, 20 March 1949; *Star*, 18 March 1949.
117 Richard Winnington, *News Chronicle*, 17 March 1949.
118 Harold Nicolson, *Spectator*, 1 April 1949.
119 See appendix.
120 *KW*, 18 December 1947, 97.
121 *Film Industry*, 4:19 (January 1948), 16.

122 For a full list of those that are available, see appendix.
123 See appendix.
124 Quoted in Jympson Harman, *News of the World*, 2 February 1950.
125 Wood, *Mr Rank*, pp. 237–9.
126 Quoted in *ibid.*, p. 234.
127 *Ibid.*, p. 235.
128 *Ibid.*, p. 244.
129 *KW*, 16 December 1948, 43.
130 'Sydney Box May Leave Shepherd's Bush', *Film Industry*, 5:37 (16 December 1948), 3.
131 *KW*, 31 March 1949, 25.
132 *KW*, 10 March 1949, 28.
133 Bright and Ross, *Mr Carry On*, p. 65.
134 Sydney Box, *KW*, 10 March 1949, 28.
135 *KW*, 16 December 1948, 43.
136 Box, *The Lion That Lost Its Way*, p. 54.
137 Bright and Ross, *Mr Carry On*, p. 66.
138 BECTU, tape 174, Maurice Carter.
139 Wood, *Mr Rank*, p. 262.
140 'Rank is Reefing His Magnificos', *Motion Picture Herald*, 4 October 1947, 42.
141 Sue Harper and Porter, *British Cinema of the 1950s*, p. 43.
142 BECTU, tape 22, Roome, transcription, pp. 156–7.
143 Diaries, 10 February 1950.
144 Diaries, 23 February 1949.
145 'Mr Box's Holiday', *Star*, 2 February 1950.
146 Jympson Harman, 'Box Leaves Rank for a Year', *Evening News*, 2 February 1950.
147 SBP, Sydney Box's 'Journals', 1 (3 April 1950–23 May 1950), entry dated 3 April 1950.
148 See Spicer, 'The BBFC Scenario Reports at the British Film Institute'.
149 See the account in *Cinema and Theatre Construction*, 15:5 (April 1948), 14–15.
150 Willis, *Evening All*, pp. 70, 72. Read's account in *Young Man in Movieland*, pp. 87–8, argues that Box did not care for their screenplay, but did all he could to smooth its passage with Balcon.
151 Read, *Young Man in Movieland*, p. 91. The planned epic adventure, *Trek*, about an overland journey from the Cape to Cairo, was another victim of the cutbacks, as was an adaptation of *Sanatorium*, Donald Stewart's powerful novel about male fears and neuroses brought on by terminal illness; the latter project was quite far advanced, see Diaries, 15 February 1949.
152 Box, 'I Challenge the Critics', *Picturegoer*, 1 January 1949, 7.
153 Gibbs, 'Sydney Box and the Problem of Production', 57.
154 Barber, 'Sydney Box', 14–15.

Precarious independence: the 1950s

7

Box's decision to take a year's leave of absence from Rank was caused by his increasing frustrations within the Pinewood hierarchy, by which his autonomy had been eroded, spurring an intense desire to regain his creative independence. In the first journal entry on his 'sabbatical', Box describes how he and Muriel were to 'begin our latest and greatest experiment ... To live as writers who may occasionally produce and direct their own work, but won't be bothered to produce and direct anyone else.'[1] The four volumes of journals he kept on his extensive travels during this 'year off' are packed with ideas for short stories, novels and plays, some quite detailed synopses, impressionistic sketches of people he met who might become characters in a tale, and anecdotes recorded with a view to development into a full narrative. The journals are a testament to the fertility of Box's invention as a writer during a period when he also completed several screenplays with Muriel and co-adapted a three-act-play version of *The Seventh Veil*.

Characteristically, despite his intention to live as a writer, Box spent part of his year trying to negotiate production deals. He had acquired the rights to Graham Greene's short story 'Across the Bridge' and had written a detailed adaptation. He spent time reconnoitring possible locations in Texas and Mexico with Muriel, who shot some exterior scenes around Laredo.[2] In September 1950 he revealed in interview that this was to be the first of four films as an independent producer, financed by Rank and by 'Anglo-Spanish interests, whose identity he will not disclose but which involves millions of pesetas which are now frozen'.[3] In the end the arrangements with the Spanish financiers fell through and Box sold on the rights and his script to John Stafford; the film was eventually made by Ken Annakin in 1957 after some rewriting by Guy Elmes.[4] Box resisted offers to work as a producer in Hollywood, made after the success of *The Seventh Veil* and now renewed during his stay in New York in March 1951 – 'I valued my freedom too much for that!'[5] But he did arrange a number of projects with American agents, worth £1 million, for consideration by Rank, along with the scripts that he and Muriel had prepared. However, on his return Box found that Davis would barely condescend to see him and rejected all the deals he had set up, declaring that he wanted everything done more cheaply.[6] As so often, Box was ahead of the game, pursuing an internationalist policy that Rank only adopted towards the end of the decade, though he was carefully to distance himself from the charge that the films would be internationalist in subject matter, as the only universal appeal was 'emotion'.[7] Faced with Davis's intransigence, Box announced in July 1951 that he was leaving Rank to set up London Independent Producers with William MacQuitty, aiming to make five to six films a year.[8]

London Independent Producers

Box and MacQuitty had worked together effectively before and had already been engaged in discussions about making films in Ireland, based on the Somerset Maugham formula.[9] London Independent Producers (LIP) was therefore a logical extension of their activities.[10] It afforded MacQuitty the opportunity to move into feature-film production and Box to work as a partner in a small organisation that could offer creative freedom. Muriel Box, the third partner, would have the opportunity to direct without interference from the Rank board. LIP was run informally, as the trio were friends and neighbours, using Box's farm at Mill Hill – where he kept a herd of pedigree Guernsey cows whose milk was sold to local dairies – as its headquarters.[11] LIP was thus a tight-knit company that tended to use the same core creative personnel: Cedric Dawe, then George Provis, as art directors; Jean Baker or Anne Coates as editors; Reginald Wyer as cinematographer; and Robert Attrill as production manager.[12]

However, the context for independent production had changed significantly since Box had worked at Riverside, when British cinema was in a phase of expansion. In a round-table discussion, reported in *Sight and Sound*, several leading film-makers painted a bleak picture of producers trammelled by high costs and limited box-office returns, which severely restricted how much could be spent, but above all by conservative distributors and exhibitors who were unwilling to take any risks, always looking to duplicate proven success.[13] Like any other independent producer, Box now had access to government funding in the form of the National Film Finance Corporation (NFFC), established in October 1948 to 'carry the independent producers until the confidence of private investors was restored'. But as a public body, the NFFC tended to play safe and avoid the risky or the controversial; its chairman, James Lawrie, was a banker.[14] Because the NFFC required that the producer obtained a distribution guarantee before loaning money, this effectively meant that the two major combines, Rank and ABPC, continued to exercise control over which films were produced. Initially at least, Box did not enjoy good relations with Lawrie and was met on several occasions by intransigence, or seemingly arbitrary rejection.[15] Box's films in this period therefore need to be seen in the context of an industry whose horizons were quite limited, one which was suffering a loss of confidence resulting from the failure of the 'prestige experiment' and Rank's retrenchment, and subject to a seemingly irreversible decline in cinema admissions.

In a speech to the National Film Association in July 1952, entitled 'Feature Films that have Influenced Public Opinion', Box attacked the timidity of an industry which failed to tackle some of the most important historical and contemporary issues: 'No film has yet been made of the Tolpuddle Martyrs, the Suffragette Movement, the National Health Service as it is today, or the scandals of patent medicines, oil control in the world or armament manufactured for profit'.[16] But he was clear that such an uncompromising socialist agenda was unrealisable in such unpropitious conditions, and that audiences might also be alienated. LIP's first film, *The Happy Family* (1952), was therefore necessarily circumspect, a modestly budgeted adaptation of a successful stage comedy. For Box there must have been a strong element of déja vu. Like *29 Acacia Avenue*, *The Happy Family*, under its working title *South Bank Story*, was begun without full financing and secure distribution.[17]

In an attempt to break away completely from Rank, Box went to Independent Film Distributors, the company set up by John and James Woolf in 1949. The Woolfs approved the script, once Stanley Holloway had accepted the leading role (after Jack Warner had turned it down), but, one week before production was set to commence, they withdrew their £50,000 because they judged that it was more like a play than a film and because they were nervous about a woman, Muriel Box, directing.[18] As Box had been unable to secure a NFFC loan, the production might have foundered if MacQuitty had not stepped in, as he had with *29 Acacia Avenue*, with his own money. This enabled shooting to continue until a deal was concluded with another independent distribution company, Apex.[19] Apex was backed by a £50,000 loan from Lloyds Bank. The film was completed at breakneck speed, in six weeks, as this money would only become available after filming had been completed.[20] However, Apex failed to secure a circuit deal, and a truncated version of the film premiered in Chicago in January 1952 as *Mr Lord Says No*. Only then was ABPC finally persuaded to show it on the ABC circuit in March 1952, almost eight months after the film had been completed in September 1951, but without a West End premiere and as the top half of a double bill. This was a come-down for Box who received a lower percentage of the gross.[21] As it was shown with Ralph Smart's *Never Take No for an Answer*, the British title had to be changed again, to *The Happy Family*, because the distributors would not allow two 'Nos' in a double bill!

The Happy Family had several of the characteristic Box trademarks: topicality, social realism focusing on the respectable working class, an economical script that retained as much of the play's dialogue as possible, and action confined largely to one set. Michael Clayton Hutton's play was a light-hearted satire set in March 1951 during the final preparations for the Festival of Britain. This national gesture of recovery and regeneration had been dogged by controversy from its inception in 1949. It was seen, in some quarters, as an ill-timed frivolity, a profligate waste of scarce raw materials, or even as just a political stunt by Herbert Morrison, 'Lord Festival', as he was dubbed by the press.[22] The opening documentary-style montage of the Festival's construction – including the famous Dome of Discovery and the Skylon – concludes with shots of the mean streets round Waterloo, where the unwitting objects of a planning error, the Lord family, live above their grocery shop. The Lord family is the Huggetts restored – which would have been even more obvious if Warner had accepted the lead role. The Lords find themselves in conflict with state bureaucrats, led by Mr Filch (Naunton Wayne), who want to demolish the 'House of Lords' in order to complete the main access road to the Festival.

The head of the household, Henry Lord (Holloway), just retired from thirty years' exemplary service on the railways, and his wife, Lilian (Kathleen Harrison), have endured the privations of the 'hungry Thirties' and the loss of a son in the war in the expectation that one day they would live in their own property. Lilian tells Filch passionately: 'all the time we dreamed of a little house of our own, a shop for me and a home we'd paid for and couldn't be kicked out of at a moment's notice ... We owe nothing to anybody and no one can take it away from us. No one, do you understand that?' Once they have fortified their property and repelled several attempts to evict them, Henry celebrates their dogged resistance to the planners by proposing: 'Let's drink to living quietly and being left alone, to our Englishman's Castle and to all the millions of little castles belonging to little people over the country. It's nicer than revolution. And let's drink to the family, our happy family and thank God for it.'

Although these sentiments echo *This Happy Breed* (1944), Noël Coward's paean to the lower-middle class as the backbone of England, their context is very different. The Lords are engaged in overt social protest, barricading their house and hurling flour and provisions at the police and the government officials trying to dispossess them. Although Henry might want to avoid the term revolution, it is his son-in-law-to-be, Cyril (George Cole), the socialist revolutionary, who spurs the family into direct action, telling them: 'You're about as free as a pig with its feet tied'. It is Cyril, whose role is more prominent in the film than in Hutton's play, who tells Joan Lord (Eileen Moore): 'England was made by revolutions. What was the 1945 result if it wasn't a revolution?'

The other complicating figure is Lilian's sister Ada (Dandy Nichols, reprising her stage role), who believes herself to be possessed of psychic powers. She understands the threat of the bureaucrats – 'Beware the men in black!' – and, in a trance, spells out 'Robespierre' on her planchette board, which spurs Cyril to recognise the need for the Lords to rebel against injustice. In the final shot she is shown floating above the Festival, a haunting reminder that in this 'fantastic comedy', there is more than one reality. In this way, the nostalgic recreation of the wartime spirit of pulling together and seeing it through is offset by a progressive post-war agenda, making *The Happy Family* a somewhat uneasy mixture of modernising socialism and mysticism.

An unanticipated problem beset the film on its British release. The hold-ups meant that it was not shown until after George VI had died on 6 February 1952, and there were strong objections from some of the critics to the actuality footage of him opening the Festival in May 1951. The *Star*'s reviewer, Roy Nash, noted that 'some people at today's show thought the glimpses of the King looking ill and tired, were a mistake'.[23] Although Box defended the footage as a 'tribute to [King George VI] and a reminder to his people of one of the jobs he did for them', he deleted the sequence after consultation with Apex and ABC before the first public showing.[24] This brouhaha aside, Nash was typical of most reviewers in his estimate that this 'rollicking, thoroughly enjoyable film' was bound to be very popular. Reg Whiteley, who, like other reviewers, saw the film in a suburban cinema, noted that 'the big laugh came when a policewoman was de-skirted by barbed wire. This audience went for the visual comedy rather than the spoken.'[25] The trade press noted the film's broad range of targets: 'The sly digs embrace everything from Festival planners, BBC outside broadcasters, policewomen, parlour revolutionaries, local government officials, spiritualists and Cockneys'.[26] *The Happy Family*, with its shrewd combination of verbal and visual humour and ambivalent values that could claim the allegiances of various groups, made a handsome profit.[27] However, Box did not receive any of it because Apex, without his knowledge, had used the proceeds to purchase the distribution rights of poor quality American 'B' features that lost money.[28]

The delays in *The Happy Family*'s release held up LIP's progress by making it difficult to approach potential financiers about other projects. It was not until January 1952 that Box felt able to open negotiations with ABPC about *Policewoman*, a drama-documentary which celebrated the sterling qualities of WPCs. Box was nervous about the details of this possible deal, as Muriel Box's diary entry records: 'We don't know quite what to think, for we know so many tales of people hating their deals with ABC that the prospect isn't too inviting'.[29] Box also approached Columbia, which demanded that the film should be made very cheaply. This was unacceptable to Box, who was determined to make an authentic and responsible film that would enhance his standing.[30] In the end a return to Rank, while possibly unwelcome, proved to be the most acceptable option. Rank's board, no doubt influenced by James Lawrie's decision that the NFFC would provide the 'end money', approved the project in July 1952.[31]

The Boxes' screenplay was made from an original story by Jan Read, who had co-written *The Blue Lamp* (1950). Read had the ear of the Metropolitan Commissioner of Police, Sir Harold Scott, who had been at school with his father.[32] Even with Read's help, gaining the support of the police to ensure accuracy and authenticity, proved to be a difficult and protracted business involving several meetings with the Chief Superintendent of the Women's Police. The screenplay went through four extensively revised drafts before it was finished and approved.[33] Even when shooting began, in September 1952, there were continual problems about getting permission for the extensive location work that was essential to the film's realism.[34] However, *Policewoman* was finished at Rank's Gate Studios in Elstree on 25 November, on schedule and £10,000 under budget.[35]

But the limitations on Box's independence were exposed when, much to his dismay, Earl St John demanded cuts totalling eight minutes, decided to change the film's title to *Street Corner*, and mount what Box thought was a rather sleazy publicity campaign.[36] What Box objected to may be gauged by the reaction of Mary Lees, an 'ordinary suburban housewife', as reported in a national newspaper:

> I saw an advertisement in a paper for this new film and it put me right off. It showed an over-rouged, underdressed pick-up girl in a slum-like background with a policewoman hanging around waiting to arrest her. It looked sordid. The film was nothing like the advertisement suggested. I

> enjoyed every moment. It's the everyday story of London policewomen, full of delightful humour, healthy excitement and with bits of first class character acting. It wouldn't harm a child. It's a pity that lurid advertisement gives quite the wrong impression.'[37]

Even the BBFC complained about the film's advertising campaign, which it felt did not promote the picture as a 'dignified successor to *The Blue Lamp*'.[38] However, Box only eventually managed to get the film's promotion changed by agreeing to pay the costs himself.[39]

Street Corner has strong continuities with the Gainsborough 'topicals'. Like *Good Time Girl*, it combines documentary realism with *film noir*, and Reginald Wyer's cinematography is equally adept at using evocative chiaroscuro lighting to depict a shadowy London underworld, and an uninflected naturalism for the routines of the police station. *Street Corner* shares with *Holiday Camp* a narrative structure that interweaves six stories, which 'cross each other, yet so dexterously is the plot contrived that they never entangle, and are always easy to follow'.[40] In the central story, a young mother, Bridget (Peggy Cummins), is lured away from home and child by the charms of a slick spiv, Ray (Terence Morgan), and becomes embroiled in crimes of escalating violence, culminating in Ray's attempt to shoot his way out of a police cordon. This plot was formulaic, but Bridget's frustrations with her tightly circumscribed life and domineering mother-in-law are shown with a degree of compassion that distinguishes this story from a routine 'delinquency' film. Altogether more original is the other main story, that of Edna (Eleanor Summerfield), who absconds from the WRAC in order to look after her disabled husband (Ronald Howard). She manages to escape censure because of her courageous rescue of a drowning boy, only to be besieged by her wastrel first husband trying to get some of the reward when he reads about her exploits in a newspaper. At her trial for bigamy, the judge takes a lenient view of her case and gives her the minimum sentence. Edna, especially in Summerfield's nuanced performance, emerges as a sympathetic, intriguing character, and the story as a whole illuminates an interesting twilight world on the margins of society, hovering between respectability and illegality.

The complex characterisation of Bridget and Edna is not matched by the portrayal of the policewomen, who tend to remain two-dimensional figures. The partial exception is WPC Susan (Anne Crawford). Susan is the central figure in the film's most gripping sequence, in which she has to climb out onto a narrow ledge to rescue a child who has been left alone on an upstairs floor of a tenement block. The incident stays with the widowed Susan, who, having lost her husband and child in a car crash, wants to adopt the little girl she saved and leave the force. Her sentiments are dismissed with a curt, 'You don't mean a word of this', by sensible Sergeant Ramsey (Rosamund John), which truncates a potentially interesting narrative development.

Despite the inept way Rank promoted the film, *Street Corner*, dubbed the 'petticoat *Blue Lamp*', did very good business.[41] There was a certain amount of carping at the policewomen's characterisation and their excessively groomed appearance: 'they look so neat and pretty tripping – not pounding – the beat'.[42] But on the whole reviewers were supportive of a film, made in the 'modern semi-documentary style', which raised awareness, not only of policewomen's work but of how these 'coppers in skirts' suffered from public prejudice and chauvinism within their own ranks.

Box was keen to capitalise on this success, but his next project, an apparently straightforward documentary thriller about the customs service, became caught up in protracted negotiations about funding with both the NFFC and Rank. Box's script had to go through several rewrites, demanded by both Michael Balcon and Earl St John, and changes of title – *Anything to Declare, Hide and Seek, Customs Story* – until it was finally approved by the Rank board in July 1954 under the title *Forbidden Cargo*.[43] It has a modest budget of £155,000.[44] By this point, Muriel Box was no longer available to direct as she was working on Box's next project, a Maugham adaptation. Box turned to the safe hands of Harold French, with whom he went to the south of France to complete the location work. Box seems to have had his own anxieties about the story, because even when the production returned to the studio, he was regularly rising at 4.30 or 5.00 a.m. to complete rewrites in order to get through the day's business.[45] At the last minute, Muriel Box was involved in shooting a more exciting climax, once permission had been obtained to use Tower Bridge.[46]

Forbidden Cargo opens with a documentary montage demonstrating the expertise of customs officers on routine inspections, but the film centres on the work of the plain-clothes branch, whose role is to foil organised criminals. The investigation is conducted by the debonair Michael Kenyon (Nigel Patrick), who wears his trilby at a jaunty angle. Kenyon picks up the trail of some clever smugglers on the East Anglian coast – where he encounters an eccentric ornithologist, Lady Flavia Queensway (a delightful cameo by Joyce Grenfell) – before decamping to Monte Carlo in pursuit of his principal suspects, brother and sister Roger and Rita Compton (Terence Morgan and Elizabeth Sellars). Morgan was cast as another sexy anti-hero after very positive notices of his performance in *Street Corner*, with Sellars as femme fatale. However, characterisation is rather sacrificed to the intricacies of the plot, in which Compton's crimes escalate from currency smuggling to drug running, culminating in an audacious attempt to smuggle thirty pounds of cocaine into Britain in a limpet mine. The finale is tense and thrilling, if predictable: Compton overreaches himself in the attempt to elude the police cordon and eventually crashes to his death trying to drive his car across Tower Bridge as the sections are being raised. Rather unconvincingly, Rita, who has distanced herself from the drug smuggling, falls into Kenyon's waiting arms.

Forbidden Cargo is no more than a competent film, a routine thriller with a veneer of authenticity, distinguished by some well-executed action sequences, as the *Star*'s reviewer acknowledged: 'no end of exciting pursuit and the under-sea photography is admirable'.[47] The production of *The Beachcomber* (August 1954), an adaptation of W. Somerset Maugham's short story 'The Vessel of Wrath', first filmed in 1938 and now shot in Technicolor, was altogether more ambitious, and part of the process of Maugham adaptation Box had initiated at Gainsborough. Although a third Maugham film, *Encore*, had been made at Pinewood under Darnborough's control, Box had every intention of returning to Maugham adaptations, but he was frustrated because, although he had the film rights, he found that Maugham had assigned the television rights to an American company, Columbia Broadcasting System. CBS presented nearly forty of Maugham's stories in a series entitled 'The Somerset Maugham Theatre', beginning in 1950, produced by Martin Ritt, and with Maugham himself opening and concluding each episode.[48] Box realised that once they had been broadcast on television, they would become useless as film properties because the public would never pay to see what was available for free in their own homes.[49]

Box had also tried to film Maugham's 1941 novella *Up at the Villa*, a typical story of fraught relationships and sexual guilt in which the heroine finally accepts that life is about taking risks and sensual excitement rather than security, industry and moral purpose. The story had been considered too explicit to broadcast on radio, but its ambiguity, irony and insight into the recesses of motivation appealed strongly to Box, who had completed a screenplay by November 1951 with Claudette Colbert earmarked for the leading role. Box managed to persuade United Artists to back the project once he had secured a co-production deal with the Italian company Panaria, but he needed a further £80,000 from a British company.[50] ABPC turned it down in January 1952, judging it to be too similar to *24 Hours in a Woman's Life*, another Italian-set romance starring Merle Oberon.[51] It was also declined by John Woolf, who thought that it was all talk and no action and refused to have Muriel Box as a director. At the NFFC, Lawrie rejected *Up at the Villa* without giving reasons, and although Earl St John had been initially keen, Rank also turned it down in March because Balcon disliked the script.[52] Box tried to revive the project after he had bought Beaconsfield Studios, initially as part of a three-film package with Margaret Leighton (see below), but it was never made.[53]

It was therefore a relief to Box to get the backing of Earl St John and the NFFC for *The Beachcomber*, which he had adapted on his own, but he had to accept John Davis's decision that the budget would not stretch to sending the principal cast on location, which meant that everything had to be shot with doubles. This severely restricted the way in which Muriel Box could shoot many of the scenes, and made marrying location and studio work very difficult, exacerbated by the notorious problems of matching Technicolor footage. A number of reviewers found *The Beachcomber*'s locations and colour photography disappointing.[54] Earl St John also insisted on several cuts and Box had to write a new voice-over commentary for the opening, in which Ewart Gray (Donald Sinden) arrives to take up his residency as governor of a remote Pacific island.[55] Once in the studio, Muriel Box had to juggle the schedules because one of the leads, Robert Newton, was too drunk to film in the afternoon.

The rewritten opening is rather at odds with Box's adaptation, because Gray does not act, as in Maugham, as the sceptical filter through which the other characters are perceived. In the manner of his previous Maugham adaptations, Box tends to soften the author's ironic approach by increasing the melodramatic pathos in key scenes and playing up the romantic and redemptive aspects of the central relationship between Martha Jones (Glynis Johns), the strait-laced sister of the missionary Owen Jones (Paul Rogers), and the Honourable Ted (Robert Newton), the feckless, womanising remittance man. A striking example occurs when Martha and Ted, initially sworn enemies, are brought together during the cholera epidemic that rages throughout the group of islands and come to trust and respect each other. Ted's kiss in acknowledgement of Martha's courage and skill has a delicacy and poignancy not in the original. Casting the attractive Glynis Johns as Martha makes her character much more desirable and feisty, no longer the pitiable ugly duckling who finally ensnares her man. However, after their marriage, Ted gives an ironic wink to the audience as, now decked out in a resplendent white linen suit, he plays the piano in the mission.

The Beachcomber found few admirers amongst the critics. Fred Majdalany, who thought the film a 'thoroughly enjoyable joke told with gusto and high humour', was decidedly in the minority.[56] Campbell Dixon in the *Daily Telegraph* thought it had 'sacrificed some of the original's cynicism and humour for a more popular story of redemption through faith and love'.[57] Several others considered that the irony and subtlety of Maugham had been replaced by farce and melodrama.[58] Most judged that the casting of Johns had been a mistake as it undermined the whole premise of Maugham's story.[59]

At this point, MacQuitty and Box went their separate ways. MacQuitty's final film for LIP was *Above Us the Waves* (April 1955), an unexceptional war film directed by Ralph Thomas. Box's was an uncompromising 'art' film, *The Prisoner* (May 1955), Bridget Boland's adaptation of her own play, a thinly veiled dramatisation of the detention and show trial of Cardinal Józef Mindszenty, the Catholic Primate of Hungary. Mindszenty had been arrested in December 1948 and put on trial in February 1949 where he 'confessed' to a series of crimes and was sentenced to life imprisonment. As Tony Shaw argues in *British Cinema and the Cold War*, Mindszenty came to be seen as a symbolic figure in the great ideological struggle between East and West, one who also had the moral authority to critique the weaker elements of Western liberalism.[60]

The driving force behind this production was a close-knit group of practising Catholics, Boland, Peter Glenville, who directed both stage and film version, and Alec Guinness, who starred in both as the Cardinal. However, Shaw is wrong to suggest that there was no creative input from Box. Box had worked with Boland on *The Lost People*, and with Glenville on *Good Time Girl*, and had been actively involved with Guinness in trying to mount a production of Shaw's *The Millionairess* in which he would star with Katharine Hepburn. Box had worked out a deal with the US producer Lester Cowan, but could not secure backing from Rank even after the budget had been ruthlessly pruned back.[61] Diary entries made during the pre-production of *The Prisoner* show that Box was intimately involved in scripting the adaptation. It was Box who put forward the radical idea that Guinness should play both the Cardinal and his interrogator, though this was too avant-garde even for this production.[62] Crucially, it was Box who brokered the financial and distribution deal with Columbia as executive producer. The details of the production were handled by Vivian Cox, a close associate of Box from the Gainsborough days, who was a friend of Guinness and had contacts with Columbia.[63] The cinematographer, Reginald Wyer, was also an LIP contract technician. At the 'wrap' party on 22 December 1954, Box received a 'delightful note' and present of wine from Guinness, who professed himself very pleased with the film.[64] The project is entirely consistent with Box's desire to engage with important issues and to be associated with serious and artistic productions.

At the heart of *The Prisoner* is the developing relationship between the Cardinal (Guinness) and his interrogator (Jack Hawkins), both of whom were heroes of the anti-Nazi Resistance but are now on opposing sides. Although the Cardinal is subject to physical privations, the interrogator does not believe in the use of torture or drugs to extract a confession, but in the techniques of psychological persecution – evoking the topical scare about Communist 'brainwashing' – probing away until he finds the weak link in the Cardinal's mental armour: his relationship with his mother. After confessing at his show trial, the Cardinal is not executed but forced to endure the humiliation of returning to the people, who no longer see him as a spiritual guide but a fallen idol that has betrayed them. The interrogator, now revolted by what he has been asked to do, offers to kill him, but the Cardinal will not agree to that, convinced that he must now endure his humiliation as a punishment for his sins. The interrogator exclaims: 'So the laugh's on me. You go out of here stronger than when you came in!' The film is stark and terrible, but offers the hope of grace and redemption through religious conviction; it is the interrogator, the political apparatchik, who is truly trapped.

The *Monthly Film Bulletin* admired 'the enterprise and courage of all concerned' in making a film that 'grapples with a vital contemporary subject' and which makes few concessions to obvious box-office appeal: 'The pace is slow, controlled, certain; there is an admirable precision about the handling of the dialogue scenes, and a consistently maintained low-key atmosphere'.[65] Derek Granger, in the *Financial Times*, judged that 'apart from some extraneous (and very half-hearted) love interest no concessions have been made to the greedy public's taste for sweets and spangles. The subject is an austere and terrible one.'[66] *The Prisoner* was a critical success rather than a commercial one, popular with film societies and the subject of specialised distribution after its initial release both in Britain and the United States.[67] It took over $100,000 in ten weeks at the Plaza Theatre in New York and was awarded the 'Best Foreign Film' accolade by the US National Board of Review.[68] For Box it provided what *The Beachcomber* had failed to: some much needed critical acclaim. But he was unable to secure Guinness's services to front the 'Alec Guinness Theatre', a series of thirty-nine television plays in a format similar to the Maugham films, to be co-produced with Columbia Broadcasting System in 1955–56, as Guinness felt it would compromise his artistic integrity. Box, who stood to gain $500,000 from the deal, was left in a parlous financial state; *The Prisoner* as a *succès d'estime* made him little profit.

Return to Rank

LIP's continuing problems with finance, distribution and box-office returns meant that both Box and MacQuitty needed to look outside the company for other offers.[69] Box had been approached by David Kingsley at British Lion to supervise five films a year by a range of separate producers.[70] British Lion, operating out of Shepperton Studios, attempted to act as a home for independent producers who wished to remain outside the Big Two: Rank and ABPC. However, at the same time, Rank made Box a more attractive offer, by which he was required to produce one or two films a year on a settled salary for two years, which removed all immediate financial worries.[71] It was a clear indication that, despite their differences, Davis considered Box to be an effective producer. In a letter to Kingsley, Muriel Box wrote: 'By concentrating on fewer films, Sydney and I feel we shall be able to do the industry more credit than by spreading our energies over a more ambitious programme'.[72] Box made three films directly for Rank, all of which were thrillers: *Lost* (January 1956), co-produced with Vivian Cox and directed by Guy Green; *Eyewitness* (July 1956) directed by Muriel Box, also based on an original screenplay by Janet Green; and *Floods of Fear* (November 1958), directed by Charles Crichton, adapted by Crichton and Vivienne Knight from the novel by John and Ward Hawkins.

Lost was the brainchild of actor-turned-journalist Peter Noble, who approached Box with his project because Box had, with characteristic generosity, 'often assured me that if I brought him the right script and stars he would do everything in his power to set me up as a producer'.[73] The intention was for Box to act as executive producer while Noble produced and Muriel Box directed. However, after Box had signed his new contract with Rank, Noble was judged to be too inexperienced to be entrusted with the film and Box was required to co-produce with Vivian Cox, while Guy Green was given his first directing assignment.[74] As usual, Box made some significant revisions to the script.[75]

Rank clearly entertained high hopes for *Lost*, made in Eastman Color, as it was extensively promoted, partly to raise the profiles of its American contract star David Knight and the Viennese beauty and former fashion model Julia Arnall, a Box protege, in her first starring role. (Arnall really needed a more experienced director in her first film role and her performance is uneven.) The promotion was targeted at women and women's groups, who might be expected to empathise with a story, written by a woman, about a mother whose child is abducted. However, Box's hand can be detected in the detailed chronicling of police procedures; the investigation is led by Inspector Craig (David Farrar), who brings a new realism to the role of the police inspector. But, as several reviewers pointed out, the attempt at authenticity is at odds with the lambent colours, which make London appear to be unreal, too shiny and picture-postcard perfect.[76]

Box felt that Green's script for *Point of Crisis* (the working title for *Eyewitness*) had a number of significant weaknesses, and despite Box's revisions, it remains an uneasy combination of crime thriller, light comedy and social realism.[77] The eyewitness of the title is Lucy (Muriel Pavlow), who sees two men, Barney (Nigel Stock) and Wade (Donald Sinden), robbing a cinema safe. In her panicked flight, Lucy is knocked down by a bus and taken to hospital, where Wade and Barney attempt to silence her. Disguised as an orderly, Wade is about to smother Lucy but the conscience-stricken Barney kills him. Wade, in particular, is a melodramatic villain, and the hospital ward where Lucy is recovering is, as *Kinematograph Weekly* observed, 'palpably understaffed'.[78] There is a tedious sub-plot concerning Nurse Penny (Belinda Lee) and her amorous boyfriend Mike (David Knight), which is designed to showcase rising Rank starlet Lee and the egregious Knight. Only Ada Reeve's comic turn as the nosy and garrulous Mrs Hudson generates much interest or conviction.

Lost and *Eyewitness* were aimed at the domestic market, while the later *Floods of Fear*, with a budget of £300,000, was part of Rank's renewed strategy to conquer the American market.[79] It exhibits all the characteristics of the Hollywood 'tough' thriller, with brutal, laconic characters and much violent action. The Hollywood lead, Howard Keel, plays Donovan, a convict serving a life sentence for a murder he did not commit, who escapes when, whilst on a working party, he is swept away in a flood created by the rising waters of the Humboldt River in Nevada. Keel's Herculean musculature is shown to good advantage in a role that has him stripped the waist for most of the film, while romantic interest is provided by doctor's daughter Elizabeth Matthews (Anne Heywood), with whom he is marooned in a deserted house along with the sadistic Peebles (Cyril Cusack), who tries to rape her. Donovan manages to reach Murphy (John Crawford), the crooked owner of a construction company who framed him and in a typically titanic struggle, he forces a confession. *The Times*' reviewer, who entitled his piece 'British Film in American Disguise', wondered what the point of pretending to be an American film was, a sentiment echoed by several others.[80] However, those who were prepared to give the film its due recognised the strengths which Box and Crichton, both ex-documentarists, brought to the project in the expert splicing of newsreel shots of real flood disasters with a fictional reconstruction.[81]

Beaconsfield Studios

The role of contract producer was as unsatisfying to Box as it always had been and these Rank thrillers may be regarded as 'rent and tax jobs', made while his main energies were engaged elsewhere on more significant projects. The first of these was the acquisition of Beaconsfield Studios in January 1956, which had become vacant because the NFFC no longer needed it as the base for Group 3 Productions, judging that the 'middle-budget' film was no longer financially viable.[82] Box had begun negotiations with the NFFC to acquire Beaconsfield as early as December 1954, in the knowledge that he would be able to produce films there at a lower cost than if he used Pinewood or Shepperton. Beaconsfield was small, with just one sound stage, but in good order as it had been handsomely refurbished after the war for the Crown Film Unit, before Group 3 took over in 1951.[83] For Box the substantial losses the NFFC had made on Beaconsfield 'might prove useful for tax purposes, but my principal object in taking over the company was to provide an outlet for another member of the family, Peter Rogers'.[84]

In many respects the establishment of Rogers as head of Beaconsfield mirrored Box's appointment of his sister at Islington a decade earlier; Rogers' principal function was to keep the studio continuously occupied. This was achieved through filming television series and low-budget second features. Typical of the latter was *Time Lock* (July 1957) directed by Gerald Thomas, filmed at headlong speed in three weeks for £30,000.[85] As these 'B' features could be produced so cheaply and quickly, it was often best to avoid bidding for NFFC funding in order to capitalise on a new trend. This tactic was exemplified by *The Tommy Steele Story* (June 1957), directed by the ex-Gainsborough scriptwriter Gerard Bryant, which Box initiated to cover a gap in the schedules. *The Tommy Steele Story*, marketed as a 'documentary about Britain's answer to Elvis' and 'The Sensational Success Story of Britain's Teenage Idol', was released only eight months after Steele's first hit record and was extremely successful. It was followed by *6.5 Special* (March 1958), adapted from the popular television series, directed by Alfred Shaughnessy. Both were scripted by Norman Hudis, who went on to the 'Carry On' series, and produced by Herbert Smith, an industry veteran whom Box persuaded to come out of retirement. They were released under the Insignia label and distributed by Anglo-Amalgamated. Shaughnessy was under contract to Rank but loaned out to Box, picking up pictures that nobody else coveted. These included the now cult horror film *Cat Girl* (November 1957), which Box wanted made as a star vehicle for Barbara Shelley, whom he had under contract.[86]

The major television series shot at Beaconsfield was *Ivanhoe*, completed during 1957 and broadcast on British and US television in 1958. *Ivanhoe* followed what had become the standard format of thirty-nine half-hour episodes, networked to all the ITV regions to spread costs and offering advertisers a national audience.[87] Producers could expect an excellent return on their investment, but such series were expensive to produce, around £8,000–£10,000 per episode, and, even if networked, could not hope to recoup more than £2,500 in the domestic market. It was therefore imperative to have a US partner which could offer finance (usually about 80 per cent) and guaranteed US distribution.[88] *Ivanhoe* was a co-production with Screen Gems, the television arm of Columbia, with which Box had established good working relations. Co-productions were attractive to the US majors because they offered a way round the tight controls on how much screen time – no more than seven hours per week – US programmes could occupy on British television.[89] Costs were also much lower: about half those incurred if series were filmed in the United States.[90] *Ivanhoe* was particularly attractive because earlier co-produced television swashbucklers had been successful both in Britain and the United States. US audiences judged them to be superior to the home product.[91]

The title role was played by the 'new Errol Flynn', Roger Moore, appearing in his first television series.[92] The directors chosen were mostly those with whom Box had worked before: Bernard Knowles, Arthur Crabtree and David Macdonald, though Don Chaffey, Lance Comfort and C. M. Pennington-Richards were also used.[93] As always, Box was keen to encourage new talent, including the Australian writer Bill Strutton, who was given his first opportunity on this series (episode 23, 'By Hook or by Crook'), before going on to script episodes of *The Avengers* and other television series. Box also employed the largely untried Bernard Coote as series producer, assisted by Herbert Smith, with Peter Rogers as executive producer.[94] It was broadcast in the early evening slot, starting at 7.00 p.m.

Ivanhoe, loosely based on Walter Scott's novel – neither all the main characters nor situations came from Scott – is a typical swashbuckler. In the first episode, 'Freeing the Serfs', Ivanhoe has returned from the Crusades to find a lawless land where 'tyranny is Lord' as the power of ruthless aristocrats is unchecked, in fact encouraged, by Prince John (Andrew Keir), scheming to supplant his brother King Richard. In a series of daring deeds, Ivanhoe frees the serf Gurth (Robert Brown), who, with his son Bart (Andrew Pike), become Ivanhoe's constant companions; restores his father Sir Cedric (Henry Vidon) to his lands and castle; and rescues the impossibly demure Lady Rowena (Norah

Gorsen). In the struggle between his love for Rowena and the stern demands of duty, duty triumphs: Ivanhoe swears an oath to fight on, knowing that 'throughout the land the people know only hardship and injustice'.

The episode is crammed with the familiar conventions of a genre that emphasised action and spectacle: much furious riding along leafy lanes and energetic sword fighting; a joust; a ceremonial banquet; two dramatic rescues; a return and leave-taking. Moore, resplendent in his white surcote, armour and plumed helmet, is a typically handsome, athletic and courageous hero fighting for freedom and justice, his actions tempered by tenderness and the desire for comradeship. Directors Macdonald and Comfort demonstrate an accomplished ability to handle action and create an engaging visual style through well chosen compositions, complemented by Stephen Dade's location photography, which is exceptionally good for a television series. According to the episode credits, 'Freeing the Serfs' was produced at the ABC Studios in Elstree, perhaps to make use of its superior facilities for the opening episode. Indeed 'Freeing the Serfs' is exceptional in its speed and scope, in the proportion of location shooting and the number of incidents crammed into the episode. It obviously functioned as the well-seasoned bait with which to hook an audience for the whole series. The others episodes I have been able to view are less ambitious and their visual style far less polished.

In addition to his work as an executive producer, the acquisition of Beaconsfield also gave Box the opportunity to produce the films he and Muriel Box wanted to make, beginning with two adult comedies about relations between the sexes – *The Passionate Stranger* (February 1957) and *The Truth About Women* (February 1958) – both based on their original screenplays. It was the first time Box had been able to do this since *The Seventh Veil*. *The Passionate Stranger* was a handsome film, with a long section in colour, a strong cast, costumes by Norman Hartnell and cinematography by Otto Heller, and Box was able to make it for only £140,000 because of the lower overheads at Beaconsfield.[95] The main difficulty was casting the 'stranger', and two French actors, Jean Denham and Jean Claude Pascal, were considered, before Box opted for the cheaper and more masculine-looking Italian Carlo Justini, though his voice had to be dubbed in post-production by Robert Rietti.[96]

Muriel Box declared *The Passionate Stranger* was 'intended to debunk the sentimental novel ... a mild satire on romance as opposed to reality and the unhappy consequences of confusing the two'.[97] Justini plays Carlo, a young Italian hired by Professor Wynter (Ralph Richardson), a wheelchair-bound scientist, to be his chauffeur. Complications arise when Carlo reads the manuscript of the latest romance written by Judith Wynter (Margaret Leighton), the professor's wife, in which the heroine has fallen in love with a handsome stranger and, tired of her husband, embarks on a passionate affair. Carlo naively assumes the novel reveals her true feelings and, as he reads on, the film modulates into colour, which distinguishes the romantic fantasy from the black-and-white real-life sections that frame it.

The colour section rolls out a succession of deliberately cliched scenes from populist romantic fiction: the uninhibited country dance culminating in the moonlight moment of rapture when the lovers kiss for the first time, the inevitable consequence of an unwanted pregnancy, and the murder of the madly jealous and domineering husband. To play two parts in the same piece is a gift for actors, and Leighton and Richardson make the most of the contrast between their 'real' and fantasy selves. Leighton changes from Judith, cool, capable and prosaic, into the shallow, befuddled Leonie, swept up in a passion she cannot control or understand. Richardson metamorphoses from the benign, if preoccupied, Roger into the sardonic Sir Clement, crippled in mind as well as body, who cannot allow his wife to have any independence.[98] In the denouement, in black and white, Carlo's misconceptions are revealed and he leaves on the bus, only to find the timid maid (Patricia Dainton), who had been in love with him all along, on the seat beside him.

Rather perversely, one or two reviewers thought that the Boxes' real interest was in the fantasy section and that the deliberate echoes of Hardy and Lawrence were unintentional.[99] Most understood that it was a burlesque of romantic fiction and the film cliche of the smouldering Latin lover, but felt that it was a good idea stretched rather too far, a criticism often levelled at Box's films.[100] There is some justice to this view; in particular, the colour section is overlong, which, as one reviewer noted, forces 'the actors to try the impossible task of making the bogus characters seem real'.[101] More positively, Peter Burnup, who considered the film's 'wit and elegance' made it the picture of the week, thought 'Margaret Leighton will make women gasp at her furs and Hartnell gowns, and touch their hearts with her serene loveliness'.[102] Box hoped to make two further films with Leighton, *Up at the Villa* (already mentioned) and *Waiting for Gillian*, adapted from the 1954 Ronald Millar play, itself based on Nigel Balchin's novel *A Way Through the Wood* (1950). Like the Maugham, it was a story about covering up a crime, anatomising middle-class deceit and guilt. But Box could not interest Rank or the NFFC in financing either project although he had written a full screenplay.[103]

Box assembled a bevy of beautiful women – Diane Cilento, Eva Gabor,

Julie Harris, Jackie Lane ('Britain's Brigitte Bardot') and Mai Zetterling – for *The Truth About Women* (February 1958). Here too the economies of filming at Beaconsfield bore fruit as, in addition to that glittering female cast and the rising star Laurence Harvey as the male lead, Box was able to afford Otto Heller, Eastman Colour, forty lavish sets, costumes by Cecil Beaton and a running time of 107 minutes, all for under £200,000.[104] The first screenplay, by Muriel Box, was something of a hotchpotch of feminist ideas loosely hung together, but Box made a complete revision, including the addition of a new commentary and a structure that focuses on the gulf that separates the sexes. After Box completed the final version in January 1957, Muriel Box commented: 'I feel he has improved it a great deal'.[105] *The Truth About Women* employs the typical Box narrative device of multiple flashbacks, which, in self-contained episodes, tell the story of Humphrey Tavistock (Harvey) through his romantic entanglements with a succession of beautiful women from different cultures.

Harvey's nondescript performance acts as a tabula rasa that allows the women he encounters to be the real centre of interest, with their markedly different demands and expectations, the ways they are valued by society and the things which prevent them from achieving equality and mutual understanding with the opposite sex. In the most overtly serious episode, Humphrey finds his greatest peace and contentment married to Helen Cooper (Julie Harris). But her sacrifice is great: she dies giving birth to twins, having already abandoned her career as a talented painter. Eventually Humphrey is reunited with his first love, Ambrosine Viney (Cilento), whose advanced ideas included a trial marriage (shades of *On Approval*), from which the more conventional Humphrey has shied away. It is Ambrosine who articulates the film's central message, telling her son-in-law Anthony (Derek Farr), who thinks that women want to be men, that women want to retain their femininity, but on their own terms: 'Women want to be women all right. They just have a different definition of what the word means. To a woman it means a person, an equal partner in the business of life, free to do what's right and best for herself.' All Humphrey can muster is the tired cliche: 'It's hell living with them but it's a damn sight worse living without them', which rather suggests that males have become bankrupt of ideas. Although the older couple seem content, the younger one, Anthony and Diana (Catherine Boyle), return to their bickering, a clear indication that the 'sex war' is far from over.

Having secured NFFC 'end money', Box approached John Davis at Rank to finance *The Truth About Women*, but was turned down.[106] David Kingsley, now managing director at British Lion, agreed to finance and distribute the film, as had happened with *The Passionate Stranger*. However, Box was dismayed when Kingsley refused to give the film a West End premiere or even a press showing because he thought it was too slow and that the joke had not come off.[107] Box was convinced that the Woolfs were behind the refusal because they were anxious that a prestigious release might jeopardise the prospects of *Silent Enemy* (March 1958), in which their contract star Harvey also starred.[108] As the film had been widely publicised during shooting, the critics made the effort to see it, several commenting on its poor exhibition. The *Manchester Guardian* talked of the 'hugger-mugger' way in which it had been released in the 'relative seclusion' of the Tottenham Court Road Odeon and the Metropole Victoria.[109] Harold Conway in the *Sketch* asked 'Why Be Ashamed of This Film?' which was to go on general release the following Monday 'still unproclaimed'.[110] Milton Shulman in the *Sunday Express* contrasted its modest release, 'bundled off like some black sheep of the family', with the 'torrential proportions' of its pre-publicity fanfare.[111] Most of the reviews were mixed, admiring the attempt to create a sophisticated comedy of manners, but finding the pace slow, the dialogue occasionally lacking in sparkle and the tone of the serious episode of his marriage to Helen at odds with the light touch of the other episodes.[112] However, even more uniformly enthusiastic reviews would hardly have compensated for *The Truth About Women*'s ignominious release, which effectively ruined its chances at the box office.

Tyne Tees Television

At the same time that Box was broadening his production interests by moving into network programming, he increased his involvement in commercial television by becoming an important shareholder in Tyne Tees television, established on 12 December 1957 as one of a number of new franchises that formed part of ITA's plans to extend the areas covered by independent television and so achieve national coverage by 1960.[113] Tyne Tees began broadcasting on 15 January 1959.[114] Although serving a region of around 2.5 million people meant that the new company would never be one of the bigger fish, such was the success of commercial television by this point that any new franchise was attractive.[115] Box was instrumental in drawing up the successful bid for a consortium led by a member of a famous Teeside family of industrialists, Sir Richard Pearse, and backed by the Daily News Corporation, Peter Cadbury and show business impresarios George and Alfred Black. This consortium won the contract from amongst eleven applicants because of its strong local links and commitment to local programming as well as more imaginative thinking about the overall balance of its programmes.[116]

Box's 20,000 shares, roughly 10 per cent of the total, made him the fifth largest shareholder, well behind the Daily News Ltd (owner of the *News Chronicle*), the Northern Mercantile and Investment Corporation and, more importantly, the Blacks, who owned 55,000.[117] Although Anthony Jelly, an experienced television executive, was appointed managing director, the Black brothers were the driving force and public face of Tyne Tees, both senior executives (George was programme director) and prominent board members.[118] Under their direction the company gained a reputation for light entertainment, especially comedy, but became the target of criticism for its lightweight populism.[119] Box succeeded Peter Cadbury as chairman of the programme committee in 1958/59.[120] But programming policy did not appear to alter significantly during his tenure. In the absence of detailed evidence, the indications are that Box regarded his involvement with Tyne Tees as a profitable sideline rather than an instrument to realise his artistic ambitions.[121]

Widening circles: Orbit Films and Sydney Box Associates

Box's decision to broaden his interests into television was based on sound economic judgement. The advent of a full national commercial television network led to a very sharp decline in cinema admissions.[122] The 300 redundancies at Pinewood announced by Rank in January 1958 were among over 1,000 jobs lost throughout the industry.[123] Rank announced postponement of four of its productions and its output fell by two-thirds during the period 1958–61. However, Alexander Walker argues that these difficult conditions 'promoted rootlessness and restlessness. And out of these flowed new amalgams of talent, fresh combinations of finance, and a much swifter recognition of any new trend that bucked the odds and found favour where it counted most – at the box-office.'[124] At the forefront of these new combinations was Sydney Box, who remained committed to film production.

Box's first initiative was the creation of Orbit Films in October 1958, in partnership with Patrick Filmer-Sankey, John Temple-Smith and John Nasht. Filmer-Sankey and Temple-Smith had backgrounds in documentaries and were looking to move into features, while Nasht, who had experience of television production in Britain, Europe and Hollywood, 'represented American interests'. Nasht was therefore integral to the company's plans to 'make four films a year aimed mainly at the international markets'.[125] This made economic sense because the steep fall in admissions meant that it was now very difficult for even modest first features to recoup their costs in the home market. Any which cost over £180,000 had to be sold abroad.

The first Orbit release was *Subway in the Sky* (February 1959), a topical psychological thriller based on Ian Main's play, set in New York, which had starred Margaret Lockwood and Zachary Scott in its West End run. As the film had been turned down by Rank, British Lion and Anglo-Amalgamated, Box struck a distribution deal with another recently created company, Britannia Films. Britannia was run by David Henley, former director of artists at Rank and a board member of City Share Trusts, and Steven Pallos, long associated with Alexander Korda, who had formed Gibraltar Film Productions.[126] Britannia agreed to distribute the film provided Van Johnson was the male lead. Box handled these protracted negotiations, as well as working on the screenplay, by the Hollywood scriptwriter Jack Andrews.[127] He had to fire cinematographer Jack Cox, whose lighting was judged 'flat' from the rushes, after only the second day of shooting; Wilkie Cooper replaced him.[128]

According to the publicity release, *Subway in the Sky* was 'aimed at worldwide markets, particularly those of America and Germany' and the cast reflected these aspirations.[129] Playing opposite Van Johnson as Baxter Grant, an American major, was the German star Hildegarde Neff, cast as a glamorous cabaret singer, Lilli Hoffman, who croons 'Love Isn't Love' in her famous 'low, smoky voice'. Katherine Kath, a French-born ballet dancer and actress, was the major's attractive but devious wife Anna, while Albert Lieven played Lilli's lawyer and unrequited suitor, Carl von Schecht. The Canadian Cec Linder completed the main cast as the hard-boiled US Army police detective, Captain Carson, investigating the major's disappearance. *Subway in the Sky* boasted one of the largest composite sets ever built in Britain (at Shepperton Studios), designed by George Provis, assisted by his daughter Pamela. It was constructed 'in the European style, rather than the American ranch type', in order to be convincing as a Berlin luxury apartment and avoid the look of a conventional Hollywood melodrama. As usual, Box insisted that every effort was made to achieve accuracy: 'To ensure complete authenticity such minor fitments as door handles, locks, taps, were flown from Germany before the set was completed'; this authenticity also extended to the electric switches, radio sets, telephones, cars, police uniforms, groceries, even the telephone directories. The exteriors were filmed at a German-designed block of flats in North London.[130]

Subway in the Sky has a dramatic cinematic opening in which a military jeep speeds along the German autobahn, through the night-time streets of Berlin, and out onto the US Army base. But the impression of fast-paced action is quickly dissipated when the narrative shifts to Grant's flat, where it settles into a wordy two-hander as he attempts to persuade its new occupant, Lilli, that he is innocent of crimes with which he has been charged.[131] Although the tension between the pair is dispelled too quickly, *Subway in the Sky* does succeed in concealing the real villain and has a dramatic climax. However, it performed quite poorly at the box office.[132]

A second film, *Treasure of San Teresa*, filmed at the National Studios in Borehamwood, retained most of the production team, except that Alvin Rakoff replaced Muriel Box as director because she was filming in Ireland. *Treasure of San Teresa* has a similarly international, vaguely Cold War milieu, set in Germany and Eastern Europe, with an American star (Eddie Constantine) in the lead role of Larry Brennan, an ex-secret service agent. Not only would the casting of Constantine facilitate a US release, he was also the biggest name in European cinema for English-language films, reflecting the importance of, in particular, the Austro-German market for the success of this film. Brennan knows the whereabouts of a Nazi general's priceless jewels and, fifteen years on, has been persuaded by Rudi Siebert (Marius Goring), a lawyer who was present at the general's death, to recover them. The jewels are hidden in a Czechoslovakian convent which has been converted into a People's Police barracks. The romantic element is provided by Heidi von Hartmann (Dawn Addams), the general's daughter, now a call-girl, with whom Brennan falls in love. The story is hackneyed, but played out against unfamiliar backgrounds. Although Wilkie Cooper's photography is distinguished, Rakoff's direction is uneven, flashy and leaden by turns, and he fails to make the most of the dramatic action scenes with which the film is loaded.

Orbit Films was a stepping stone towards a much more far-reaching initiative: the creation of Sydney Box Associates (SBA) in December 1958.[133] SBA consisted of Sydney Box, Muriel Box, Betty Box, Peter Rogers, Ralph Thomas, William MacQuitty and David Deutsch, son of Oscar Deutsch (who had been an associate producer on a number of Box productions), together with affiliated members John Nasht and Patrick Filmer-Sankey, and Norman Williams the television producer, who also had a small stake in the company.[134] Box described SBA's formation as a 'tangible expression of our faith and belief in the future of the cinema as a family entertainment. Between us we have made a lot of successful pictures over the past 15 years. Now we are putting back into the film industry a substantial proportion of the money we have taken out of it.'[135]

SBA was a production and distribution company financed by investment from its individual members, but it also had a deal with Rank which enabled it to have a rolling or revolving production fund that spread risk over a number of films. This revolving fund was one in which a bank agrees to withdrawals from a fund on deposit in order to finance new productions. The revenues from films released are paid straight into this fund keeping money available for the next production. According to a diary entry, Box received £125,000 capital from Rank for future film production and a further £600,000 from the National Provincial Bank, making SBA the biggest independent film company in Europe.[136] As Rank still needed a substantial number of British films to fulfil the exhibitor's quota (30 per cent) on its two cinema circuits, Box realised that, having cut back on its own production, Rank would be prepared to back an independent company which could make films more economically (because SBA's overheads were much lower) and without Rank having to bear the full financial risks. However, as Rank had no *direct* financial interest in SBA, the Rank board would not be able to interfere in the films made by or through SBA. Although Rank handled domestic distribution, SBA's overseas distribution was handled by Alliance Film Distributors (International), a company run by William Gell and Michael Bromhead. Gell had extensive experience in film distribution through running Monarch Films, and his expertise in preselling SBA films abroad became an important factor in the company's ability to keep the revolving fund operational.

SBA's independence, its revolving fund (offering up to 75 per cent of a film's costs) and guaranteed distribution, made it attractive for other film-makers to make their films under its auspices, and therefore it could become an important outlet for independent producers. As Box later recalled: 'I calculated that I could afford to back two million pounds' worth of production without using too much of my own money and without doing more than listening to other producers' proposals and deciding whether or not they were worth financing.'[137] Overall, SBA was a characteristically ambitious manoeuvre that set out to break free from a potentially crippling accountability to Rank, circumvent the NFFC and become a rival to British Lion, attracting film-makers who, like Box himself, had found these organisations difficult or capricious.

Box ensconced himself in suitably plush offices on Park Lane and, for the first time since his appointment as head of Gainsborough Pictures, found himself the subject of extensive press coverage: 'Sydney Box is apparently as energetic, as resourceful and as confident as he looks. With the figure of a wrestler, a short, sharp, and forthright manner of expressing himself, and a broad smile, he gives the impression that he knows what he is about and intends to succeed.'[138] *Kinematograph Weekly* reported that in its initial year of production, SBA proposed to finance 'at least six British features and six co-productions with Continental producers'. £1 million had been earmarked for the British productions, but more would be needed for the co-productions; half the British films would be in colour and 'top American and international stars' would always be used unless the film was 'typically British' like *Carry on Sergeant*.[139]

SBA was also poised to become substantially involved in television series co-productions. In conjunction with Rank and Sol Lesser, Box had undertaken to produce a minimum of four thirty-nine-part series, to be shot at Pinewood for network sale and syndication, in a £2 million deal believed to be one of the biggest of its kind ever struck.[140] SBA, represented by John Nasht, was in talks with ZTV to co-produce a seventy-eight-part thirty-minute British detective series starring Broderick Crawford, the star of ZTV's *Highway Patrol* series as well as a new series, *A1 at Lloyds*.[141] SBA had also bought the rights of thirty Edgar Wallace novels, to be filmed as 60–75 minute second features, produced by Norman Williams and shot at Twickenham Studios. Each adaptation would bring the story up to date with contemporary settings and characters, and be on the floor for three weeks.[142] Williams also produced *White Hunter*, an African jungle adventure series starring Rhodes Reason, filmed at Twickenham and Beaconsfield. SBA thus had significant television as well as film interests; not only was Box director of an ITV company, but Betty Box and MacQuitty were directors of Ulster Television. Box stated in interview that he was convinced that the two industries could 'live happily – and profitably – side by side'.[143]

SBA's film production was to begin with a 'modern comedy', costing around £160,000, and two 'international' productions directed by Joseph Losey, the first of which was to be *SOS Pacific*.[144] Losey had already written the screenplay in conjunction with screenwriter Ben Barzman (both were on the Hollywood blacklist), 'intended as a warning about the dangers of the bomb and the moral consequences of exploding it'.[145] But this project fell through when Columbia refused to distribute the film internationally. Box told Losey: 'There's no point discussing the script because Columbia will not have you'.[146] The production's star, Hardy Kruger, who had worked closely with Losey, left because he feared that a new script would dilute a subject in which he believed passionately.[147] Despite this hiatus, Gell made a deal with Kurt Ulrich Films in Berlin to co-produce *SOS Pacific*, in return for a share of the European market and the casting of two German actors in fairly prominent roles.[148] The overall budget was £150,000 and shooting was to begin on 13 April 1959.

The new script, by Robert Westerby, while it retains vestiges of the original message, is essentially *Broken Journey* revisited: how a motley group of people react when disaster strikes. In place of Kruger, Eddie Constantine was cast in the lead, playing a hard-bitten tough guy, Mark Reisener, who holds his nerve under pressure, a very similar role to the one he played in *The Treasure of San Teresa*. Although he is being deported for smuggling offences, Reisener takes charge of a group which has crash-landed on a small Pacific island after their pilot, Jack Bennett (John Gregson), his nerve irreparably damaged by being an observer at Hiroshima, proves inadequate. Once they have realised that the island is an observation post for an imminent nuclear test explosion, Reisener swims across to the adjacent island where the bomb is located, overpowers the villain, the vicious and weaselly informer Whitey (Richard Attenborough), saves the day and gets the girl (Pier Angeli). Wilkie Cooper's photography is excellent and, although the characters are rather two-dimensional, the replacement director Guy Green manages to orchestrate the action effectively. When the film was released in October 1959, the *News Chronicle*'s critic, Paul Dehn, admitted that the 'conventional race against time was so enthrallingly handled that I was often betrayed into making a fool of myself by uttering little cries of foreboding and dismay'.[149]

In an adroit manoeuvre, Box managed to retain the services of both Losey and Kruger by using them in a medium-budget thriller, *Blind Date* (August 1959). This was a co-production with Independent Artists (Julian Wintle and Leslie Parkyn); Box had sold them Beaconsfield Studios in March 1959, where the film could be shot rapidly and economically. The producer, David Deutsch, had made a deal with a German producer, Luggi Waldtleitner, who put up £40,000; and a further £98,000 came from SBA.[150] Box had agreed that Losey could rewrite what he considered to be a poor script (Eric Ambler's adaptation of Leigh Howard's novel), if he could do this in four weeks. Losey managed by collaborating with Barzman and another blacklisted writer, Millard Lampbell, who wrote the love scenes.

Blind Date is a romantic murder mystery which Losey turns into an incisive exploration of the class-based corruption of British society. Kruger plays a somewhat naive Dutch painter, Jan Van Rooyen, who becomes suspected of a murder he did not commit through the cunning of his former lover Jacqueline (Micheline Presle), who has killed her husband's mistress. It is only the bloody-minded persistence of Inspector Morgan (Stanley Baker), who is an outsider of a different kind, the self-made son of a chauffeur in a profession still dominated by the old school tie, which eventually proves his innocence. In defiance of the warning from his boss, Deputy Commissioner Sir Brian Lewis (Robert Flemyng), who tries to make him understand the 'deeper meaning of public service', Morgan reveals that Jacqueline is Lady Fenton, who is being protected because her husband is a senior civil servant engaged on important government business.

It was the SBA board which had insisted on casting Baker (a 'name') as Morgan and, although he was initially antagonistic, Losey elicits an absorbing performance from Baker, concentrating on Morgan's wary but gradually deepening relationship with Van Rooyen and placing the emphasis on characterisation and motivation rather than plot machinations.[151] *Blind Date* achieved considerable critical acclaim, but its profitability stemmed from Box's business acumen. Losey recalled: 'Box, who is an extraordinary salesman, went to New York before the picture was ever released in England, and sold the American rights to Paramount Pictures for a sum which was nearly double what the picture cost. So it was immediately in profit.'[152] In fact it was Gell who handled the Paramount negotiations in New York on Box's behalf.[153] Unfortunately, *Blind Date*'s chances of earning a substantial amount from the American box office (under the title *Chance Meeting*) were scuppered when it provoked a furore because of its blacklisted director; the film was withdrawn from circulation.[154] However, its success and critical acclaim were important in attracting other producers to SBA.

Box was more directly involved in the production of *Too Young to Love* (January 1960), which explored female delinquency. It was based on Elsa Shelley's play *Pick-up Girl*, which had caused a sensation during its London production in 1946.[155] Box acquired the rights to the play in order to provide Muriel Box with a film subject she wanted to direct.[156] He collaborated on the script with Muriel and Shelley; it has a typical multiple flashback structure. It gives greater prominence than the play to the most controversial aspects of the story: under-age sex, abortion and venereal disease. Muriel was determined to produce a serious and adult film that dealt uncompromisingly with the uncomfortable issues surrounding under-age sex.[157] She had to fight numerous battles with the censors in order to obtain even an 'X' certificate.[158] *Too Young to Love* reflected the internationalism of SBA, being set in Brooklyn, with Hollywood veteran Thomas Mitchell in the leading role of Judge Bentley.[159] The critics recognised that it was neither sensationalised nor salacious, but found the characters inauthentic, the writing and acting poor and the direction 'irresolute'.[160] This would not have helped the film's box-office chances but, above all, *Too Young to Love* had missed its moment, as the interest in the cinematic representation of delinquency, on both sides of the Atlantic, was now well past; it performed weakly at the box office.[161]

A number of other independent producers released through SBA. One was Brian Rix, with *The Night We Dropped a Clanger* (September 1959), the first of three films to be produced by his company, Four Star Films, to be released on the National Film Circuit, which Rank had created as a dumping ground for its less profitable cinemas.[162] Basil Dearden and Michael Relph made *Desert Mice* (December 1959), a service comedy set during the Second World War. Five were made by Norman Williams using Twickenham Studios: the marital comedy *Your Money or Your Wife* (March 1960) directed by Anthony Simmons (possibly the 'contemporary comedy' referred to at SBA's inception), and four crime thrillers. These were *Witness in the Dark* (December 1959), directed by Wolf Rilla, with a screenplay by Leigh Vance and John Lemont; *The Shakedown* (January 1960), directed and scripted by John Lemont; *And Women Shall Weep* (April 1960), directed by Lemont and scripted by Leigh Vance; and *Piccadilly Third Stop* (September 1960), scripted by Leigh Vance and directed by Wolf Rilla.

This level of activity allowed the *Evening News* in August 1959 to describe Box as 'Britain's top independent producer', and SBA as 'fantastically successful', with films being made at four different studios.[163] A week earlier, in a much more abrasive article in the *Evening Standard*, Thomas Wiseman referred to Box as the 'great corn merchant', but recognised that he had 're-emerged as a major figure in British films. While the big companies are cutting down on production and sacking their contract artists, Box is expanding and signing up.'[164] He quotes Box: 'When other people are getting out that is the time to get in. When other people are not making pictures and there is a shortage of product that is the time to make pictures.' Wiseman reported that SBA had plans to make thirty films during the next two years, as many as Rank and ABPC combined, and had also negotiated a contract to produce 120 half-hour television-series episodes at the cost of £1,500,000 with another 'huge contract' in the pipeline. Wiseman notes acidly that the 'new Box programme has a sprinkling of what he calls pretty subjects, films which have an air of class about them' – including *No Love for Johnnie*, bought for £10,000 as a vehicle for James Mason, and two Somerset Maugham adaptations – but that would be supported by the revenues from 'less classy' films, the crime thrillers and comedies. According to Wiseman, Box and his associates had invested £300,000 of their own money in the company, which was planned to operate for five years, after which Box would retire to write plays.

Thus ten years after he had left Gainsborough and taken a year out to devote himself to writing, Box was again an executive producer, one who was even more deeply embroiled in the hurly-burly of the film industry. Muriel Box recorded in exasperation in her diary:

> he is really happy working out astonishingly cunning deals, encouraging new people to make film and inspiring new writers to write them ... He seems to thrive on the constant contact with people of all sorts, distributors, producers, artists, writers and promoters. He likes to control their activities because, somehow, he always seeks to short-cut their objections and sets them working with renewed vigour and intensity'.[165]

She also noted that her husband had worked out a new method of shooting second features that was modelled on television production. The film was rehearsed for a week like a television play and shot live on 'visual tape' [sic] then transferred to celluloid, thereby saving time and laboratory processing charges. Box had calculated that £5,000 was saved by this method, a substantial proportion of a 'B' feature's budget.[166]

The end of Sydney Box Associates

Box was indeed a gifted producer, but the diversification and expansion of his interests, the fifteen-hour days that he regularly worked and the constant travelling, placed ever-greater strain on his health. In August 1959, at the age of 52, he suffered a cerebral haemorrhage after a gruelling flight back from New York following four days intensive negotiations during which he had secured a deal with Cinerama to make three 'spectaculars', costing $2 million each, beginning with *William the Conqueror*.[167] On doctor's advice, Box relinquished nearly all his film and television interests, with Peter Rogers placed in charge of SBA.[168] Although *Kinematograph Weekly* reported in October 1959 that SBA's twenty-film programme would continue, it soon became clear that this was not the case.[169] A letter from Betty Box and Peter Rogers in late October made it plain that they did not want to run SBA any longer than was necessary and did not want to invest their own or Ralph Thomas's money in films made by others.[170] In her autobiography, Betty Box justifies their decision on the grounds that continuing would have been impossible anyway: 'His affairs were in a very complicated state, with several film projects in various stages of preparation and no one in a position to take over from him. In fact, as with so many tycoons of his calibre, too many of the details of his various deals were known only to him, and he was in no state of health to be worried with it all.'[171]

Incapacitated, Box was powerless to stop three years work from unravelling. The Cinerama contract collapsed, along with the other planned television series. The Edgar Wallace adaptations were sold to Merton Park, produced by Jack Greenwood and distributed by Anglo-

Amalgamated; forty-two were made between September 1960 and November 1964. Projects that Box was hoping to set up with prominent screenwriters James Kennaway – a thriller with an international cast – and Bryan Forbes – an epic war film about the D-Day landings – also broke down.[172] For Rank, SBA's place was taken by a new consortium, Allied Film Makers (founded in September 1959), which was offered a similar financial deal, though more favourable to Rank, which retained the rights over overseas distribution. Indeed, according to Alexander Walker, the original idea for this consortium came from Box and when he dropped out because of ill health, he was never replaced as the fifth partner.[173] Several of the films that *Kinematograph Weekly* had reported were about to go into production – *The Challenge, Love Birds, The Day of the Triffids, Watch It Sailor!* and *Conscience Bay* – were eventually made by a range of producers. Peter Rogers made *Please Turn Over* (December 1959, directed by Gerald Thomas) for SBA, while Betty Box completed *No Love for Johnnie* (directed by Ralph Thomas) in January 1961. But several others, *No Concern of Mine, Not in the Book, Milk and Honey* and *Time to Kill*, were never made.[174] It is impossible to know how many of the other twenty films that were not named in that article were also unrealised.[175]

The difficulties Box experienced in his attempts to become a genuinely independent producer after he left Rank reveal a great deal about the constraints and pressures that film-makers were under in the 1950s, a decade of anxious retrenchment dominated by the power of the distributors. Although Box managed to produce thirteen films, the Diaries and Journals reveal that over twenty projects were unrealised. Several of the most important have been mentioned; the other that most rankled with Box was his failure to make a film with Leslie Caron, whom he 'discovered' whilst reading a copy of *Paris Match* in 1952. Box judged her ideal to star in a balletic version of *The Seventh Veil* that he had scripted with Muriel. Neither Earl St John nor Lawrie was prepared to back the proposal, and Balcon judged Muriel Box insufficiently experienced to direct what appeared to be a major production. Box had negotiated a five-year contract with Caron on very favourable terms, but Rank declined to take it up.[176] Several years later, Box prepared a full shooting script of Norman Collins's historical novel *Anna*, set during the Franco-Prussian war, seeing in it a choice role for Caron as a woman whose life and love are torn apart by the conflict. The production was announced in the trade press, but after complications arose with the direction and scripting, Davis cancelled the project in March 1958, costing Box £9,500.[177] This was another reminder of the precarious and compromised nature of Box's status as an 'independent' producer and his ultimate dependence on Rank which, along with ABPC, largely controlled production finance, distribution and exhibition, a fact which no producer, even with NFFC support, could circumvent.

Box's activities in the 1950s may therefore be read as a series of attempts to break the stranglehold of the combines. LIP gained him a degree of autonomy and creative freedom, but because he always needed to negotiate with Rank to obtain distribution and a circuit release, he was forced to accept its interference. He achieved more freedom with *The Prisoner*, distributed by Columbia, but that was a special case. The acquisition of Beaconsfield Studios at least gave Box a production base in which he could juggle the schedules to suit his own purposes, but the studio was too small for him to mount a real challenge to the existing commercial arrangements. The poor release of *The Truth About Women* showed that British Lion was also not a genuine alternative to Rank, at least as far as Box was concerned.

The move into television production and the formation of SBA were a more radical stratagem, though one which took Box ever further away from his ambitions as a writer, the 'great experiment' with which he had begun the decade. It also largely occluded his working relationship with Muriel Box, the basis of LIP.[178] It involved seeking American partners and a frankly commercial and international orientation, but to dismiss Box as the 'great corn merchant' would be wrong, as Thomas Wiseman did, echoing Richard Winnington a decade before. There are clear signs that SBA was also prepared to nurture more 'artistic' projects exemplified, not so much by *Blind Date* – which was really a tribute to Losey's inventiveness – but by *No Love for Johnnie*, which examined the struggle between socialism and the marketplace, between the man of conscience and the man of ambition. Box was also intending to return to further Somerset Maugham adaptations, always for him the union of art and box-office appeal. A more generous view would recognise that, as at Gainsborough, Box was seeking to create a healthy indigenous film industry that, while it had to be financially viable, could, in the longer term, support more experimental and challenging work. Unfortunately, the strains of holding together such a complex and rapidly expanding enterprise broke Box's health, and SBA unwound before it could really make its mark.

However, Box's achievement, albeit truncated, has not yet received its proper recognition. Even Alexander Walker fails to recognise the significance of SBA in leading the way towards those 'new amalgams of talent' – which he discusses solely in relation to Bryanston (formed April 1959) and Allied Film Makers (formed September 1959) – which attempted to switch control from the distributors to the producers themselves, and which gave a renewed impetus to a rather moribund British film industry and helped to create the New Wave.[179] In December 1959 *Kinematograph Weekly* celebrated 'a new pattern of production and distribution in which creative individuals have as much say as impersonal, mammoth corporations'.[180] Sydney Box may be said to have contributed much to this decisive shift which began to weaken the stranglehold of the combines.

Notes

1 SBP, journals, 1, entry 3 April 1950.
2 Muriel Box, *Odd Woman Out*, p. 208.
3 'Box Starts Film in Texas', *KW*, 31 August–21 September 1950, 3, 11.
4 Annakin, *So You Wanna Be a Director?*, p. 72.
5 Box, *The Lion That Lost Its Way*, p. 55.
6 Diaries, 4 February 1951.
7 'Box Starts Film in Texas', 11.
8 *The Cinema*, 11 July 1951, 3, 22.
9 Diaries, 31 January 1951.
10 The company was incorporated on 27 January 1950, some eighteen months before the announcement indicating that plans had been made to go independent before Box left for his 'year off'. See the file on LIP at Companies House, 00811808.
11 MacQuitty, *A Life to Remember*, p. 309. As the staff consisted of two personal assistants, and most of the business was conducted on the telephone, little remains by way of company records. There is an LIP file in the Sydney Box Papers, but this dates from the 1970s and 1980s.
12 See BECTU, tape 229, Cedric Dawe, transcript, p. 27. Alfred Roome and Maurice Carter stayed at Pinewood, working mainly for Betty Box.
13 *Sight and Sound*, 19:8 (May 1950), 114–22.
14 Harper and Porter, *British Cinema of the 1950s*, pp. 5–34.
15 Diaries, 28 February 1952, 1 March 1952. Muriel Box commented: 'its surveillance gets more despotic as it goes on'.
16 Reported in *Workers' Party News*, 27 July 1952. The National Film Association represented the Labour Party, the TUC and Co-operative organisations on matters concerning film. See Bert Hogenkamp, *Film, Television and the Left 1950–1970* (London: Lawrence and Wishart, 2000), pp. 32–5.
17 'Sydney Box Back in Production', *KW*, 12 July 1951, 7.
18 MacQuitty, *A Life to Remember*, p. 308.
19 'Apex to Release Sydney Box Films', *KW*, 13 September 1951, 9.
20 Diaries, 28 July 1951.
21 Diaries, 26 January 1952, 13 and 17 February 1952.
22 Harry Hopkins, *The New Look: A Social History of the Forties and Fifties in Britain* (London: Secker & Warburg, 1963), p. 269.
23 Roy Nash, *Star*, 12 March 1952.
24 Nash, *Star*, 15 March 1952.
25 Reg Whiteley, *Daily Mirror*, 12 March 1952.
26 *Today's Cinema*, 13 March 1952, 5.
27 Diaries, September 1952.
28 When accounts came to be settled, Apex threatened liquidation and the case went

to arbitration for the £9,000 Box said he was owed; Diaries, 23 February 1954. Apex was wound up by court order in March 1954; *KW*, 18 March 1954; *KW*, 10 March, 1954; *KW*, 25 March 1954, 8.
29 Diaries, 12 January 1952.
30 Diaries, 24 June 1952.
31 Diaries, 20 June 1952; 26 July 1952.
32 Read, *Young Man in Movieland*, p. 86.
33 Diaries, 31 March 1952, 6 and 13 June 1952.
34 Diaries, 5 September 1952.
35 Diaries, 25 November 1952.
36 Diaries, 26 April 1953.
37 R. Nunn, *Daily Sketch*, 13 March 1953.
38 *Today's Cinema*, 5 March 1953, 5.
39 Diaries, 12 February 1953.
40 *Sunday Dispatch*, 15 March 1953.
41 *Daily Film Renter*, 23 April 1953, p. 7. A diary entry, 28 April 1953, noted that *Street Corner* broke the Gaumont Circuit record on its London release; Davis rated its initial returns as 'excellent'; see appendix.
42 *Daily Herald*, 13 March 1953.
43 Diaries, 27 July 1953.
44 MSBC, box 5, undated item.
45 Diaries, 4 September 1953.
46 Diaries, 31 March 1954.
47 *Star*, 23 April 1954.
48 Calder, *Willie*, p. 316.
49 In the late 1950s, Box tried to make a film by combining two short stories, 'Neil Macadam' and 'The Outstation', in one script, *A Matter of Temperament*. Box reasoned that the stories' exotic setting and difficult subject matter would make a television screening unlikely. The production was scripted, cast and studio space booked before Maugham wrote informing him that he had sold the rights to these stories some years before. Maugham declined to compensate Box for the £27,000 he had spent (*The Lion That Lost Its Way*, p. 74; Diaries, 30 April 1959, 19 July 1959).
50 Diaries, 12 January 1952.
51 *Ibid.*
52 Diaries, 18 March 1952.
53 Box had also tried to interest Ingrid Bergman in the role, but without success.
54 The location work was completed in Ceylon, which MacQuitty knew well.
55 Diaries, 26 and 29 April 1954.
56 Fred Majdalany, *Daily Mail*, 6 August 1954.
57 Campbell Dixon, *Daily Telegraph*, 7 August 1954.
58 See, *inter alia*, *The Times*, 7 August 1954.
59 For instance, Roy Nash, *Star*, 6 August 1954.
60 Tony Shaw, *British Cinema and the Cold War: The State, Propaganda and Consensus* (London: I. B. Tauris, 2001), pp. 77–8.
61 Diaries, 31 March 1954 and 12 April 1954.
62 Diaries, 4, 7, 11, 13, 21, 27 October 1954 and 9 December 1954.
63 Author's interview with Vivian Cox, 10 June 2003.
64 Diaries, 22 December 1954.
65 *Monthly Film Bulletin*, 22:257 (June 1955), 84–5.
66 Derek Granger, *Financial Times*, 25 April 1955.
67 See *Columbia Studio News*, 28 February 1956; BFI microfiche for *The Prisoner*.
68 It was also politically controversial: *Tribune*, 28 October 1955; *Daily Telegraph*, 12

November 1955.
69 MacQuitty had a major success with his film about the sinking of the Titanic, *A Night to Remember* (July 1958).
70 Diaries, 13 October 1954.
71 Diaries, 8 December 1954.
72 Diaries, 27 December 1954.
73 Peter Noble, *Reflected Glory: An Autobiographical Sketch* (London: Jarrolds, 1958), p. 159.
74 *Ibid.*, pp. 159–60.
75 Diaries, 13 September 1955.
76 *Evening Standard*, 26 January 1956.
77 Diaries, 12 and 26 November 1955 and 2 December 1955. See also the second draft screenplay with rewrites (February 1956), MSBC, box 2, item 4.
78 *KW*, 12 July 1956, 17.
79 £300,000 is the figure quoted in a diary entry, 25 March 1959; for Rank's policy shift. See Harper and Porter, *British Cinema of the 1950s*, pp. 52–5.
80 *The Times*, 17 November 1958.
81 Isabel Quigly thought *Floods of Fear*'s best moments were 'those in which we are given almost documentary treatment of a flood'; *Spectator*, 21 November 1958.
82 See David Kingsley, 'Out of the Crisis', *Films and Filming* (August 1955), 7.
83 Warren, *British Film Studios*, p. 13.
84 Box, *The Lion That Lost Its Way*, p. 57. Box had already assisted Rogers' post-Gainsborough career when he co-produced, with the American Ben Schrift, the marital comedy that Rogers had adapted, *To Dorothy a Son* (November 1954). Box invested £15,000 of his own money into this production, which was released through a separate company, Welbeck Films; Muriel Box directed.
85 Bright and Ross, *Mr Carry On*, p. 72.
86 Alfred Shaughnessy, *Both Ends of the Candle* (London: Peter Owen, 1978), pp. 126–8. Shaughnessy also produced a Beaconsfield film, *Heart of a Child* (April 1958), directed by Clive Donner.
87 Peter Black, *The Mirror in the Corner* (London: Hutchinson, 1972), p. 55.
88 Tony Gruner, 'The Growth of TV Production', *KW*, 29 May 1958, vi, xi.
89 Bernard Sendall, *Independent Television in Britain, vol. 1: Origin and Foundation, 1946–62* (London: Macmillan, 1982), pp. 106–9.
90 Gruner, 'The Growth of TV Production', vi.
91 Jeffrey S. Miller, *Something Completely Different: British Television and American Culture* (Minneapolis and London: University of Minnesota Press, 2000), pp. 21–2. *Ivanhoe* had been preceded by *The Adventures of Robin Hood*, first broadcast in 1955, and *The Adventures of Sir Lancelot* in 1956. For further discussion see Steve Neale, 'Adventure, Exchange and Identity: British, American and Un-American Involvement in Costume Adventure Television Series and Films in the Postwar Era'. I am grateful to Professor Neale for allowing me to see this article in manuscript.
92 James Green, 'Ivanhoe – knight with the Adonis look', *TV Times*, 10:115 (12–18 January 1958), 20–1.
93 Macdonald only jointly directed the first episode, with Comfort. For directorial credits and a breakdown of episodes see Dave Rogers, *The ITV Encyclopedia of Adventure* (London: Boxtree/TV Times, 1988).
94 See Peter Noble (ed.), *The British Film and Television Year Book 1957–8* (London: British and American Press, n.d.), p. 320.
95 Figure given in Anthony Carthew's review of *The Passionate Stranger*, *Daily Herald*, 15 February 1957.
96 Diaries, 13 and 26 January 1956.

97 Muriel Box, *Odd Woman Out*, p. 221.
98 There are clear echoes of Nicholas in *The Seventh Veil*.
99 'A Film That Wastes Its Own Ingenuity', *The Times*, 18 February 1957.
100 See, *inter alia*, C. A. Lejeune, *Observer*, 17 February 1957.
101 Peter Forster, *Financial Times*, 18 February 1957.
102 Peter Burnup, 'What a Week for the Ladies', *News of the World*, 17 February 1957.
103 Box also wanted to make an adaptation of Lesley Storm's 1949 play *Black Chiffon*, another powerful tale of middle-class duplicity and shifting moral and sexual allegiances. Although a deal with the American producer Sol Lesser was announced in the trade press, Box could not obtain Davis's approval for a co-production. See *KW*, 3 July 1952, p. 29; Diaries, 8 February 1953.
104 *The Truth About Women* cost £183,000 (Muriel Box, *Odd Woman Out*, p. 222).
105 Diaries, 19, 24 August 1957, 17 December 1957, 14 January 1958.
106 Diaries, 19 August 1957.
107 Diaries, 15 January 1958.
108 Diaries, 11 and 16 February 1958.
109 *Manchester Guardian*, 15 February 1958.
110 Harold Conway, *Daily Sketch*, 15 February 1958.
111 Milton Shulman, *Sunday Express*, 16 February 1958.
112 See, *inter alia*, *The Times*, 17 February 1958.
113 'Box Moves into ITV', *KW*, 19 December 1957, p. 3; Bernard Sendall, *Independent Television in Britain, vol. 2: Expansion and Change, 1958–68* (London: Macmillan, 1983), p. 3.
114 Box was also instrumental in helping shape MacQuitty's successful bid for the Ulster Television franchise; Betty Box was a prominent board member. See Diaries, 16 January 1958, 19 September 1959.
115 See Burton Paulu, *British Broadcasting in Transition* (London: Macmillan, 1961), pp. 66–71; Clive Jenkins, *Power Behind the Screen: Ownership, Control and Motivation in British Commercial Television* (London: MacGibbon and Kee, 1961), p. 230.
116 Sendall, *Expansion and Change*, p. 4.
117 Jenkins, *Power Behind the Screen*, pp. 230, 235.
118 Antony Brown, *Tyne Tees Television: The First 20 Years* (Newcastle: Tyne Tees Television Limited, 1978), p. 4.
119 Sendall, *Expansion and Change*, pp. 8–10.
120 Noble (ed.), *British Film and Television Yearbook 1957–8*, p. 397.
121 See Thomas Wiseman, 'Mr Box (and All the Other Boxes) See the Money Come Rolling in', *Evening Standard* (7 August 1959). In its second year, Tyne Tees made a profit of £400,000; see PRO HO 244/575, Tyne Tees submission to the Pilkington Committee, 18 May 1961, p. 6.
122 See John Spraos, *The Decline of the Cinema: An Economist's Report* (London: Allen and Unwin, 1962).
123 Walker, *Hollywood, England* (London: Harrap, 1986), pp. 68–9.
124 *Ibid.*, p. 70.
125 *KW*, 9 October 1958, 28.
126 Diaries, 3, 10 and 19 September 1958; *KW*, 9 October 1958, 28.
127 See the revisions and annotations to Andrews's screenplay, MSBC, box 3, item 6, 18 September 1959.
128 Diaries, 30 September 1958, 1 October 1958.
129 Orbit Films press release, BFI microfiche for *Subway in the Sky*.
130 *KW*, 9 October 1958, 28.
131 In the play, Grant was on the run because of his Communist tendencies, but Box decided to alter this to make the drama less specifically political; see Muriel Box's comments, *KW*, 9 October 1958, 28.

132 According to a letter to Muriel Box (then Lady Gardiner) from Pawley and Malyon, Box's accountants, 16 March 1977, the film still showed a 'very considerable loss', grossing under £35,000. Box thought Britannia had grossly mishandled its distribution. (SBP).
133 The articles of association were drawn up on 11 December 1958; see the records at Companies House, 617975G.
134 Diaries, 24 November 1958.
135 'Sydney Box Group Lines up 12 Films for 1959', *KW*, 4 December 1958, 7.
136 Diaries, 23 July 1959.
137 Box, *The Lion That Lost Its Way*, p. 58.
138 *Manchester Guardian*, 28 November 1958. See also Edward Goring, 'Star-Maker', *Daily Mail*, 28 November 1958.
139 'Sydney Box Lines up 12 Films for 1959', 7. Box had purchased the rights to R. F. Delderfield's story *Bull Boys*, the basis of *Carry on Sergeant* (Bright and Ross, *Mr Carry On*, p. 75).
140 *Daily Mail*, 20 November 1958, p. 3.
141 *KW*, 13 August 1959, 3.
142 *Ibid.*
143 Quoted in Goring, 'Star-Maker'.
144 *KW*, 4 December 1958, 7.
145 Losey, quoted in Michel Ciment, *Conversations with Losey* (London: Methuen, 1985), p. 169.
146 *Ibid.*
147 Edward Goring, *Daily Mail*, 17 April 1959.
148 SBP, agreement dated 3 March 1959.
149 Paul Dehn, *News Chronicle*, 16 October 1959.
150 David Caute, *Joseph Losey: A Revenge on Life* (London: Faber and Faber, 1994), p. 132.
151 For casting issues see *ibid.*
152 Ciment, *Conversations with Losey*, p. 170.
153 Interview with William Gell, 28–29 July 2003.
154 Ciment, *Conversations with Losey*, p. 171.
155 See Peter Coates, *No Star Nonsense* (London: Rockliff, 1949), pp. 47–61.
156 Diaries, 28 April 1959.
157 See MSBC, box 3, item 8, 'Information Folder Compiled by Edna Tromans and Publicity Notes by Muriel Box'.
158 See the file on *Too Young to Love* held by the BBFC.
159 Muriel Box had gone to America in July 1959 to cast the film (Diaries, 18 July 1959). The only British actor used was the pop star Jess Conrad.
160 Alexander Walker, *Evening Standard*, 3 March 1960.
161 See the letter to Lady Gardiner, 16 March 1977 mentioned in note 132 above.
162 'Conyers Doesn't Want to Drop a Clanger', *KW*, 11 June 1959, 9; Brian Rix, *My Farce from My Elbow: An Autobiography* (London: Secker & Warburg, 1975), pp. 171–2.
163 'Four at Once', *Evening News* 15 August 1959.
164 Wiseman, 'Mr Box'.
165 Diaries, 23 July 1959.
166 *Ibid.*
167 Box, *The Lion That Lost Its Way*, p. 58.
168 See, *inter alia*, 'Sydney Box Says: I Am Leaving Films', *Daily Express*, 26 September 1959.
169 *KW*, 1 October 1959, p. 6. Jimmy Sangster recalled that although Box had encouraged him to produce a film from an original script he had written, *See No*

Evil, Peter Rogers was reluctant to support the project after he had taken over. Sangster took it to Michael Carreras at Hammer Films and it was released as *Taste of Fear* in April 1961, the first of a successful series of psychological thrillers (Sangster, *Do You Want It Good or Tuesday? A Life in the Movies* (Baltimore: Midnight Marquee Press, 1997), p. 69).

170 Diaries, 23 October 1959.

171 Betty Box, *Lifting the Lid*, p. 202.

172 See Trevor Royle, *James and Jim: A Biography of James Kennaway* (Edinburgh: Mainstream Publishing, 1983), p. 143; Bryan Forbes, *Notes for a Life* (London: Everest Books, 1977), pp. 294–5.

173 Walker, *Hollywood, England*, p. 102.

174 The first three were adaptations of comedy plays – from Arthur Watkyn, Jeremy Kingston and Philip King respectively; *Time to Kill* was an original story by Leigh Vance.

175 Two others, which could have been part of the twenty and were produced by film-makers linked to SBA, were the Cold War thriller *Beyond the Curtain* (April 1960), produced by John Martin and directed by Compton Bennett, and *Faces in the Dark* (March 1960), a gripping thriller based on the novel by Pierre Boileau and Thomas Narcejac, produced by Jon Penington and directed by David Eady.

176 Box, *The Lion That Lost Its Way*, pp. 92–4.

177 Diaries, 9 March 1958; Rank lost £60,000.

178 Muriel Box's diary entries in 1958 and 1959 are full of lamentations about their estrangement, including: 'the bigger he has grown as an entrepreneur and financial chess player the wider the gap that has opened up between us' (30 August 1958).

179 Walker, *Hollywood, England*, pp. 40–6, 68–75.

180 Quoted in *ibid.*, p. 468.

Lion hunt and after

8

Box only recovered slowly from his cerebral haemorrhage in August 1959. In an interview he admitted that he had 'dropped out altogether' for a year, spending four months on a world tour, and lost fifty pounds in an attempt to improve his health and fitness.[1] Box resumed writing in late 1960, composing various outlines for plays, short stories, novels and screen adaptations with Muriel, much as he had done a decade earlier when he took his 'year off'. Few of these came to fruition, but their three-act marital comedy, *Stranger in My Bed*, begun in June 1963 and performed during 1964–65, proved moderately successful, especially in provincial theatres. Box continued to act as an agent for various film-makers, including Ken Annakin, Betty Box and Gerald and Ralph Thomas.[2] Box also had an ultimately unsuccessful sojourn in Hollywood from April to September 1961. In typical fashion, he tried to combine making a deal for six Cinerama features and a remake of *The Seventh Veil* while he was working for MGM on an original screenplay about the life of Baden Powell and the relief of Mafeking. Despite telling Sol Siegel, head of MGM, that Mafeking was 'like the Alamo but with a happy ending', Box's efforts were rejected because the subject matter was felt to be 'too English' for US audiences.[3]

As he recovered Box began to resume his role as producer of films which, as with *Too Young to Love*, Muriel was keen to direct. In March 1963 he paid £50,000, a record sum, for the rights of Charles Dyer's play *Rattle of a Simple Man*.[4] He invested £10,000 of their money in the story of a thirty-nine year old virgin northerner, Percy Winthram, who finds romance with a Soho prostitute, Cyrenne, when he and his mates come down to London for the Cup Final. Box was actively involved in revising the screenplay prepared by Dyer, though William Gell took on the main production duties, including mollifying ABPC's worries about the budget, which was finally pegged to a very modest £141,500. Box had wanted Peter Sellers as the male lead, but he was too expensive and the eventual choice of Harry H. Corbett was something of a compromise.[5] Box also had to intervene when the female lead, Diane Cilento, expressed her unhappiness about certain deleted scenes.[6]

However, the most protracted problems, even in 1963, were with the censors. The BBFC's secretary, John Trevelyan, informed William Gell that in the adaptation 'sensationalism should be avoided ... If the film is shot with tenderness and sensitivity it will be acceptable; if it contains any degree of exploitation, and it appears to be aimed at commercial exploitation, it will run into trouble.'[7] Although the BBFC had certain problems with the language, especially the line 'Stuff that up your old mill chimney', it was much more exercised about nudity and 'suggestiveness'. In particular the board: 'would not want to have shots which emphasised [Cyrenne] taking her panties off; nor would we want nudity or titillating semi-nudity'. Gell was told to delete any shots of Cyrenne with a whip, 'as many as possible of her in soft black boots' and that her 'bra and panties must be reasonably adequate ... We would not want shots of long black suspenders cutting into plushy thighs, or anything of that kind.'[8] There was a further exchange of correspondence in which Gell was told to remove any suggestion of incest between Cyrenne and her brother or father (it was to be made clear that he was her stepfather).[9] More general tidying up took place ('suggestive noises' on the sound track were replaced with pigeons cooing, shots of nudes on posters round Soho strip clubs, and even nude dummies, were taken out) before the film was passed with an 'X' certificate and exhibited in July 1964. Trevelyan had already told Gell that, because Cyrenne was quite clearly a prostitute, an 'A' certificate was ruled out.

The 'X' certification did not help *Rattle of a Simple Man*'s commercial chances and it was rather unsuccessful, neither a box-office success nor critically applauded.[10] As one representative commentator argued: 'All the impact that the story could have had is destroyed by the inevitable opening up of the film beyond just the one set. This disrupts the tension between the two main characters which is the only thing that could have saved the film, as it did the play.'[11] But at least the film had been made. Box's parallel attempts to produce an adaptation of Giles Cooper's 1962 play *Everything in the Garden* was abandoned after pre-consultation with Trevelyan. He took the view that its subject matter – a group of suburban wives earning extra income as 'high-class' prostitutes, whose actions are endorsed by their cash-strapped husbands – was unacceptable even for an 'X'.[12]

Characteristically, Box was not satisfied to be a writer-cum-occasional-producer: 'I was not content to face the future without something challenging to occupy my rapidly reviving energies and my deep interest in the health and wealth of the British film industry'.[13] He re-entered the fray with an ambitious scheme that encompassed acquiring an ITV franchise – London Weekday Television – and the purchase of a major distribution company, British Lion, and with it the ownership of the large and well-equipped Shepperton Studios. It was Sydney Box Associates revived, but on a grander scale. Box sought to construct nothing less than a genuine third force that would have the size and industrial muscle to take on the Big Four (Associated Television, Associated-Rediffusion, ABC Television and Granada) and the Big Two (Rank and ABPC), which, of course, were interconnected: ABPC owned ABC Television.[14] Although he had to bid separately, Box's overall scheme was 'predicated on the realisation that film and television were in fact interchangeable and indivisible'.[15] And, as always with Box, it was a scheme designed to place film and television production in the hands of creative talent.

The bid for the London Weekday franchise

The opportunity to bid for a new television franchise occurred because the initial ten-year contracts awarded by the Independent Television Authority expired in July 1964. Box formed a new company – London Independent Television Producers (LITP) – to make the bid. His was one of eight new groups to apply, along with all the existing companies; bids had to be submitted by November 1963.[16] Lord Hill, chairman of the ITA, had announced a two-stage plan: there was to be an 'interim phase' (1964–67) in which some modifications to the existing franchises were to be made, followed by a more drastic reshaping when a second ITV channel was introduced in 1967.[17] Box took the view, like most of the new companies bidding for franchises in 1964, that this was a limbering-up exercise in preparation for 1967, but he had some hopes of success even at this stage, as Hill had indicated that some changes could be made.[18] Box was anxious to gain control of London Weekday Television, one of the major franchises belonging to the big four (in this case Associated-Rediffusion), because the television companies operated as a restrictive oligopoly, which meant that only they could produce or acquire programmes in the expectation that they would be nationally networked, and hence made a handsome profit. However well made or innovative, a programme produced by an independent company had no chance of recouping its costs unless the big four allowed it to be networked, which it was not in their interests to do. As Box observed: 'It was the stranglehold of the circuits all over again!'[19]

Box's bid was an attempt to end this stranglehold based on a conception of broadcasting as a 'ministry of all the talents'. LITP's structure consisted of a small group of seven directors, who would be responsible for the day-to-day running of the company, including Box, William MacQuitty, Ted Willis, ex-Verity colleague James Carr (now head of World Wide Pictures) and Norman Fisher, who had been chairman of the BBC's advisory council for seven years. The directors were to be advised on matters of policy by a board of governors that consisted principally of notable writers and actors.[20] But the radical and innovative feature of LITP's bid was a group of 126 'associates',

> who, although not in many cases intending to become members of staff, were bound to it by their enthusiasm for its general policy and had pledged themselves to provide special programmes at intervals on a fee basis, without any sort of retainer. These associates were mostly well-known film and television producers and directors, performers or writers.[21]

They included writers (T. E. B. Clarke, Willis Hall and Keith Waterhouse, Robin Maugham, Frank Muir and Denis Norden); directors (Ken Annakin, Roy Ward Baker, Ken Hughes); and actors (Stanley Baker, Anthony Quayle, Richard Todd).[22] Thus Box's company was to have adopted a method of broadcasting used nearly twenty years later by Channel 4: commissioning programmes from a wide and diverse group of freelance creative personnel, able to draw on their talents without incurring the stifling overheads that would accrue if they had been contract staff. Other innovations included a much larger and more comprehensive news service; links with leading theatres to provide actors and plays for adaptation; and drastic shortening of drama serials to about eight weeks, as Box felt that long-running serials, such as *Emergency Ward 10*, became stale and repetitious; an in-house symphony orchestra under the direction of Muir Mathieson (an 'associate'); more flexible scheduling so that programmes were not cut to fit a rigid timetable; more serious programmes at peak hours; and late night open-ended discussions. Box felt that 'ITV at present underestimates the public's taste and ability to absorb' serious programming.[23] LITP's bid also had a solid commercial foundation. Box had secured £500,000 from directors and associates who were subscribing personally to back his scheme, and £3 million from the City. He had also negotiated a contract with Marconi to supply £1.5 million of equipment and the necessary engineering staff to service it, and had options on three stages at Shepperton with a further call on three more and the use of two smaller studios in the West End at World Wide's premises.[24]

The recently ennobled Lord Willis, president of the Screen Writers' Association, was the public face of Box's bid, as he was widely respected throughout the industry. Willis argued that LITP's structure would ensure a 'new and more equal partnership between producers and management', which would 'disrupt the established order.'[25] The *Observer* saw this bid as a 'revolt of the intellectuals', and recognised that Box had been able to command the support of his associates because of the deep dissatisfaction that creative people felt with the business ethos of commercial broadcasting.[26] Although his scheme was radical, Box could have anticipated a sympathetic hearing of his proposals with some confidence because, after the swingeing criticism of commercial television programming as trivial and low-brow in the Pilkington Report (1962), the ITA was anxious to impose stricter and more rigorous conditions on the general programming policy of the applicants in order to ensure more diverse and innovative programmes.[27] And indeed, Lord Hill and his colleagues on the board admired the 'vigour and freshness of approach and liveliness of imagination' in the LITP bid's plans for programming, but they judged it weak financially, especially in comparison with the incumbent, Associated-Rediffusion.[28] As a compromise, Hill wanted Associated-Rediffusion to share the equity and control with LITP on an equal basis. Unsurprisingly Associated-Rediffusion was strongly opposed to such an arrangement, arguing that it should be awarded the contract outright and emphasising the difficulties that such a merger would create.[29] Box, disappointed, but not surprised, announced that he would now concentrate his efforts on making a new bid when a second commercial channel was introduced.[30] Box had been heartened by the ITA's tacit assurance that 'we had an excellent chance of success' in the next 'round'.[31] And it was reported in the press that Box had nearly succeeded.[32] Bernard Sendall suggests that LITP's bid was probably turned down on 8 January 1964 because the ITA was wary of the 'complicated and time-consuming negotiations' that such a forced marriage with Associated-Rediffusion would have created and concerned that Box might be overreaching himself, as he was also bidding for British Lion.[33]

Lion hunt

Box was able to make a parallel bid for British Lion (BL) because the government was selling it off. British Lion had had a chequered post-war history, becoming a wholly owned subsidiary of the NFFC in January 1955 after the demise of Alexander Korda. BL did not produce its own films, but continued to operate Shepperton Studios and a distribution agency to provide facilities for independent producers. However, the Conservative administration and in particular the Board of Trade regarded this arrangement as an interim measure until a sale could be negotiated, taking the view that 'the film industry is one of the least appropriate for Government ownership or Government direction. It remains our desire to sell British Lion to private interests.'[34] The City financier, Sir Nutcombe Hume, who had been appointed as chairman of both the NFFC and British Lion in 1956, was determined to privatise the company. In October 1958 he wrote to Box, and several other prominent film-makers, asking if they were interested in buying the company.[35] At this point Box was absorbed in his activities with SBA and did not make a formal offer.[36] Throughout the protracted attempts to dispose of BL, the timing, the price of the sale, and the occupation of the purchaser were sensitive issues because the government was mindful that BL was regarded, both by disinterested observers and industry insiders, as the principal agency through which independent producers could operate with some hope of profit. The Board of Trade had ruled out a sale to Rank, ABPC, any of the major television companies or a US concern.[37]

The situation was complicated when David Kingsley, who had moved across from his post as managing director of the NFFC to become BL's chief executive in December 1957, invited five independent film producers – Frank Launder and Sidney Gilliat, the Boulting Brothers, and John Woolf (who left in October) – to become members of the British Lion Board in February 1958. The directors were allowed to acquire shares in the company so that 'their interests will in future be linked with the prosperity and development of the business as a whole'.[38] However, their own attempt to buy BL in March 1960 for £611,000 was rejected because they had been too successful – both the Boultings and Launder and Gilliat had had several major box-office hits – and the new president of the Board of Trade, Reginald Maudlin, decided in December 1960 that the company's financial health meant that the sale was no longer justified at that price.[39] Although the BL board had been given a qualified assurance by Maudling that there would be no further move to sell until the expiry of their contracts on 31 March 1964, Hume told Kingsley on 27 November 1963 that the NFFC intended to sell the company for £1,590,000, the valuation provided by an independent City financier, Sir William Lawson.[40] On 19 December the NFFC acquired the equity shares of the five executive directors, ensuring that the sale could go ahead, having notified the directors on 13 December 1963 that if they wished to buy the company they would have to pay the valuation fee by 8 January 1964.[41] However, before that date, on 20 December 1963, Hume had sold British Lion to Sydney Box.

Box had made an initial approach in November, intimating that, backed by the Standard Industrial Trust (SIT), an issuing house for industrial corporations and an offshoot of the Standard Industrial Group which had connections with the leading merchant banks Lazards and Warburgs, he was prepared to pay the valuation price. The use of Shepperton Studios was an important part of his bid for the London Weekday franchise and it was only through an overall scheme that embraced both film and television production that Box felt he could challenge the existing oligopolies. In a detailed letter accompanied by supporting documentation, dated 15 January 1964, to C. H. Scott, the deputy chairman of the NFFC, Box described his plans for the reconstituted BL, which showed a deliberately close resemblance to his scheme for the television franchise.[42] MacQuitty and Willis would also be directors of BL, together with Kenneth Shipman, son of Box's old associate Alfred Shipman and managing director of Twickenham Studios. In addition there were two promoted BL executives, Michael Bromhead, who was to take charge of Lion International, the overseas arm of BL, and Victor Hoare, who was to become managing director, replacing Kingsley. The final board members were to be John Cuckney from SIT, as a financial adviser, and John Terry, or another representative, from the NFFC. Like LITP's board of governors, Box's British Lion was to have an advisory panel consisting of a similar group of people who could advise the board about projects submitted by independent producers, and act as a 'court of appeal' for those who felt the BL board had ignored them. It was to be chaired by Lord Archibald, president of the Federation of British Film Makers.[43] Box was clear that, under his direction, BL was to become a 'service studio for independent production run *for* film producers, and not *by* them'.[44] Therefore, in contradistinction to the existing management structure, no one asking for production finance and distribution should sit on the board.

Box made, as always, particular provision for writers, through Willis, who was to have 'special responsibility for writers'. Willis stated that under Box, BL 'would launch a pre-production fund to give the best opportunities to film script writers. It would commission a dozen scripts simultaneously from different writers, making an advance payment of £2,000.' This was designed to encourage writers at present outside the small circle of established screenwriters and therefore never given the opportunity to develop their ideas or outlines.[45]

In this way Box felt he could clear the way for a wide range of independent producers to use BL's studio and distribution facilities, supported by a guarantee of 70 per cent of the production costs. The new BL was to have an initial outlay of £1.5 million and a revolving fund of £3 million, which needed to handle 8–12 films per year to operate profitably. At least half of these were to be 'prestige pictures', co-productions (with US partners), costing £500,000 each, 'on a scale which could not be matched by television', while the remainder would be comedies and 'unusual local subjects' [sic], costing £150,000 each, produced for domestic consumption. As a testament to the seriousness of his intentions, Box had actually put in place a provisional programme of fifteen films for the fiscal year 1964/65. The prestige pictures would be provided (one each) by Richard Attenborough and Bryan Forbes, Betty Box, Ivan Foxwell, Jack Hawkins and Colin Lesslie, John Mills, and the Woolfs, while the modestly budgeted films (three each) would be provided by Peter Rogers ('typical British comedies'), James Carreras ('his traditional line', i.e. horror) and BL's satellite companies (Britannia, Bryanston, Bryanston-Seven Arts, Magna and Pax) – presumably these were to be the 'unusual local subjects'.[46] Box stated that there had been additional co-production offers from US companies, which he expected to increase once BL had been re-established.

In interview, Box revealed that he had ambitious plans for Shepperton to become 'a multi-purpose studio properly equipped to make feature films, television films, productions for Pay-TV Limited, and, eventually, capable of handling live television'.[47] Box referred to 'Pay TV' because BL owned shares in Telemeter, a pay-per-view company, and because Box expected to form an alliance with Lord Brabourne, chairman of British Home Entertainment and Pay-TV Limited. Box recognised that there was over-capacity in British studios for feature-film production, therefore the production of television programmes would ensure work for the studios in the intervals between feature films. Box argued that LITP, if successful in obtaining the London Weekday franchise, would use Shepperton as the base for its productions. He added that even if this bid was unsuccessful, he was confident of obtaining the proposed ITA second channel, which would keep Shepperton fully occupied. Indeed, he thought that the whole future of Shepperton was 'bound up with ancillary production of this sort' – and that British Lion itself could only hope to become a true third force by 'extending its ramifications in this direction'.[48] Box judged that writers, producers and directors could work effectively in both media, and that both film and television production would halve the financial risk and double the turnover, making the company more attractive to investors.

Box also had a strategy to overcome the notorious problem of exhibition. The weakness of BL was that it did not own a chain of cinemas and had to negotiate with Rank and ABPC to obtain a circuit release for its films. Kingsley and others had drawn attention to the problems BL had had obtaining a circuit release for a number of its films in 1963, and also the very poor return that could be expected if any of its films were released on the so-called third circuit, earning on average only half the revenue that could be expected from a release on the main circuits.[49] In order to get round these recurring difficulties, Box argued that, rather than completing a film and then negotiating for its release, a better alternative was to approach the circuits with script, stars and budget ready, seeking a tentative exhibition date before production commenced. However, he was determined to resist 'any interference on their part with scripting, production, casting, or artistic integrity of our product'.[50] He also thought that the backlog of feature films in the BL vaults would provide a powerful bargaining counter if his company also owned a television station. New features that the circuits would not book could be released on television 'in open competition with the circuit which refused them'.[51] Box also contended that the joint selling arrangement with Columbia, which BL had operated since March 1961, should continue, as this was essential to its financial viability in the international marketplace.

Hume had agreed to Box's purchase at the valuation figure because, at that point, he was the only suitable purchaser. But this verbal agreement was overridden when a huge furore erupted as news leaked out that Box was going to be the owner of BL without, apparently, having to compete for it. The five ex-executive directors of BL, who strongly opposed the sale, did their best to ensure that there was extensive press coverage. They were fully supported by Michael Balcon, who had learned of Box's bid from Roy Boulting and who made much of what he considered to be the secretive and high-handed attitude of the NFFC in trying to dispose of public assets: 'It seemed to me a very unusual procedure for a para-Government institution to sell government property other than by competitive tender and, as justice had to be seen to be done, I decided to take action'.[52] Accordingly, he wrote to NFFC saying that, given time, he could make a bid, and gave this information to the press. Balcon had a direct interest in the sale of BL because he was chairman of several of its 'satellite' companies which supplied more films for distribution through BL than any other group of independents.[53] Balcon's intervention, as a highly respected elder statesman, ensured that the sale to Box was not only made public, but became a *cause célèbre* in which the various factions who were against the sale and the government's withdrawal from the film industry sensed an opportunity to go onto the attack.

The news of the sale to Box came within the context of a general concern about the power of the combines and the problems of independents and prompted a Commons debate on 20 December 1963. Labour MPs demanded that any action by the government should be delayed until the Commons reassembled after the Christmas recess.[54] Several backbench Tory MPs also opposed the sale to Box, disliking what they referred to as 'backstairs trading'.[55] Eric Lubbock, the Liberal MP for Orpington, accused Box of having been put up to it by the NFFC behind closed doors.[56] Because of Box's extensive involvement with the Rank Organisation, there were frequently repeated accusations that he was merely the front man for Rank's anti-competitive move to gain control of the one company that was a genuine alternative to combine power. There were protests from the Federation of British Film Makers, and the Federation of Film Unions, whose chairman, Sir Tom O'Brien, suggested that the 'unsavoury haste' with which the government was trying to dispose of British Lion to Box suggested ulterior motives.[57] Both organisations were opposed to the sale per se, arguing that the NFFC should retain full ownership, but with a seat on the board for Box. However, Alan Sapper of the ACTT wanted to know the names of the 'faceless ones' who were backing Box.[58] The overriding fear was that Box, or whoever acquired BL, would asset-strip the company and sell off Shepperton Studios, which occupied prime residential land.

Lord Willis was again put forward as the acceptable face of Box's bid, and he made repeated press statements designed to allay fears that Box was acting in association with Rank and/or ABPC. Willis stated that Box's group looked to government help to give British Lion equal rights and opportunities for distribution with Rank and ABC and to set up an independent distribution committee, accepted by all sides, to which problems of distribution could be referred and which would have the power to overrule any local distributor.[59] However, Box was drawn into the fray and tried to present himself in the press as open, reasonable and disinterestedly concerned with the well-being of the British film industry:

> I am coming back into the industry after four years retirement merely because I love the film business and want to do what I can to help in the present crisis.
>
> My associates and I intend to continue to operate British Lion as a completely independent company roughly along the same lines as at present and with the present staff.[60]

Of course, his second point referred to executives such as Hoare and Bromhead, not the board of directors that had been bought out by the

NFFC. Box also argued that government ownership was not a necessary condition for independent production to thrive:

> We agree that Government financial help through NFFC is absolutely necessary to the future of independent production. We do not agree that the Government should be implicated in production directly through British Lion, or any other organisation, particularly so long as private capital is available.[61]

Box also insisted that there would be no quick sale of the company or its assets, and that if his group eventually wished to sell, the NFFC would have first option to repurchase it.

However, Box made an error of judgement when he stated in an interview on 30 December that,

> if the present directors had wanted to go on running British Lion they might have shown their confidence by purchasing the company when it was offered to them. Since they were not prepared to do so one is entitled to ask whether their present protestations are really genuine or merely a smokescreen intended to hide the fact that they are taking something like £800,000 of risk capital out of the industry.[62]

This figure was a reference to the profit that the directors had made on their shares in the company when it was bought by the NFFC, in which each received a tax-free dividend of £158,735. At the High Court, the plaintiffs, Kingsley and his co-directors, argued that the statement was doubly libellous. Not only had it been the NFFC's decision, not theirs, to purchase their shares, but it was not lack of confidence that made them reluctant to purchase the company, but a genuine belief that the sale was not in the best interests of the film industry. Box was forced to apologise and to retract his statements, which was accepted without his incurring damages.[63]

However, Box enjoyed the backing of John Terry, who had been sceptical about how BL had been run and thought that the sale to Box

> will mean that substantial private finance will be introduced into the film industry at a time of difficulty and unemployment and should have a stimulating effect on future independent production. Moreover, the NFFC has received assurances from Mr Box that he would continue to operate British Lion as an independent force in the industry outside Rank and ABC.[64]

However, neither Terry's nor Hume's support was sufficient to allow the sale to Box to proceed. Box received a letter from Hume, dated 3 January 1964, which informed him that the verbal agreement Hume had made on behalf of the government was no longer considered binding, and the sale of BL was to be opened to any bidder, with a closing deadline of 4 March. In a lengthy Commons debate on 4 February, Edward Heath, the new secretary of the Board of Trade, revealed that the NFFC was to have a place on the board of a reconstituted BL and, through the device of a single 'golden' share, would retain certain crucial rights that included preventing the disposal of Shepperton Studios, stopping the company going into voluntary liquidation and vetoing the sale of any significant part of the company's operations. He reiterated:

> our policy will be to ensure that the Company will continue to provide finance, distribution and studio facilities for British Independent Producers of cinematograph films so far as the condition of the market permits and that we will continue to preserve the Company's independent trading position in the interests of British film production.[65]

As Box reflected ruefully, a company in which no interest had been shown suddenly became the subject of a latter-day gold rush.[66] Six other contenders emerged in addition to Box: the Grade Organisation; John Bloom, the washing machine and refrigerators manufacturer; the Federation of Film Unions; Edward Martell's ultra-right-wing Freedom Group; a shadowy group negotiating through Stanley Dubens, the theatrical agent; and a wide-ranging consortium led by Michael Balcon. Balcon argued that the best people to run the company were those who had been running it before, 'plus some strengthening from outside interests'.[67] In addition to Kingsley, the Boultings and Launder and Gilliat, Balcon brought in Walter Reade, the American exhibitor and distributor; Woodfall Films (Tony Richardson and John Osborne), with whom Balcon had already been associated, and who were supported by Border Television in which Balcon was a substantial shareholder; the producer-director team of Joseph Janni and John Schlesinger; Peter Sellers; and Brian Epstein, the Beatles' manager. Balcon's bid was supported by Hambros Bank and the Edinburgh Investment Trust.

In this volatile situation, Box was himself approached by Leslie Grade, John Brown, Sam Spiegel and John Woolf for various combinations.[68] However, he declined to alter his application and, by the closing date of 4 March, only three bids remained: Balcon, Box and Martell. Martell's bid had always been considered marginal, while Box's had continually lost ground to Balcon in public estimation. The trade press commented that Balcon's group 'now represents the most formidable assembly of creative talent to come together under one banner'.[69] *The Times* endorsed such sentiments and raised the problem of Box's fitness:

> There were indications yesterday that there might be considerable reluctance in certain quarters of the film industry to cooperate with Mr Box if he were the successful bidder. This cooperation might also be difficult

> for some of Sir Michael Balcon's backers, and certainly without the wholehearted support of the majority of those who now oppose him it would not be an easy task for Mr Box to make a success of British Lion.[70]

It was therefore no great surprise when Edward Heath announced on 17 March that Balcon's group had been successful. The day after, Box revealed that in fact his group had never made a formal offer for BL.[71]

Box, under pressure from SIT, was unhappy with the details of the conditions of sale imposed by the NFFC, although he accepted the basic principles. SIT's interest in backing Box's scheme was to raise revenue through a large share issue. In a letter to Hume on 9 March, SIT argued that it made financial and ethical sense to have a broad spread of equity capital rather than to have the shares vested in a few hands. It wanted the issued capital increased to £700,000 ordinary shares and £300,000 preferred shares. The former would be purchased in cash from the board (for £1,300,000) and then put up for public sale, no doubt for a substantial profit. SIT also wanted greater flexibility about the future of Shepperton Studios and BL's accrued tax loss, which, under the conditions set out by the government, went entirely to the NFFC. Without these assurances, SIT took the view that the sale was 'too restrictive to make it a suitable proposition to which to invite members of the public to subscribe, and to give the directors a reasonable degree of commercial and financial discretion in running the business'.[72] Although Terry indicated that the NFFC would not necessarily oppose the sale of Shepperton if 'alternative studio facilities are available', or if it could only be run at a loss, he would not vary the conditions of the sale significantly.[73] Box wrote on 9 March, just two days before the deadline, to Terry, assuring him that even the major shareholders – Max Rayne, Kenneth Shipman, David Brown and LITP – would not hold more than 10 per cent of the total, and to Hume, that he had 'lost none of my enthusiasm for the project'. But in the end the gap between the two sides could not be bridged and the bid was not made.[74] Box maintained that the conditions insisted on by the NFFC were more severe than would have been imposed without a scramble for the company, and that the public furore made it adopt an inflexible position.[75] Box was tempted either to insist publicly that BL be sold by auction – he was prepared to go to £2 million or even £2.5 million – or to risk signing the document as it stood 'and seek our revisions later when the dust of the contest had settled'.[76] However, the NFFC rejected Box's private enquiry as to whether the sale would made to the highest bidder out of hand, and he decided that to go public 'would almost certainly produce further misunderstandings'.[77] Reluctantly, Box informed the NFFC that he was withdrawing his bid which left the way clear for Balcon.

Final projects

After the disappointment over British Lion, Box returned to his role as writer-cum-occasional-producer. He spent considerable time preparing a screen treatment of the life of Edward VIII, based on the Duke of Windsor's ghosted memoirs. Ironically, *A King's Story*, narrated by Orson Welles, was one of the few films distributed by British Lion/Columbia in 1965. Box had been commissioned by the producer, Jack le Vien, who had gained a reputation as the 'world's top screen biographer'. He had made a biography of Hitler, *Black Fox* (1962), an award-winning twenty-six-part television series, *The Valiant Years* (1961), and a two-hour colour film, *The Finest Hours* (1964–65), both based on the memoirs of Winston Churchill. Le Vien had begun negotiations with the Duke of Windsor late in 1961 and the Duke had given over his private film footage, including rare and never before publicly viewed footage shot by friends, family photographs and his personal correspondence concerning the abdication crisis. However, if le Vien had privileged access to material, this was used to construct an anodyne account, as le Vien put it: 'a story with no villains, in which everyone acted for what he thought to be the best. I believe it will convince the world that democracy, the British form of government, is a fine and honourable thing.'[78] The premiere of *A King's Story*, advertised as 'perhaps the most poignant, intriguing, and dramatic love story of modern times', was held at the Royal Festival Hall on 3 May 1965, in the presence of the Duke and Duchess. The general critical verdict was, unsurprisingly, that *A King's Story* was engaging and interesting, but not revelatory. *The Times*'s reviewer thought it 'steers with remarkable skill a middle course', offering no new insight into the abdication, but conveying something genuine about the character of the Duke himself and his life.[79] The whole process disappointed Box, who, when he spent time with couple at their country residence at Gif-sur-Yvette to gather information for his treatment, found both the Duke and Duchess extremely courteous, but impenetrable: 'everything was sweetness and light and shiny, enamelled dignity'.[80]

In the mid-1960s, the fortunes of Betty Box suffered a downturn, and once again big brother stepped in. He negotiated a deal with the Australian Bruce Newbery, managing director of Santor Film Productions, to co-finance *Deadlier than the Male* (November 1966), distributed by Rank and Universal. Betty Box produced, with Ralph Thomas as director. *Deadlier than the Male* was part of the plethora of 1960s secret-agent films inspired by the success of the James Bond films, with Richard Johnson as an ersatz Sean Connery. Johnson played Hugh

'Bulldog' Drummond, tough, resourceful and urbane but only a distant echo of Sapper's creation, in Jimmy Sangster's story, set partly in a fictitious Mediterranean country (and filmed in Italy) and not based on any of the books. Its distinctiveness was to have a pair of merciless female assassins, played by Elke Sommer and Sylvia Koscina, in the pay of criminal mastermind Petersen (Nigel Green).

This provoked another lengthy exchange between Box and the BBFC. The board was 'not entirely happy about beautiful, sexy girls committing a series of ruthless murders. It would be easier from our point of view if Petersen employed some male thugs, and used his beautiful girls for more decorative and less homicidal purposes.'[81] The board was also insistent that *Female of the Species* (the working title), if it was to obtain an 'A' certificate', should treat sex and violence in the same way as Bond, defined as 'lightly and unrealistically'. Although Box assured Trevelyan that this would indeed be the case, and Betty Box wrote to insist that Drummond, who never uses weapons or violence except as self-protection, was 'a copybook Boys' Own Paper hero', the board continued to take a severe line with the script.[82] Considerable dislike was expressed for its 'emphasis on promiscuity, which is largely based on nymphomania'; 'it is permeated with sadism'.[83] Certain scenes were singled out for revision or removal, but despite this the board was adamant that 'the element of female sadism and callous attitude to killing and death, treated with a cynical gloss' meant an 'X' certificate. It was 'Not a film which, in our view, should be seen by young teen-agers (girls particularly)'.[84] The Boxes reluctantly decided to accept this certification rather than fight on and try to make the further cuts required for an 'A', as these would be 'extremely detrimental'.[85]

The reception of *Deadlier than the Male* was quite cool. One reviewer saw it as 'a film of a now familiar kind. International spies, supermen with super gimmicks, passed the point of burlesque several films ago and it's slightly surprising to see so straight a version at this late date.'[86] Another felt the Boxes had missed a trick by not reviving the 1920s ambience for their depiction of Drummond, since this tactic had been so successful in the recent television adaptation of P. G. Wodehouse's Jeeves and Wooster.[87] There was some comment about the 'X' certification: Gerard Fairlie, writer of many latter-day Drummond stories, pointed out the censors' clear double standards in singling this film out for harsh treatment.[88] However, *Deadlier*'s restricted certification did not seem to undermine its box-office success: it grossed £4,729 in its first four days and £1,400,000 worldwide.[89] Cinema managers were exhorted to emphasise the 'brigade of bikini-clad beauties seen in the film' including constructing a 'glamour peep show' in the foyer.[90]

After the frustrations of the abortive purchase of BL, Box scored a notable success with the launch of his own publishing company, Triton Books, in April 1964. It was a typical mixture of astute commercial logic and a way for Box to encourage young or relatively unknown writers to get published. Box recalled:

> I had always been intrigued by the fact that a film producer was expected to pay much more for a story that came to him in hard covers, with an attractive jacket, than for the same story presented in sober typescript in a manila folder. The prior acceptance of the story by a publisher apparently lent the whole transaction some sort of respectability – almost the equivalent of a *Good Housekeeping* seal of approval.[91]

Triton was set up to test this theory, and within its first year had been used to negotiate the film rights of five novels, including Hugh Mill's *Prudence and the Pill* and Andrea Newman's *Three into Two Won't Go*, all for over £10,000, twice as much as would have been paid for a typescript.[92] Triton caused 'something of a sensation in the literary world', seen as 'under-capitalised, over-gentlemanised and generally difficult for outsiders to break into'.[93] Box used his company to promote new writers, including Roland Starke and John Warwick, or those, like Noel Langley and Jimmy Sangster, who were looking to branch out. Box encouraged Sangster to write a novel, and Triton published *Private I*, a hard-boiled secret agent thriller, in 1967.[94]

Box was less successful in his efforts to resurrect himself as a film and television impresario. In December 1964 the grandly named National Film Corporation (NFC) was launched, with Box as chairman and William Gell as managing director, and with headquarters at 35 Piccadilly.[95] The NFC was a way of bundling together their various interests in some thirteen production and distribution companies. Steven Pallos, representing Pax and Britannia Films, joined them on the board. William MacQuitty had introduced Box to George Livanos and Stavros Niarchos, Greek shipping billionaires who were prepared to venture the finance, establishing a permanently revolving fund of £800,000, and who were represented on the NFC board by the Marquis of Blandford and David D'Ambrumenil, son of the Lloyds' chairman.[96] A complete screenplay was prepared by Ian Stuart Black from Virginia Cowles' book *The Phantom Major*, the story of Lieutenant Colonel David Stirling, commander of the first SAS regiment during the Desert Campaign, a latter-day Scarlet Pimpernel; but the budget of £750,000 required a US partner, and the story was again 'too English' to attract investment from Hollywood.[97] No further projects were developed because, although MacQuitty remembers that Box 'was in his element, a magnificent catalyst in the humming machinery of creation', the NFC was virtually stillborn.[98] As Box recalled, 'The new company had an influential board and enough money to make and distribute three or four prestige pictures a year, but lacked a guiding force, largely because I was by then a very sick man and had perforce to pack my bags and retire for good.'[99] Box's ill health – he suffered two hearts attacks in February and September 1966 – also meant that his plans to relaunch his bid for an ITV station were frustrated. He had resigned from the board of Tyne Tees Television in September 1965 in order to leave himself free to make another attempt, backed by City money and 200 creative writers, producers, directors and musicians who felt 'stifled' by the BBC or frustrated by the regimentation of ITA programmes.[100] But by December 1966, when the franchises became vacant, he was too ill to mastermind a bid.[101]

Box also had to withdraw from a joint production he had negotiated on behalf of LIP between a group of Indian financiers, backed by the Maharaja of Batoda, and Rank, to make *The Long Duel* (March 1967), an empire adventure film set in India in the 1920s, in which a liberal police officer (Trevor Howard) finds himself reluctantly having to hunt down a tribal chieftain (Yul Brynner). When the Indian money did not materialise, Box was too ill to sort out the problems, but Ken Annakin, who took on the role of producer as well as director, salvaged the project by switching the location shooting to Spain and convincing Rank to finance the entire production.[102] Box formally resigned his chairmanship of LIP on medical grounds in July 1967.[103]

Retirement: the writer reborn

Relations between Muriel and Sydney Box had gradually deteriorated over a long period. Their interests had begun to diverge significantly, and Muriel had always been unhappy with what she took to be his increasingly entrepreneurial attitude – the triumph, in her eyes, of the businessman over the creative writer – and by the revelation of his infidelity.[104] Their marriage was effectively over before he departed for Australia in November 1966. Box wrote in March 1967 urging Muriel to accept that 'the Sydney you knew died two years ago. Don't try to disinter him. It won't do any good. Nobody can live with a corpse.'[105] Box tried residing in Spain, Cap Ferrat, New York, California, and then back in England in April 1967, but all of these proved to be unsatisfactory as he was too easily accessible to people from the film industry seeking his advice. He returned to Australia and in October 1967 settled in Perth with Sylvia Knowles, whom he married in July 1969 after his divorce from Muriel had been finalised.[106]

Although Box at first refused to have a telephone installed so that he would be 'no longer prey to its siren call and agree to something that's bad for me', inevitably, he did not completely relinquish his involvement in films, revising or commenting on various scripts that were sent to him.[107] The newly elected Labor premier of Western Australia persuaded Box, in April 1971, to become a member of the Arts Council of Western Australia (1974–77).[108] Through his membership, Box made contacts with workers in the Australian film industry, and he helped and advised on various projects and chaired TVM-7's Young Film Makers' award.[109] Box prepared an adaptation of his unpublished novel *The Nurse's Story* and an original screenplay, *Bitter Grapes*, for Australian International Films in 1979–80, but these were not taken up. He continued to write almost every day: short stories, plays (including *All Alone* – 'a sextet of plays for one actress and nine telephones' – in 1979–81), and further screenplays, most of which were not published. He did have success with several novels, beginning with *Diary of a Drop-Out*, published by Triton in 1969, about a rebellious teenage girl. *Golden Girls* (1971) was more openly sensationalist and its soft-porn descriptions of fornication more frequent. The Sphere paperback edition quotes the *Evening Chronicle* – 'Harold Robbins and Jacqueline Susann must be green with envy – they couldn't have done it better themselves' – and the cover features a curvaceous nude. Box was embarrassed by the success of *Golden Girls*, but pleased to bank the proceeds.[110] *Alibi in the Rough* (1977) was a rather hackneyed thriller about the perfect crime that goes wrong, but Box's last novel, *Second Only to Murder* (1978) was his best, exposing the social hypocrisy surrounding rape in ways that recalled his 1930s plays.

Although no further work was published, not even his autobiography, *The Lion That Lost Its Way*, completed in 1977, Box continued to write until his death on 25 May 1983. In a profile in *The Australian*, published a month before he died, the writer discerned that, although Box was in a wheelchair crippled by 'the slow sinister onset of osteo-arthritis', he was still mentally as agile and energetic as ever, valued for his 'animated disposition, his cheer, the constant flashes of conversational brilliance, the rich diversity of his intellectual interests ... the company of Sydney Box is a coveted privilege'.[111]

What might have been

Although it was generally believed at the time that BL had been sold to the right people, that the good guys had won, the reconstituted company soon gained an unenviable reputation as the producer of unexciting and unadventurous films, and was castigated for only making a handful of films rather than the 10–15 a year that had been promised.[112] Balcon quickly became disillusioned, realising that his 'principal colleagues' were not interested in sustaining high production levels, fearing that they could not obtain a release for their films. As this was contrary to what Balcon regarded as their mandate to support independent production in general, he resigned in 1966.[113] As Alexander Walker argues, BL's position was weakened by the increasing penetration of US finance into the British film industry; US methods of financing were both more generous – offering 100 per cent financing (as opposed to BL's 70 per cent) – and far less complex.[114] Balcon's colleagues, notably Woodfall, took their projects to US companies. The government seemed unable, or unwilling, to intervene, and the recommendations of the long-awaited report of the Monopolies Commission into restrictive practices within the film industry, published in October 1966, fought shy of the radical action that was needed.

In his autobiography, Balcon concluded:

> If I had known how the whole adventure into British Lion was going to turn out there would have been no justification, except on principle, for my interfering over the original Sydney Box deal for control of the company. I could have saved myself a great deal of work and worry, and in the end severe disappointment. I have no reason to believe that Mr Box would not have done just as much by way of actual film-making as was now the official policy of British Lion.'[115]

Could Box have fared any better than Balcon in the face of the American 'invasion'? It is impossible to say with any confidence, but had *both* Box's bids been successful, he would have been in control of a closely interconnected media conglomerate whose size would have made it a formidable force, and one predicated on an innovative conception of production that was ahead of its time. One cannot but agree with Box's own judgement that it was a pity that he was not allowed to create this third force, which might have changed the course of British film and television production.

Notes

1 'Mr Box's Boredom', *Evening Standard*, 30 December 1963. Box's weight had been a recurrent issue since he was quite a young man; there are constant references to periods spent in a clinic trying to reduce his weight in the Diaries.

2 Annakin rated his services as an agent very highly (*So You Wanna Be a Director?*, pp. 96, 153, 169, 190, 197).

3 See the correspondence with Muriel Box in MSBC, box 5; the Alamo reference is in a letter to Muriel Box, dated 15 June 1961.
4 '£50,000 Paid for Film Rights', *Daily Telegraph*, 1 March 1963.
5 MSBC, box 4, Item 10.
6 See 'Film Cuts Make Diane Furious', *Sun*, 25 September 1964.
7 BBFC file on *Rattle of a Simple Man*, letter from Trevelyan to Gell, 5 June 1963,
8 *Ibid.*
9 *Ibid.*, letter from Trevelyan to Gell, 27 July 1963.
10 *Rattle of a Simple Man* eventually broke even. See MSBC, box 5, letter from Box to Muriel Box, 3 January 1967.
11 Jonathan Gill, *Isis*, 17 October 1964, 27.
12 Muriel Box, *Odd Woman Out*, p. 193.
13 Box, *The Lion That Lost Its Way*, p. 4.
14 Rank had a substantial 37.5 per cent holding in Southern Television.
15 Box, *The Lion That Lost Its Way*, p. 7.
16 Sendall, *Expansion and Change, 1958–68*, p. 211.
17 'Two-Stage Plan for Future of Commercial TV', *Financial Times*, 2 August 1963.
18 'No certainty of "As You Were" on TV Contracts, Says ITA', *Sunday Times*, 15 December 1963.
19 Box, *The Lion That Lost Its Way*, p. 5.
20 'Show Business Group Seek and ITV Contract', *The Times*, 12 December 1963. The board of governors was to consist of: Dame Peggy Ashcroft, Anthony Asquith, John Betjeman, Dame Edith Evans, Christopher Fry, Jack Hawkins, Ivan Foxwell, Rose Heilbron QC, Benard Miles, John Mills, Mrs JB Priestley (Jacquetta Hawkes), Sir Michael Redgrave, Dame Flora Robson, Sir John Rothenstein (Director of the Tate Gallery) and Peter Ustinov.
21 Sendall, *Expansion and Change*, p. 214; see also Diaries, 27 October 1963.
22 *The Times*, 12 December 1963.
23 John Ardagh, 'The Box Rebellion', *Observer*, 5 December 1963.
24 *Ibid.*
25 Quoted in Sendall, *Expansion and Change*, pp. 214–15.
26 Ardagh, 'The Box Rebellion'.
27 Sendall, *Expansion and Change*, p. 214.
28 *Ibid.*, p. 215. The *Sunday Telegraph* reported on 15 December 1963 that LITP's submisssion had 'much impressed the authority'.
29 Sendall, *Expansion and Change*, p. 215.
30 'Mr Box to Seek ITV-2 Programme Contract', *Financial Times*, 10 January 1964.
31 Box, *The Lion That Lost Its Way*, p. 9.
32 'Film Men to the Fore', *Observer*, 18 December 1966.
33 Sendall, *Expansion and Change*, pp. 215–16.
34 PRO, BT 258/160, E. V. Marchant [films branch at the Board of Trade], 'Reorganisation of British Lion in the Spring of 1958', undated.
35 PRO, BT 258/160, copy of Hume's letter sent to Herbert Andrew at the BoT, 13 October 1958.
36 PRO, BT 258/160, letter from John Terry to E. V. Marchant, 30 December 1958. Terry reported that although various discussions had been held between the NFFC and Box, they 'never advanced very far'. The only film-maker to make a formal bid at this point was Herbert Wilcox, but his submission was judged unsatisfactory by the BoT.
37 PRO, BT 258/160, G. S. Knight [films branch, BoT], memo dated 7 October 1958.
38 'The British Film Industry 1958', *Political and Economic Planning*, 24:424 (1958), 148.
39 PRO, BT 258/162, Reginald Maudling, letter to Sir Nutcombe Hume, 21 September 1960.

40 Bernard Husra, 'Patterns of Power', *Films and Filming*, 10:7 (April 1964), 53.
41 *Ibid.*
42 SBP, Box, letter to C. H. Scott, 15 January 1964, p. 3.
43 The British Lion advisory panel consisted of: Ken Annakin, Stanley Baker, Ernest Betts, Norman Fisher, Ivan Foxwell, Christopher Fry, Jack Hawkins, George King (president of the Cinematograph Exhibitors Association), Joan Werner Laurie (critic and editor of *She*), the Countess of Longford, Roger Manvell, Lord Maugham, James Quinn (director of the BFI), Richard Todd, Lord Westwood (past president of the CEA), and John Wood (exhibitor).
44 Box, quoted in Philip Oakes, 'Has the Kill Been Made?, *Sunday Telegraph*, 19 January 1964; original emphasis.
45 Willis, quoted in 'Storm Over Proposal to Sell British Lion', *KW*, 2 January 1964, 15.
46 Box claims that nine of these films were eventually made, but does not list their titles (*The Lion That Lost Its Way*, p. 14).
47 Quoted in Oakes, 'Has the Kill Been Made?'
48 SBP, Box, letter to Mr Scott (Deputy Chairman, NFFC), 15 January 1964.
49 Husra, 'Patterns of Power', p. 51.
50 SBP, Box, letter to Mr Scott (Deputy Chairman, NFFC), 15 January 1964.
51 Box, *The Lion That Lost Its Way*, p. 7.
52 Michael Balcon, *Michael Balcon Presents ... A Lifetime of Films* (London: Hutchinson, 1969), p. 204.
53 Balcon was chairman of Bryanston and Bryanston-Seven Arts.
54 'Storm Over Proposal to Sell British Lion', 3, 15.
55 'Tory MPs Now Opposing British Lion Sale', *The Times*, 2 January 1964, 8.
56 'Conditions Imposed on British Lion Sale', *The Times*, 5 February 1964, 15.
57 'Renewed Effort to Stop British Lion Sale', *The Times*, 31 December 1963, 10.
58 'New Labour Peer in Bid for British Lion Films', *The Times*, 1 January 1964, 6.
59 Quoted in 'Rival Ready to Outbid Mr Box', *The Times*, 6 January 1964, 8.
60 Quoted in 'Storm over Proposal to Sell British Lion', 3.
61 Quoted in *The Daily Cinema*, 1 January 1964, 6.
62 See 'Libel on British Lion Directors', *The Times*, 7 February 1964, 12.
63 *Ibid.*
64 Quoted in Husra, 'Patterns of Power', p. 53.
65 Quoted in Mark Shivas, 'British Lion', *Movie*, 14 (Autumn 1965), 2.
66 Box, *The Lion That Lost Its Way*, p. 10.
67 'Renewed Effort to Stop British Lion Sale', 10.
68 See the diary entries for this period, 29 December 1963 to 31 January 1964.
69 'Government Not to Retain Its Interest in British Lion', *The Daily Cinema*, 18 January 1964, 9.
70 'New Support for Balcon Bid', *The Times*, 10 March 1964, 12.
71 *The Daily Cinema*, 18 March 1964, 1.
72 SBP, Andre de Breyne, chairman of SIT, letter to Hume, 24 February 1964.
73 SBP, Terry, letter to de Breyne, 28 February 1964.
74 SBP, Box, letter to Terry, 9 March 1964; letter to Hume, 9 March 1964.
75 Box insisted his backers were seeking that 'the tax loss position should not be followed by the imposition of any other tax impost that would adversely affect the profitability of the company'. Draft version of the opening chapter of *The Lion That Lost Its Way*, SBP, p. 30.
76 *Ibid.*, p. 32.
77 *Ibid.*
78 Quoted in 'Putting a King's Story on Film', *Sunday Telegraph*, 12 July 1964.
79 *The Times*, 4 May 1965.

80 Box, *The Lion That Lost Its Way*, p. 103.
81 BBFC file on *Deadlier than the Male*, letter from Trevelyan to Box, 27 August 1965.
82 BBFC file on *Deadlier than the Male*, Box, letter to Trevelyan 31 August 1965; Betty Box, letter to Trevelyan, 7 October 1966.
83 BBFC file on *Deadlier than the Male*, letter from Trevelyan to Betty Box, 5 October 1966.
84 BBFC file on *Deadlier than the Male*, letter from Trevelyan to Betty Box, 4 November 1966.
85 BBFC file on *Deadlier than the Male*, Betty Box, letter to Trevelyan, 15 November 1966.
86 Ian Wright, *Manchester Guardian*, 30 December 1966.
87 Felix Barker, *Evening News*, 29 December 1966.
88 Gerard Fairlie, 'Why "Bulldog" Gets an X', *News of the World*, 18 December 1966.
89 MSBC, box 5, Box, letter to Muriel Box, 19 February 1967; SBP, Box's note on Rank's box-office returns, undated. Box includes a fascinating analysis of where the profits from the film actually went in his autobiography, pp. 117–20.
90 Campaign booklet, author's collection.
91 Box, *The Lion That Lost Its Way*, p. 154.
92 *Ibid.*, p. 155.
93 'Box's Books', *Sunday Times*, 12 April 1964.
94 Sangster, *Do You Want It Good or Tuesday?*, pp. 103–4.
95 *KW*, 10 December 1964, 3.
96 William Gell, interview with author, 28–29 July 2003; MacQuitty, *A Life to Remember*, p. 347.
97 Gell interview. A copy of the screenplay is held in the Sydney Box Papers.
98 MacQuitty, *A Life to Remember*, p. 348.
99 Box, *The Lion That Lost Its Way*, p. 155.
100 'Mr Sydney Box Plans to Tun "Creative TV"', *Financial Times*, 30 September 1965.
101 There was, of course, no second ITV channel created in 1967. The ITA contented itself with some limited redrawing of the franchise areas.
102 For the details see Annakin, *So You Wanna Be a Director?*, pp. 197–206; see also David Watkins, *Sun*, 18 November 1966. Vivian Cox, who wrote the original (uncredited) story based on a tale he had heard during his childhood in India, recalled that the money was available and that he had prepared all the locations ready for shooting to begin. However, for personal reasons, Annakin wanted to film in Europe. Interview with author, 10 June 2003.
103 See *KW*, 29 July 1967, 3. Box was also involved in the initial stages of *Accident*, but this was left to William Gell to complete. See Caute, *Joseph Losey*, pp. 185–6, 202.
104 Muriel Box, *Odd Woman Out*, pp. 230–5, 242–8.
105 MSBC, box 5, Box, letter to Muriel Box, 4 March 1967.
106 See Sylvia Box's afterword to *The Lion That Lost Its Way*, pp. 157–67.
107 For instance *The Limbo Line*, an LIP spy thriller released in November 1968.
108 MSBC, box 5, Box, letter to Muriel Box, 22 April 1971.
109 See Graham, 'Let's Forget the "Art" of Film Making', 43–4.
110 MSBC, box 5, Box, letter to Muriel Box, 26 April 1976, in which he admits: 'I still disown the book, if anyone asks about it I pretend it was written by some other chap of the same name! But I take the money without blushing!'
111 Max Harris, 'Perth's Fugitive from Fame', *The Australian*, 2 April 1983, 6.
112 Shivas, 'British Lion', p. 3.
113 Balcon, *Michael Balcon Presents*, p. 208.
114 Walker, *Hollywood, England*, pp. 334–8.
115 Balcon, *Michael Balcon Presents*, pp. 208–9.

Conclusion

9

One of the motivations for writing this study was to try to define with some precision the complex nature of the producer's role and to demonstrate its importance in the film-making process. I hope that the case has been made, but a more comprehensive analysis would, as suggested in the introduction, need to both comparative – weighing Box's career against those of his contemporaries including Anthony Havelock-Allan, Michael Relph, Herbert Wilcox, John Woolf and indeed Michael Balcon – and historical, situating Box within a long-term analysis of the fluctuating role of the producer in British cinema history. That is beyond the scope of the present study, and therefore I wish to conclude by assessing Box's own achievements.

Taken as a whole, what is striking about Box's career is its episodic nature, the product of particular circumstances, especially ill-health, as has been detailed, but also of temperament. All those who worked with Box are agreed that he possessed gargantuan energy, charm and a remarkable range of abilities, but that what he enjoyed most was to initiate projects rather than see them through. As William MacQuitty observed, Box 'never seemed happier than when he was in the thick of complicated negotiations sandwiched between writing scripts and doctoring other people's'.[1] In a deleted section of his autobiography, Box revealed: 'One of my greatest pleasures has always been to throw out an idea – preferably a slightly nonconformist idea – for dealing with any given situation; one of my greatest tortures has always been to carry out that idea to its logical conclusion'.[2] This pleasure explains his motivation for setting up new companies and devising new systems – including Verity Films, London Independent Producers and Triton Books – and then leaving them once they were running effectively in order to find something new to absorb his extraordinarily fertile mind. Undoubtedly he would have also have moved on from Gainsborough Pictures, Sydney Box Associates and British Lion/London Weekday Television had they too continued (or started) and left the 'logical conclusion' of running them to others.

However, to make this observation is not to concur with Charles Drazin's verdict that, although Box was 'one of the most gifted people working in British films. The pity was that he never applied himself at anything for long enough to make a permanent mark. He was the Man Who Did Too Much.'[3] Box only abandoned his creations once he was fully convinced that others were capable of continuing them, and his achievements are real and substantial. As an executive producer he was highly successful. Verity Films, created out of nothing, made upwards of 100 short films during the war, and retained over forty people in continuous employment because of Box's ability to secure commissions and ensure a cost-effective service. The volume and range of Verity's output made an important contribution to the government's propaganda effort. At Gainsborough, despite shoddy studio conditions, Box's skill as a planner and organiser meant not only a steady supply of British films during a production crisis, but full employment for the studio staff. It was a triumph of cost-effective rational ordering, which showed how to construct a profitable domestic film industry which could deliver consistently, one a month, a range of different types of film, and secure an overall profit. The Box era was a distinctive one, in which the studio engaged with topical issues in a number of films and created an innovative form of literary adaptation in the Maugham 'trilogy', in which one can discern the attempt to create a writers' studio in which the writer would be the key figure. There is no gainsaying that Box's output at Gainsborough was uneven, and that there was a marked falling off in invention and execution after a bright start, and much has been made of the faults of *Christopher Columbus* and *The Bad Lord Byron*, but this should not obscure what he did accomplish.

However, these two periods as an executive producer were extended interludes in Box's attempt to be a creative independent producer along pre-war French lines, espousing a socialist agenda that was idealistic but in touch with progressive change. This came closest to fulfilment in the two years at Riverside Studios, and it is no coincidence that most of his best films were made during this period, including *The Seventh Veil*, which, in various ways, explored the profound social and psychological changes that the war had created. The constraints were more severe in the 1950s, and Box's achievements more patchy, because this was precisely the wrong time to be an independent producer in a British cinema dominated by the entrenched power of the circuits, which made it very difficult for filmmakers to maintain creative control and artistic integrity; hence the number of aborted or unrealised projects that Box endured. It was also a period in which audience tastes were changing rapidly and unpredictably, making it very difficult for any producer to anticipate what might work. London Independent Producers faltered in the face of combine power, but Sydney Box Associates spearheaded changes that attempted to wrest control away from the distributors and put it back into the hands of the producers. Unfortunately, Box's poor health meant that SBA, which gave every indication of being a success, unravelled before it could make its mark.

It is at this point that an assessment of Box's career shifts from the real and substantial to what-might-have-been. Box's foresight meant that SBA enshrined the interconnectedness of the film and television industries, and this was at the heart of his imaginative parallel bids for the London Weekday franchise and British Lion. They showed the skill and daring of Box as a deal-maker, organising disparate elements into a coherent package which was consistent with everything he did in his career: seeking to give control over the production process to creative people, notably writers, and forging the conditions under which their creativity could flourish with a high degree of autonomy. These bids were the culmination of his continued struggle with the corporations, the big two and the big four, which controlled film and television production. Had both succeeded, then a genuine third force would have been created which could have had a significant impact on the subsequent course of both British cinema and British television. That, of course, is speculation, but the bid itself needs to be recognised as highly imaginative and not the sign of diminished energy and inventiveness. His career was not, as some of the obituaries suggested, a long decline from the peak of *The Seventh Veil*; rather it is the story of Box's protean ability to adapt and reinvent himself, to make a series of strategic moves in an industry that was changing radically.

Drazin's verdict also obscures Box's achievement, not only in providing work for hundreds of people within the industry, but also in creating opportunities for new, untried talent. This included those closest to him, Muriel Box, Betty Box, Peter Rogers – Box was as protective of his family's interests as any Hollywood mogul – and many others who played a significant role in the post-war British film industry – including Ken Annakin, Compton Bennett, Antony Darnborough, David Deutsch, Terence Fisher, Guy Green, Ken Hughes, William MacQuitty, Jan Read, Ralph and Gerald Thomas and Julian Wintle. One of Box's best qualities was that of inspiring others to give of their best, and those he helped remained sensible of their debt. The most eloquent was David Deutsch, who recalled 'the complete impresario' always capable of 'providing the right environment for creative people to work, welcoming, encouraging, and subtly influencing'.[4] Deutsch's tribute acts as a reminder that a producer's achievement often resides in the work of a corpus of creative people rather than a body of films. Overall, as both creator and enabler, Box was a major presence in the British film industry who deserves far more recognition than he has been accorded.

Notes

1 MacQuitty, *A Life to Remember*, p. 280.
2 Quoted in Andrew Spicer, 'Introduction', Sydney Box, *The Lion That Lost Its Way*, pp. xxiv–xxv.
3 Drazin, *The Finest Years*, p. 212.
4 David Deutsch, letter in *Screen International* (4 June 1983), 4.

Appendix

Costs and box-office revenues of Box's films distributed by Rank, where available

Title	*Cost £*	*Net revenue £ 24 Dec. 1949*	*Expected total revenue £ 24 Dec. 1949*	*Estimated profit/loss £*	*Net revenue £ July 1953*	*Comment by John Davis*
The Seventh Veil	92,000				253,000	Exc't
The Years Between					143,000	Good
Daybreak	150,000				130,000	Avge
The Man Within	161,800	128,100	128,200	–6,500	105,000	Avge
The Brothers	162,900	111,000	111,100	–55,700	110,000	Good
Dear Murderer					139,000	Avge
The Upturned Glass	196,000	211,300	211,300	+45,800	170,000	Exc't
Holiday Camp	150,400	184,300	184,300	+16,000	149,000	Exc't
Jassy					200,000	Exc't
When the Bough Breaks					125,000	Good
Easy Money	116,800	125,300	127,700	+2,200	117,000	Good
Snowbound					120,000	Avge
Miranda	170,400	181,300	182,200	+5,600	182,000	Exc't
Broken Journey	197,000	118,200	119,500	–63,900	116,000	Avge
Good Time Girl	180,000				177,000	Exc't
The Calendar					92,000	Avge
My Brother's Keeper	113,600	96,300	105,000	–9,400		
The Blind Goddess	143,000				88,000	Avge
Quartet	168,000				122,000	Avge
Here Come the Huggetts	100,000				127,000	Good

Portrait from Life	132,800	100,200	120,000	+4,100	150,000	Good
Vote for Huggett					143,000	Good
Once upon a Dream					79,000	Poor
The Bad Lord Byron	223,900	22,400	45,000	−179,200	75,000	Poor
It's Not Cricket						
A Boy, a Girl and a Bike					61,000	Poor
The Huggetts Abroad					113,000	Good
Christopher Columbus	500,000				121,000	Poor
Marry Me!	117,900	21,100	50,000	−67,600	63,000	Poor
Helter Skelter					84,000	Poor
Don't Ever Leave Me						
The Lost People					80,000	Poor
Diamond City					97,000	Poor
Traveller's Joy					68,000	Poor
Boys in Brown					94,000	Avge
The Astonished Heart					93,000	Poor
So Long at the Fair					132,000	Good
Trio					147,000	Good
Encore					172,000	Exc't
Street Corner					49,000 [incomplete]	Exc't

Sources: PRO, BT 64/4490, data on production costs and distribution returns for Rank films up to December 1949; BFI, Michael and Aileen Balcon Collection, Papers H3, undated list prepared by John Davis, with an attached covering letter dated 16 July 1953. I am grateful to Professor Vincent Porter for bringing the latter source to my attention.

Filmography

For reasons of space, this is a list of Box's films rather than a comprehensive filmography.

Non-fiction films

[It has proved to be impossible to establish a definitive list of Box's films for Publicity or Verity; I have listed those that can be included with confidence.]

Publicity films

Precision Makes Perfect, 1937.
Sweet Success, 1937.
The World Rolls On, 1938.

Verity films

[co-productions where indicated]

1940
Herring; *Oatmeal Porridge*; *Potatoes*; *Steaming*; *Casserole Cooking.*

1941
A-tish-oo; *Breast Feeding*; *Canteen on Wheels* [a longer, non-theatrical version was released as *Mobile Canteen*]; *Dai Jones*; *The English Inn*; *Everybody's Business*; *Food Advice Centre*; *HM Minelayer*; *Roots of Victory*; *Salvage Sense*; *Shunter Black's Night Off*; *The Sixteen Tasks of Maintaining Motorised Vehicles*; *The Soldier's Food*; *Switchover*; *Tea Is Served*; *Telefootlers*; *Ten Tips for Tackling Tanks*; *'UXB'* [Unexploded Bombs]; *Women at War.*

1942
Action; *Ask CAB*; *Cookers in the Field*; *Cooks*; *House*; *HMS George V*; *Jane Brown Changes Her Job* [Verity-Technique]; *The Job that Fits* [The ATS];

Men of Tomorrow; *Summer on the Farm*; *The Sword of the Spirit*; *Techniques of Bomb Disposal I, II* and *III*; *Teeth of Steel* [Verity-Technique]; *Three Cadets*; *Twelve Days*; *Vehicle Mastership*; *A Way to Plough*; *We Serve*; *WVS*.

1943

Anti-Personnel Bomb; *Black Diamonds*; *Common Cause*; *The Crown of the Year* [Greenpark-Verity]; *Decontamination of the Streets*; *Factory Fireguard*; *It Began on the Clyde*; *Jigsaw*; *The Job that Fits the Facts*; *London 1942*; *March Discipline*; *Meet the Ship*; *Power on the Land*; *Off Duty*; *Summer on the Farm* [Verity-Greenpark]; *Youth*.

1944

Anti-Personnel Bomb; *Butterfly Bomb*; *Catholics in Britain*; *A Cautionary Tale*; *Conquest of a Germ*; *Danger Area*; *A Flying Start*; *Fuel and the Tractor*; *Harness Your Horsepower*; *Harvest Uplift*; *Men of Rochdale*; *Other Men's Lives*; *Piping Hot*; *A Ride with Uncle Joe*; *Unit Messing*; *You Too Can Get Malaria*.

1945

Battledress; *Best Feet Forward*; *A City Reborn* [Gryphon-Verity]; *Country Town*; *Frame Concrete Housing*; *General Election*; *The Hospital Team*; *Know Your Enemy: The Japanese Army and How It Became What It Is Today*; *Night and Day*; *Pacific Thrust*; *Post-War Road Safety*; *Public Opinion*; *Resettlement Advice Service*; *The Second Freedom*; *A Solder Returns Home* [Greenpark-Verity]; *Song of the People*; *To Be a Farmer's Girl*.

1946

Julius Caesar; *Macbeth*; *The Story of Money*; *'Twas on a Monday Morning*.

Feature films

[pc. = production company] Box's role is given in brackets.

Alibi Inn, 1935, 53 mins, b/w, pc. MGM-British [co-screenwriter]
The Flemish Farm, 1943, 82 mins, b/w, pc. Two Cities [producer]
On Approval, 1944, 80 mins, b/w, pc. Independent Producers [co-producer]
English without Tears (US title: ***Her Man Gilbey***), 1944, 89 mins, b/w, pc. Two Cities [co-producer]
Don't Take It to Heart, 1944, 91 mins, b/w, pc. Two Cities [producer]
29 Acacia Avenue (US title: *The Facts of Love*), 1945, 83 mins, b/w, pc. Boca [producer; co-screenwriter]
The Seventh Veil, 1945, 94 mins, b/w, pc. Theatrecraft-Ortus [co-producer, co-screenwriter]
The Years Between, 1946, 100 mins, b/w, pc. Sydney Box [producer; co-screenwriter]

The Man Within (US title: ***The Smugglers***), 1947, 95 mins, col., pc. Production Film Services [producer; co-screenwriter]
The Brothers, 1947, 98 mins, b/w, pc. Triton [producer; co-screenwriter]
Dear Murderer, 1947, 94 mins, b/w, pc. Gainsborough [executive producer; co-screenwriter]
The Upturned Glass, 1947, 86 mins, b/w, pc. Triton [executive producer]
Holiday Camp, 1947, 97 mins, b/w, pc. Gainsborough [producer; co-screenwriter]
Jassy, 1947, 102 mins, col., pc. Gainsborough [producer]
When the Bough Breaks, 1947, 81 mins, b/w, pc. Gainsborough [executive producer; co-screenwriter]
Easy Money, 1948, 94 mins, b/w, pc. Gainsborough [executive producer; co-screenwriter]
Snowbound, 1948, 85 mins, b/w, pc. Gainsborough [executive producer]
Broken Journey, 1948, 89 mins, b/w, pc. Gainsborough [producer]
Miranda, 1948, 80 mins, b/w, pc. Gainsborough [executive producer]
Daybreak, 1948, 81 mins, b/w, pc. Triton [producer; co-screenwriter]
Good Time Girl, 1948, 93 mins, b/w, pc. Triton [producer; co-screenwriter]
The Calendar, 1948, 80 mins, b/w, pc. Gainsborough [executive producer]
My Brother's Keeper, 1948, 91 mins, b/w, pc. Gainsborough [executive producer]
The Blind Goddess, 1948, 87 mins, b/w, pc. Gainsborough [executive producer; co-screenwriter]
Quartet, 1948, 120 mins, b/w, pc. Gainsborough [executive producer]
Here Come the Huggetts, 1948, 93 mins, b/w, pc. Gainsborough [executive producer; co-screenwriter]
Portrait from Life (US Title: ***The Girl in the Painting***), 1948, 90 mins, b/w, pc. Gainsborough [executive producer; co-screenwriter]
Vote for Huggett, 1949, 84 mins, b/w, pc. Gainsborough [executive producer]
Once upon a Dream, 1949, 84 mins, b/w, pc. Triton [executive producer]
The Bad Lord Byron, 1949, 85 mins, b/w, pc. Triton [executive producer; co-screenwriter]
It's Not Cricket, 1949, 77 mins, b/w, pc. Gainsborough [executive producer]
A Boy, a Girl and a Bike, 1949, 92 mins, b/w, pc. Gainsborough [executive producer]
The Huggetts Abroad, 1949, 87 mins, b/w, pc. Gainsborough [executive producer]
Christopher Columbus, 1949, 104 mins, col., pc. Gainsborough [executive producer; co-screenwriter]
Marry Me!, 1949, 97 mins, b/w, pc. Gainsborough [executive producer]
Don't Ever Leave Me, 1949, 85 mins, b/w, pc. Triton [executive producer]
Helter Skelter, 1949, 84 mins, b/w, pc. Gainsborough [executive producer]
The Lost People, 1949, 88 mins, b/w, pc. Gainsborough [executive producer]
Diamond City, 1949, 90 mins, b/w, pc. Gainsborough [executive producer]
Traveller's Joy, 1949, 78 mins, b/w, pc. Gainsborough [executive producer]

Boys in Brown, 1949, 85 mins, b/w, pc. Gainsborough [executive producer]
The Astonished Heart, 1950, 89 mins, b/w, pc. Gainsborough [executive producer]
So Long at the Fair, 1950, 86 mins, b/w, pc. Gainsborough [executive producer]
Trio, 1950, 91 mins, b/w, pc. Gainsborough [executive producer]
Happy Family (US title: ***Mr Lord Says No***), 1952, 86 mins, b/w, pc. London Independent Producers [co-producer; co-screenwriter]
Street Corner (US title: ***Both Sides of the Law***), 1953, 94 mins, b/w, pc. London Independent Producers [co-producer; co-screenwriter]
Forbidden Cargo, 1954, 85 mins, b/w, pc. London Independent Producers [producer; screenwriter]
The Beachcomber, 1954, 90 mins, col., pc. London Independent Producers [screenwriter]
To Dorothy a Son (US title: ***Cash on Delivery***), 1954, 84 mins, b/w, pc. Welbeck [co-producer]
The Prisoner, 1955, 95 mins, b/w, pc. London Independent Producers-Facet [co-producer]
Lost (US title: *Tears for Simon*), 1956, 89 mins, col., pc. Rank [executive producer]
Eyewitness, 1956, 82 mins, b/w, pc. Rank [producer]
The Passionate Stranger (US title: ***A Novel Affair***), 1957, 97 mins, b/w & col., pc. Beaconsfield [co-screenwriter]
The Truth about Women, 1958, 107 mins, col., pc. Beaconsfield [producer; co-screenwriter]
Floods of Fear, 1958, 84 mins, b/w, pc. Rank [producer]
Subway in the Sky, 1959, 86 mins, b/w, pc. Rank [co-producer; co-screenwriter]
Too Young to Love, 1960, 88 mins, b/w, pc. Welbeck [executive producer; co-screenwriter]
Rattle of a Simple Man, 1964, 95 mins, b/w, pc. Martello [executive producer]
A King's Story, 1965, 102 mins, col., pc. Le Vien Films [original screen treatment]
Deadlier than the Male, 1966, 98 mins, col./scope, pc. Santor [executive producer]
The Long Duel, 1967, 115 mins, col./scope, pc. Rank-London Independent Producers [associate producer]

Films made by Sydney Box Associates

Blind Date, 1959; *The Night We Dropped a Clanger*, 1959; *SOS Pacific*, 1959; *The Treasure of San Teresa*, 1959; *Desert Mice*, 1959; *Witness in the Dark*, 1959; *Your Money or Your Wife*, 1960; *The Shakedown*, 1960; *Piccadilly Third Stop*, 1960.

Television series

Ivanhoe

39 30-minute episodes, broadcast on ITV 5 January 1958–7 May 1959 (syndicated in USA 1957).

Select bibliography

Archival and unpublished document sources

Public Record Office, Kew, London (PRO)

BT 64: Board of Trade Manufactures Department
HO: Home Office Entertainment Files
INF 1: General Memoranda, correspondence and records of the Ministry of Information

British Film Institute London (BFI)

Special collections

The Michael and Aileen Balcon Collection
The Muriel and Sydney Box Collection
The Clive Brook Collection
The Filippo Del Giudice Collection
The Joseph Losey Collection

Other BFI material

Carter, Maurice, 'The Darker Side of the Screen', unpublished autobiography (1981)

Hurst, Brian Desmond, 'Brian Desmond Hurst', unpublished autobiography (1986)

Film Script Collection: *The Man Within* (S17411); *Daybreak* (S12909); *The Blind Goddess* (S13922); *The Bad Lord Byron* (S13913); *Christopher Columbus* (S13986; S19247; S901); *Quartet* ('The Alien Corn', S6294; 'The Kite', S7231; 'The Colonel's Lady', S6293)

British Board of Film Censors' Scenario Reports: 1941–47, 1949 (incomplete)

BECTU Oral History Tapes: Muriel Box (177); Maurice Carter (174); Jill Craigie (363); Cedric Dawe (229); Ray Elton (67); Harold French (179); William

MacQuitty (223); C. M. Pennington-Richards (122); Alfred Roome (14); Peter Tanner (13)
Microfiche of reviews for each of Box's films
Press Books for each of Box's films

The Imperial War Museum, London

Interview with David Macdonald (4654/3)

In the possession of the author

Papers and other material lent by Leonora Dossett and William Gell, principally consisting of: *The Lion That Lost Its Way*, Autobiography, 1977, and supporting documentation, especially concerning the sale of British Lion; material on Box's early career as a playwright; five journals solely by Box (January 1950–March 1954); numerous unpublished short stories, plays and novels; several unproduced screenplays; miscellaneous documentation relating to various films and companies.
Oral interviews conducted by the author: Ken Annakin (15 May 2001); Lord Attenborough (26 November 2002); Sylvia Box (18 May 2003); Vivian Cox (10 June 2003); Leonora Dossett (6 May 2003); John Franks (28 July 2004); Bill Gell (28–29 July 2003); Jean Kent (17 April 2003); William MacQuitty (9 April 2003); Jan Read (13 June 2003); Peter Rogers (7 May 2003); Dinah Sheridan (14 April 2003); Carolyn Whitaker (19 November 2003); Googie Withers (30 April 2003)

Published documentary sources

Parliamentary Debates: House of Commons, Fifth Series (Hansard)
National Film Finance Corporation, *Annual Reports of the National Film Finance Corporation to 31st March* (London: HMSO, 1950–65).
Monopolies Commission, *Films: A Report on the Supply of Films for Exhibition in Cinemas* (London: HMSO, October 1966).
Future of the British Film Industry: Report of the Prime Minister's Working Party (London: HMSO, 1976) (Cmnd 6372)
British Lion, *Annual Reports* (1958–65)
Rank Organisation, *Annual Reports* (1948–67)

Newspapers and Periodicals

Daily Express; Daily Graphic; Daily Herald; Daily Mail; Daily Mirror; Daily Sketch; Daily Telegraph; Daily Worker; Evening News; Evening Standard; Financial Times; Leader Magazine; Manchester Guardian; News Chronicle; News of the World; Observer; Picture Post; Reynolds News; Spectator; Star; Sunday Chronicle; Sunday Dispatch; Sunday Express; Sunday Graphic; Sunday People; Sunday Pictorial; The Times; Tribune; Weekly Illustrated

Film journals and trade papers

British Film Review; British Picture News; British Studio Newsletter; Cinema and Theatre Construction; Cinetechnician (Film and TV Technician); Cinema Today; Contemporary Cinema; Daily Cinema; Daily Film Renter; Documentary Newsletter; Film Fashionland; Film Forum; Film Illustrated Monthly; Film Industry; Film Mirror; Film Miscellany; Film Monthly Review; Film World; Films and Filming; Focus; Hollywood Quarterly; Kinematograph Weekly [KW]; The Living Cinema; Monthly Film Bulletin; Motion Picture Herald; Penguin Film Review; Picturegoer; Picture Show; Screen International; Sequence; Sight and Sound; Today's Cinema; Variety; World Review

Memoirs

Annakin, Ken, *So You Wanna Be a Director?* (Sheffield: Tomahawk Press, 2001).

Balcon, Michael, *Michael Balcon Presents ... A Lifetime of Films* (London: Hutchinson, 1969).

Box, Betty, *Lifting the Lid* (Lewes: The Book Guild, 2000).

Box, Muriel, *Odd Woman Out* (London: Leslie Frewin, 1974).

Box, Sydney, *The Lion That Lost Its Way: And Other Cautionary Tales of the Show Business Jungle*, edited with an introduction and notes by Andrew Spicer (Lanham, Maryland and Oxford: Scarecrow Press, 2005).

Coates, Peter, *No Star Nonsense* (London: Rockliff, 1949).

Constanduros, Mabel, *Shreds and Patches: Autobiographical Memoirs* (London: Lawson & Dunn, 1946).

Dors, Diana, *Dors by Diana* (London: Macdonald Futura, 1981).

Forbes, Bryan, *Notes for a Life* (London: Everest Books, 1977 [1974]).

Francis, Anne, *Julian Wintle: A Memoir* (n.p.: Dukeswood, 1984).

Guest, Val, *So You Want to Be in Pictures* (London: Reynolds and Hearn, 2001).

Guinness, Alec, *My Name Escapes Me: The Diary of a Retiring Actor* (London: Hamish Hamilton, 1996).

Lockwood, Margaret, *Lucky Star* (London: Odhams Press, 1955).

MacQuitty, William, *A Life to Remember* (London: Quartet Books, 1991).

Mason, James, *Before I Forget* (London: Sphere, 1982 [1981]).

McCallum, John, *Life with Googie* (London: Heinemann, 1979).

Noble, Peter, *Reflected Glory: An Autobiographical Sketch* (London: Jarrolds, 1958).

Owen, Bill, *Summer Wine and Vintage Years: A Cluttered Life* (London: Robson Books, 1994).

Read, Jan, *Young Man in Movieland* (Lanham, Maryland and Oxford: Scarecrow Press, 2004).

Redgrave, Michael, *In My Mind's Eye: An Autobiography* (London: Weidenfeld & Nicolson, 1983).

Rix, Brian, *My Farce from My Elbow: An Autobiography* (London: Secker & Warburg, 1975).

Sangster, Jimmy, *Do You Want It Good or Tuesday? A Life in the Movies* (Baltimore: Midnight Marquee Press, 1997).

Shaughnessy, Alfred, *Both Ends of the Candle* (London: Peter Owen, 1978).

Sherriff, R. C., *No Leading Lady* (London: Gollancz, 1969).

Todd, Ann, *The Eighth Veil* (London: William Kimber, 1980).

Willis, Ted, *Evening All: 50 Years Over a Hot Typewriter* (London: Macmillan, 1991).

Zetterling, Mai, *All Those Tomorrows* (London: Cape, 1985).

Secondary sources

Aspinall, Sue and Robert Murphy (eds), *Gainsborough Melodrama* (London: BFI, 1983).

Box, Sydney, *Film Publicity: A Handbook on the Production and Distribution of Propaganda Films* (London: Lovat Dickson, 1937).

Box, Sydney and Vivian Cox, *The Bad Lord Byron* (London: Convoy Publications, 1949).

Bright, Morris and Robert Ross, *Mr Carry On: The Life and Work of Peter Rogers* (London: BBC Worldwide, 2000).

Chapman, James, *The British at War: Cinema, State and Propaganda, 1939–1945* (London: I. B. Tauris, 1998).

Cook, Pam (ed.), *Gainsborough Pictures* (London: Cassell, 1997).

Drazin, Charles, *The Finest Years: British Cinema of the 1940s* (London: André Deutsch, 1998).

Geraghty, Christine, *British Cinema in the Fifties: Gender, Genre and the 'New Look'* (London: Routledge, 2000).

Gifford, Denis, *The British Film Catalogue 1888–1994: Non-fiction films* (Fitzroy Dearborn, 2001).

Gifford, Denis, *The British Film Catalogue 1888–1994: Feature Films* (London: Fitzroy Dearborn, 2001).

Harper, Sue, 'Historical Pleasures: Gainsborough Costume Melodrama', in Christine Gledhill (ed.), *Home Is Where the Heart Is* (London: BFI, 1987).

Harper, Sue, *Picturing the Past: The Rise and Fall of the British Costume Film* (London: BFI, 1994).

Harper, Sue and Vincent Porter, 'Cinema Audience Tastes in 1950s Britain', *Journal of Popular British Cinema*, 2 (1999).

Harper, Sue and Vincent Porter, *British Cinema of the 1950s: The Decline of Deference* (Oxford: Oxford University Press, 2003).

Jenkins, Clive, *The Power Behind the Screen: Ownership, Control and Motivation in British Commercial Television* (London: MacGibbon & Kee, 1961).

Kelly, Terence, with Graham Norton and George Perry, *A Competitive Cinema* (London: Institute of Economic Affairs, 1960).

Macnab, Geoffrey, *J. Arthur Rank and the British Film Industry* (London: Routledge, 1993).

McFarlane, Brian, *An Autobiography of British Cinema* (London: Methuen, 1997).

McFarlane, Brian (ed.), *The Encyclopedia of British Film* (London: Methuen/BFI, 2003).

Murphy, Robert, *Realism and Tinsel: Cinema and Society in Britain 1939–49* (London: Routledge, 1989).

Porter, Vincent, 'The Context of Creativity: Ealing Studios and Hammer Films', in James Curran and Vincent Porter (eds), *British Cinema History* (London: Weidenfeld & Nicolson, 1983).

Pronay, Nicholas and D. W. Spring (eds), *Propaganda, Politics and Film, 1918–45* (London: Macmillan, 1982).

Richards, Jeffrey and Dorothy Sheridan (eds), *Mass-Observation at the Movies* (Routledge and Kegan Paul, 1987).

Robertson, James, *The British Board of Film Censors: Film Censorship in Britain, 1896–1950* (London: Croom Helm, 1985).

Sendall, Bernard, *Independent Television in Britain, vol. 1: Origin and Foundation, 1946–62* (London: Macmillan, 1982).

Sendall, Bernard, *Independent Television in Britain, vol. 2: Expansion and Change, 1958–68* (London: Macmillan, 1983).

Slide, Anthony, *Banned in the USA: British Films in the United States and their Censorship, 1933–1960* (London: I. B. Tauris, 1998).

Spicer, Andrew, *Typical Men: The Representation of Masculinity in Popular British Cinema* (London: I. B. Tauris, 2001).

Spicer, Andrew, 'Extending People's Minds for a Short Time Every Day: The wartime propaganda short', *Journal of Media Practice*, 4:2 (2003).

Spicer, Andrew, 'The Production Line: Reflections on the Role of the Film Producer in British Cinema', *Journal of British Cinema and Television*, 1:1 (Autumn 2004).

Street, Sarah, *Transatlantic Crossings: British Feature Films in the United States* (London: Continuum, 2002).

Thorpe, Frances and Nicholas Pronay, *British Official Films in the Second World War: A Descriptive Catalogue* (Oxford: Clio Press, 1980).

Walker, Alexander, *Hollywood, England: The British Film Industry in the Sixties* (London: Harrap, 1986 [1974]).

Wood, Alan, *Mr Rank: A Study of J. Arthur Rank and British Films* (London: Hodder & Stoughton, 1952).

Index

EU authorised representative for GPSR:
Easy Access System Europe, Mustamäe tee 50,
10621 Tallinn, Estonia
gpsr.requests@easproject.com

www.ingramcontent.com/pod-product-compliance
Lightning Source LLC
Chambersburg PA
CBHW070941230426
43666CB00011B/2516

* 9 7 8 0 7 1 9 0 6 0 0 0 7 *